DEMOCRATIC SOCIAL EDUCATION

TEACHING AND THINKING
VOLUME 3
GARLAND REFERENCE LIBRARY OF SOCIAL SCIENCE
VOLUME 1156

DEMOCRATIC SOCIAL EDUCATION
SOCIAL STUDIES FOR SOCIAL CHANGE

DAVID W. HURSH
E. WAYNE ROSS

FALMER PRESS
A MEMBER OF THE TAYLOR & FRANCIS GROUP
NEW YORK & LONDON
2000

Published in 2000 by
Falmer Press
A member of the Taylor & Francis Group
29 West 35th Street
New York, NY 10001

10   9   8   7   6   5   4   3   2   1

Library of Congress Cataloging-in-Publication Data

Hursh, David W., 1948–
    Democratic social education / social studies for social change /
David W. Hursh, E. Wayne Ross.
        p.   cm. — (Garland reference library of social science ; vol.
1156. Teaching and thinking ; vol. 3)
    Includes bibliographical reference and index.
    ISBN 0-8153-2855-9 (alk. paper)
        1. Social Sciences—Study and teaching—United States.
2. Critical pedagogy—United States.   I. Ross, E. Wayne, 1956– .   II. Title
III. Series: Garland reference library of social science ; v. 1156.   IV. Series:
Garland reference library of social science.
Teaching and thinking; vol. 3.
LB1584.H87 2000
300'.71'2—dc21   99-39027
                                                                    CIP

Printed on acid-free, 250-year-life paper.
Manufactured in the United States of America

Contents

Acknowledgments

Wayne thanks Jeffrey W. Cornett, Stephen C. Fleury, Rich Gibson, Perry Marker, Susan Noffke, Valerie Ooka Pang, Ceola Ross Baber, Kevin Vinson, and, of course, David Hursh—all comrades in the effort to reconstruct schools and society along more humane and democratic lines. Sandra Mathison is the most important person in my life—I am forever grateful that she shares her love, intellect, and life with me. To my son, John Colin Mathison Ross, and daughter, Rachel Layne Ross: "I love you both with all my heart."

David thanks Camille Martina, Michelle Erklenz-Watts, Susan Noffke, and Wayne Ross for their vision and tireless efforts to make a difference in the world. I also want to thank my mom, Helen Hursh, and wife, Kathleen, for their support over the years of working on this book. Lastly, I want to acknowledge my sons, Asa and Austin, for continually reminding me why this work is so necessary.

Finally, chapters by Henry A. Giroux, Joe L. Kincheloe, Wendy Kohli, Shirley Steinberg, and E. Wayne Ross (Chapter 13) first appeared in a special issue of the *International Journal of Social Education* (1996, Vol. 11, No. 1) on democratic education. Sandra Mathison's chapter is adapted from an article that appears in the same issue of *IJSE*. Perry Marker's chapter originally appeared in *Social Science Record*. Thanks to both journals for allowing the inclusion of these chapters here.

DEMOCRATIC SOCIAL EDUCATION

CHAPTER 1

Democratic Social Education
Social Studies for Social Change

DAVID W. HURSH

E. WAYNE ROSS

In 1932 George Counts, in his speech "Dare the School Build a New Social Order?"[1] explicitly challenged teachers to develop a democratic, socialist society. In this book we take seriously the question of what social studies educators can do today to build a democratic society, in a society that is currently marked by antidemocratic impulses of greed, individualism, and intolerance. The essays in this collection respond to Counts' question with theoretical analyses of education and society, historical analyses of efforts since Counts' challenge, and practical analyses of classroom pedagogy and school organization.

The chapters that follow can be situated within three broad perennial debates that have been central to social studies and education. The first debate focuses on the social purposes of education, primarily examining the relationship between education and work and conceptions of citizenship. The second debate focuses on the social studies curriculum, primarily whether it should be narrowly defined around the traditional social sciences—history, political science, and geography—or more broadly defined to include multicultural perspectives, media, and the arts. The last debate looks at the process of educating students: whether students are to be indoctrinated and instilled in particular ways of looking at the world or whether we are to develop democratic spaces within school and the larger social order.

It is, of course, oversimplifying to see these debates as distinct from one another, and the following sections necessarily intertwine and overlap. Education as the preparation for the workplace complements narrow conceptions of social studies emphasizing, as in William Bennett's or

Diane Ravitch and Abigail Thernstrom's recent publications,[2] calls for conventional military and political history and reverence toward our nation's founding fathers and documents. In this approach, the student receives historical knowledge as passed down from the experts and aims to be a productive worker who works with other workers from different backgrounds. In contrast, as presented in this volume, critical conceptions of social studies problematize the nature of society, the economy, and social studies itself. Social studies under this conception is not limited to the traditional social sciences but expanded to include art, culture, and identity.

The contributors to this book call for social studies to become central to the elementary and secondary school curriculum. Although no one, including the authors, can draw a blueprint for a new social studies (or a new society!), the contributors raise questions and make suggestions for developing a new social studies curriculum. They regard social studies as crucial to revitalizing a critical citizenship that situates political decisions within an analysis of economic and political issues, to reintegrating the curriculum subjects, and to reconnecting the student's public experience of media and culture to education. The authors invite the reader to collaborate in creating and enacting a new vision.

Of course, calls for developing a critical citizenship, such as those presented here, have not gone uncontested. While Counts and his contemporaries like Dewey[3] advanced social education for its potential to develop critical democratic citizens and cultural diversity, conservatives, reflecting the interests of capitalists and cultural conservatives, have promoted social education as a means of supporting economic productivity, nationalism, and conservative morality. In this introduction we begin by situating the chapters within these debates and then give an overview of the chapters in terms of their central points, links with other chapters, and implications for practice.

CONCEPTIONS OF CITIZENSHIP: EDUCATION FOR ECONOMIC PRODUCTIVITY AND POLITICAL PASSIVITY OR CRITICAL WORKERS AND CITIZENS

Because education necessarily provides students with knowledge, skills, and values that they will apply in their vocational careers and as citizens, education necessarily prepares students for both work and citizenship. The question becomes, then, what kind of workers and citizens?

The answer to this question has always been contested. On the one hand, writes historian Fones-Wolf, schools have been seen as a "means of socializing workers for the factory, and as a way of promoting social and political stability."[4] In opposition, progressives throughout the twentieth century have promoted education to develop the social conditions and intelligence that enable citizens to make social and vocational decisions that support their own and the community's welfare.

The conflict between schooling for economic productivity and schooling for critical, informed citizenry has raged throughout the twentieth century. Kliebard,[5] in his history of the American curriculum, recounts conflicts at the beginning of the century between proponents of scientific efficiency and reconstructionists such as Counts. In the early 1900s, "productivity expert" Frederick Winslow Taylor promoted scientific efficiency as a way of increasing worker productivity.[6] Taylor's principles and techniques were quickly adopted by curriculum theorists and education policy makers as a way of improving educational productivity. David Snedden of Massachusetts, a powerful state commissioner in the early part of the century, argued that schools should aid the economy to function as efficiently as possible by sorting and training students for their "probable destinies" in the workforce.[7] The efficiency movement emphasized hierarchical decision making, with experts conceptualizing educational goals, curriculum, and pedagogy to be carried out by teachers. Social studies teachers, under social efficiency theorists such as Snedden, would be required to be neutral, "disinterested" presenters of the opinions of the majority or to withdraw from teaching. Social studies exist to prepare students to be productive workers.

In contrast, Dewey was not interested in making students' interests subservient to those of business. He argued instead for the development of such intelligence, ingenuity, and capacity as shall make workers, as far as possible, masters of their own industrial fate.

> The kind of vocational education in which I am interested is not one which will "adapt" workers to the existing industrial regime . . . but one which will alter the existing industrial system and ultimately transform it.[8]

During the Depression of the 1930s, the debate continued. Counts' call for schools to create a new social order came when many were questioning whether capitalism was tenable. In the journal *The Social Frontier* (1934–1939), reconstructionists such as Dewey, Counts, Charles Beard, and Harold Rugg called for reforming the economic system to serve the needs of people. Rugg believed that society required a "thorough going social reconstruction . . ." and that "there is no social institution known to the mind of man that can encompass that problem except education."[9] Teachers, working with a curriculum that promoted a critical study of contemporary economic, social, and political problems, could "remake the world."[10] To this end, Rugg, seeing the curriculum as central to what could be accomplished, developed a series of social studies textbooks that, rather than presenting the United States as the democratic beacon for the world without faults, raised social issues and problems.[11]

Of course, the ideas and activities of the social reconstructionists were not unopposed. Conservative educators and corporate leaders denounced the reconstructionists and the critical emphasis in education. During the Depression, the U.S. Chamber of Commerce led a campaign to reduce school taxes and slash school budgets. Leaders of the National Association of Manufacturers and the Chamber of Commerce joined the [American] Legion in charging that collectivists were indoctrinating students through [Ruggs' textbooks] and reducing the younger generations' trust in the free enterprise system."[12] Organizations, supported by the Daughters of the Colonial Wars and Bertie Forbes of *Forbes* magazine, successfully forced the removal of Ruggs' texts from the schools.

After the Depression, the National Association of Manufacturers teamed with the National Education Association (then primarily an organization of school administrators) to promote corporate interests in schools. For example, at a jointly sponsored 1945 conference, the schools were urged to "indoctrinate students with the American way of life" and teach that "the American system of free enterprise has done more for human comforts than any other system."[13] These efforts aimed to rid schools of any criticisms of the U.S. economic system and to prepare students through teaching and tracking for their "appropriate" place in the workforce. After the war, this meant that women would leave their paid work to return home, thus ending the career of "Rosie the Riveter," and that men would have to be satisfied in jobs at the socioeconomic level of their families.

After World War II, the mild support for an expanded welfare state, including support through the G.I. Bill for returning veterans, "roused the ire of all but the most moderate business leaders . . . [who] disliked the liberal agenda and feared that the New Deal traditions associated with the labor movement and the Democratic Party continued to appeal to many American workers."[14] Business leaders aimed to reshape the ideas of Americans so that they would see that success required nationalism, individualism, competition, and a weak welfare state.

The emphasis on individualism and the attack on welfare have intensified during the current post-Fordist era of global corporate expansion. Government and corporations continue to redesign education around the needs of business. Undersecretary of Education Marshall Smith calls for schools to be reformed to meet "ever changing challenges of international competition and a changing workplace."[15] In the spring of 1996, the nation's governors held an educational summit in the headquarters of corporate giant IBM. A working paper, developed in cooperation with IBM's CEO, stated:

> We believe that efforts to set clear, common, and community-based academic standards for students in a given school district or state is a necessary step in any effort to improve student performance. . . . We are convinced that technology, if applied thoughtfully and well-integrated into the curriculum, can be used to boost student performance and ensure a competitive edge for our workforce.[16]

Governmental and privately funded groups, such as the National Center for Education and the Economy, focus their reform efforts on developing students' knowledge and skills to be productive workers. These efforts replace social studies as a discipline to exercise critical thinking with an emphasis on incorporating "appropriate" workplace values.

As a result, some school districts have redesigned social studies curricula to emphasize social studies as preparation for the global economy rather than as liberal, critical education. For example, *Preparing for the 21st Century*, developed by the East Irondequoit (New York) School District and the Eastman Kodak Company, orients the district "learning outcomes" in terms of success in the workplace. "Global viewpoint," one of the eight outcomes, with the subcategory of multiculturalism, focuses on serving business interests. Multiculturalism becomes necessary as

> [e]ducation and industry recognize the impact of changing demographics and increased global awareness. Therefore, it is imperative that people understand the world more effectively from a geographic, environmental, economic, political, and cross-cultural perspective. This understanding will promote greater productivity in increasingly diverse school and work settings.[17]

The Rochester City School District similarly redefines multicultur-alism in terms of economic productivity. In a handout given to district teachers, multiculturalism appears only within the context of improving students' abilities to work with "diverse populations."[18]

Contributors to this volume criticize the global emphasis on post-Fordist conceptions of work and individual economic productivity rather than overall social welfare. Under this new global order, write the critics, the emphasis is on cultivating "more social obedience and commonness of purpose and less democracy and liberty."[19] Citizenship is redefined as individual responsibility for economic productivity without regard for existing economic and social inequalities that undermine overall social welfare.

Further, the authors decry the impact economic interests have had on social education. The current economic and political climate is domi-nated by corporate and neoconservative efforts to shape politics, work, culture, and education to serve the interests of capitalism. Under post-Fordism, workers have even less control over their work, as they compete for fewer high-skilled jobs with less security and fewer benefits. Corpo-rations continually counter employees' demands for increased pay and security by threatening to shift jobs to more business-friendly states or countries. Workers are less likely to have careers, as they move from temporary position to temporary position.

Instead, we argue for a broader, more encompassing conception of social education, one that promotes a "revitalization of civics. Such a civics . . . focus[es] its attention on the appreciation of the diverse ways economic, political, and social forces shape lives and structure unequal power relations."[20] Such a social education would raise issues "in order to begin developing pedagogies dedicated to the creation of democratic spaces within school and the larger social order."[21]

By calling for a proactive social education, we also call for a new conception of citizenship and civics. Rather than a passive citizenship limited to pulling voting booth levers every few years, social education develops the foundation of a questioning, active citizenship that makes problematic not only social outcomes but also social structures them-selves, including economic ones.

CURRICULUM CONTENT: THE UNCRITICAL CANON OR CURRICULUM DIVERSITY

What we should teach in school has been and will continue to be de-bated. Throughout the history of education in the United States, what counts as knowledge has been contested. Not only did white progressives like Dewey and Counts critique the conservative views that supported corporate interests but also African American educators have always critiqued the curriculum as reflecting the interests of those in power. Jessie Fauset and Helen Whitty are two forgotten African American educators of educators who, in the 1920s, integrated a progressive social studies with the history of the African American community. The work of W. E. B. Du Bois and Carter Woodson revealed the silences and biases in the dominant white history written at the time. Woodson, in 1926, was also central in promoting the adoption of Negro History Week in the schools and in publishing the *Negro History Bulletin*.[22] In 1935, Horace Mann Bond, in much the same way as Dewey, critiqued "scientific curriculum making" for its emphasis on scientific efficiency.[23]

James Banks has described elsewhere the evolution throughout this century of historical research on African Americans and multicultural education.[24] The debates over social studies intensified over the last three decades as people of color and women rightfully demanded to be represented in the curriculum, contributing to what many have called the "culture wars."[25]

Efforts to incorporate diverse views into the curriculum have been resisted. Conservatives such as Diane Ravitch attack multiculturalism as distorting history, emphasizing differences rather than similarities, and threatening the social fabric by promoting "group rivalry."[26] Historian Arthur Schlesinger, in *The Disuniting of America,* argues that multiculturalism threatens the social fabric through social difference.[27]

Others, such as E. D. Hirsch and William Bennett, question the inclusion of non–Western European history and culture in schooling. Hirsch does not so much argue for the moral superiority of Western European culture as state that its prevalence makes it the basis for discourse and knowledge in the United States. Hirsch claims:

> Without appropriate, tacitly shared background knowledge, people cannot understand newspapers. A certain extent of shared canonical knowledge is inherently necessary to a literate society.[28]

Our everyday interactions, Hirsch claims, require knowledge of Mother Goose nursery rhymes, patriotic songs, Bible stories, and famous people, who are almost always white men. Therefore, it is these things that children should be taught if they are to participate equally in society. Hirsch's resistance to developing more inclusive history and social studies courses seems to rest on arguing that knowing about Betsy Ross is not necessarily superior to knowing about Malcolm X, only that one needs to know about Betsy Ross in order to be "literate" in our society.[29]

In contrast, Bennett does argue for the superiority of Western civilization as the main contributor to "our" history. Therefore, Western European knowledge and values should be emphasized; to do otherwise would risk inclusion of less worthy ideas. This leads him and other conservatives, such as Edward Wynne, to argue not only that European history should be taught, but so should "Western" values. Bennett has pushed for teaching particular, "traditional" values and has worked to develop material for that teaching. For example, his *Book of Virtues* includes stories intended to teach particular values such as honesty; fairness; self-discipline; fidelity to task, friends, and family; responsibility; and love of country.[30]

Conservative Wynne not only wants to teach particular values to students but also explicitly calls for schools to indoctrinate students in those values. Wynne has pushed for character education to indoctrinate students into the "great tradition." Wynne states that "on the whole, school is and must be inherently indoctrinate."[31] As an example of what might be done, Wynne offers the example of an inner-city elementary school that provided a "charm class" for African American girls who caused discipline problems. The "charm class" stressed proper dress, makeup, poise, good grooming, posture, and etiquette.[32]

Landon Beyer and Daniel Liston, in their book *Curriculum in Conflict: Social Visions, Educational Agendas, and Progressive School Reform,*[33] critique Wynne for his deficit model, which attributes student failure entirely to the students and their culture and not to the larger social structure, and for his aim to indoctrinate students into a particular system of values. We return to the progressive debate over indoctrination later in this introduction.

Although some conservatives completely dismiss multiculturalism by reasserting the superiority of Western European civilization and traditional values, others recognize that U.S. society is becoming more diverse and, therefore, seek to embody multiculturalism within the corporate agenda. Just as schools have redefined multiculturalism as learning to work with others from diverse backgrounds, corporations have redefined multiculturalism as preparing management to manage employees from diverse backgrounds. For example, Angela Davis[34] cites Linda Mitchell's article "Get Ready to Manage a Salad Bowl," written for corporate leaders. Mitchell writes:

In the past, managing a labor force really meant managing white males. However, experts tell us we have jumped out of the "melting pot" and into the "salad bowl." The once-homogeneous workforce is becoming decidedly heterogeneous, and the parts of the whole are determined to retain their own cultures and customs. . . . How is corporate America dealing with this? A number of megacompanies have complex training programs. . . . These multicultural programs generically are termed "workforce diversity management". . . . Progressive firms want every employee to receive diversity training.[35]

Davis responds to such proposals by noting:

"Diversity management" assumes that a racially, ethnically, and culturally heterogeneous workforce needs to be managed or controlled in ways that contain and suppress conflict. This process is precisely a means of preserving and fortifying power relations based on class, gender, and race. Such discipline of diversity is, in fact, a strategy for more exhaustive control of the working class.[36]

The contributors to this volume decidedly disagree with the neo-conservatives on multiculturalism. We can ask what united America Schlesinger fears multiculturalism will disunite when, we would argue, we already have deep divisions in our society. We have the greatest income disparity since the Depression, our schools are decidedly segregated and unequal, and women and people of color are marginalized. We have little hope of developing a common civic culture if we fail to take into account the current conditions. We can ask Hirsch if a poem or aphorism that has become prominent should remain so. We can ask Bennett whether his abbreviated version of the story of Rosa Parks and the Montgomery bus boycott in *The Book of Virtues,* in which she is presented as a tired seamstress to exemplify the virtue of "courage," has a different political message than a more accurate history that acknowledges Parks' previous work as a civil rights activist in the NAACP.[37]

The contributors call for not only a social studies curriculum that incorporates history beyond "great white males" but also one that integrates history with examination of media, culture, and identity. The kind of multiculturalism proposed here is not devoting one month of the year to teaching the contributions of African Americans. Nor is it teaching the foods, fashions, and festivals of different racial and ethnic groups.

Rather, multicultural social education requires rethinking the entire school curriculum and organization, with emphasis on social education. Although the neoconservatives fear multicultural education because it doesn't teach "our" values and might emphasize differences, the contributors to this volume welcome different historical and cultural perspectives. The authors would support Kohl's[38] contention that Rosa Parks and the Montgomery bus boycott is misportrayed so as to sanction individual action rather than the collective activity of group organization. The former approach, Kohl argues, besides being historically inaccurate, promotes social passivity in students by presenting social change as the consequence of individual heroism rather than "a community effort to overthrow injustice."[39] While not every child, writes Kohl, can imagine her or himself to be a Rosa Parks, "everyone can imagine her or himself as part of a community working for social change."[40]

In this volume, we argue not only for including historical perspectives that have been excluded but also for broadening the definition of social studies to make it become the organizing principle for the curriculum. Rather than relegating social studies to a supporting role in schools (or, worse, using social studies to produce docile citizens), we can broaden social studies to include multicultural, media, artistic, and literacy studies in order to analyze and transform the economic, political, and cultural forces in our society. Indeed, in the chapters that follow, the authors suggest that when schools become places where students and teachers together raise questions about issues important to their lives—such as questions about students' racial, gender, and class identities, or about local community issues—the larger historical and political questions gain significance. Students begin to learn how to develop questions and gather information in ways that enable them not only to better understand society but also to change it.

In fact, because social studies make it possible to link the social sciences, art, culture, literacy, and identity, social studies becomes central to the curriculum. Such a conception requires rethinking and reforming what and how we teach in ways that are neither easy nor predictable. It requires teachers and students to raise questions of whose knowledge is in the curriculum and how power and inequality are maintained. It requires students and teachers to give voice to their own experiences and for social education to become a crucible within which students give voice to their own concerns and lives.

Social studies can become central to not just schools but other educational institutions as well, such as museums. The New Museum of

Contemporary Art, for example, has linked art and multiculturalism as illustrated by Susan Cahan and Zoya Kocur in *Contemporary Art and Multicultural Education.*[41] They developed a curriculum that specifically links popular culture, multiculturalism, and identity. They describe multiculturalism as a new "cultural politics of difference" that aims

> to challenge monolithic and homogeneous views of history in the name of diverse, multiple, and heterogeneous perspectives; to reject abstract, general, and universal pronouncements in light of concrete, specific, and particular realities, and to acknowledge historical specificity and plurality.[42]

Media and art can be used in this politics of difference to help students understand "their own place in history" and emphasize "the capacity and ability of all human beings, including those who have been culturally degraded, politically oppressed, and economically exploited."[43] Art serves "as a reservoir of 'unofficial knowledge,' a critique of history, and an affirmation of life. It is a primary source material for interdisciplinary education in which art is understood as both a product of history and a potential agent for social change."[44]

THE EDUCATIONAL PROCESS: INDOCTRINATION OR CRITICAL THINKING

We referred earlier to Wynne's call for education to indoctrinate students into conservative values. Similarly, those on the political left have sometimes called for indoctrinating students into particular values. They include Counts, whose call for a new social order we echoed at the outset of this introduction. The issue of indoctrination has a long history in social education that will not be repeated here.[45] In this volume, we offer some alternative ways of thinking about issues that transcend choosing between indoctrination and critical thinking.

All the contributors would probably agree that efforts by teachers to remain neutral are impossible and likely to end in indoctrination for the status quo. Such a stance, for Counts, meant "clothing one's deepest prejudices in the garb of universal truth and the introduction into the theory and practice of education an element of obscurantism."[46]

Some of the contributors take a more cautious, postmodern, antifoundational view, arguing:

Education can play a crucial role in the process of providing genuine
experiences wherein students can acquire both a thorough understanding of society, the means to critique it from various perspectives, and
the opportunity to propose alternative forms of social action and
arrangements.[47]

In this view, teachers and students can aim to confront problematic
situations and work toward solutions, while remaining modest in our
goals. We must be careful not to impose solutions to social problems on
the students.

Other contributors begin from an ethical foundation that schools
should be places where students begin to analyze how oppression operates "through exploitation, marginalization, powerlessness, cultural imperialism, violence, and oppressive ecological consequences of other's
actions."[48]

One author explicitly tackles the issue of whether social studies can
be neutral and apolitical by critiquing Leming's[49] defense of traditional
social studies and the status quo. Leming dismisses "peace," "poverty,"
and "multiculturalism" as possible organizing topics because they represent "particular ideological perspective[s]."[50] Leming assumes that the
traditional organization of topics is somehow neutral and apolitical.

Dewey would contend that such a traditional curriculum is little more
than indoctrination, "especially with reference to narrow nationalism under the name of patriotism, and with reference to the dominant economic
regime."[51] Students and teachers should ask questions about the nature and
behavior of our own society, and social studies education should provide
"countersocialization" that gives students the opportunity to ask questions that cannot be asked of traditional social studies subject matters.

John Marciano, in *Civic Illiteracy and Education: The Battle for the
Hearts and Minds of American Youth,*[52] describes efforts by teachers to
foster civic literacy regarding the Vietnam War and the 1991 Gulf War.
He describes, among others, Bill Bigelow's efforts to have his fourth-
grade students raise questions and conduct research regarding the causes
of the Gulf War. Bigelow admits that, like most teachers, he was ill prepared to examine events beyond the newspaper headlines. But "with the
help of others, he educated himself about it, and engaged his students in
a rigorous dialogue to help them sharpen their civic literacy skills."[53]
Bigelow's aim was to have the students and teachers become "truth seeking reporters who try to ask tough but fair questions that challenge the

dominant explanations for the war which were passed on by the media and schools to secure uncritical approval of a foreign policy."[54]

The aim of this approach to social studies is not to indoctrinate students in a particular way of seeing the world but to have teachers and students together realize that they do not know what they need to know, pose questions, and diligently pursue answers to those questions with a critical eye toward the sources of information. To create a critical literacy, students have to have access to views other than those provided by the people in power and must be able to situate current issues within their historical context. In much the same way that we have situated social studies within its historical, political, and economic context, teachers and students need to be able to situate and connect social studies to the wider culture.

THE CHAPTERS

Continuing the Tradition of Democratic Social Education

We begin with Wendy Kohli (Chapter 2) because in her narrative she raises many of the questions tackled throughout this volume. We connect the questions she has raised over the last thirty-five years to those of the other authors and, we hope, to those of the reader.

Although she began college acquiescing to the expectations of women in the late 1950s—she entered teaching because it was one of the careers women were expected to choose—the dichotomy between what was taught in school and what was discussed in the world led her to question what and how she was being taught. Specifically, as a teacher she observed how debates and even discussions of the Vietnam War were excluded from the social studies curriculum in the school. She had previously thought of schools as neutral conveyors of information. When she saw what was included and excluded from the curriculum, however, she realized that schools taught a "selective tradition," one that led students to a particular passive conception of citizenship.

Kohli began to work to develop classrooms where students and teachers could raise questions about democracy and be able, as she writes, to face "our history and *our present* squarely, [so that] we will be able to create the kind of society that our people, *all our people,* deserve."[55] We need to create space where students not only can recognize differences in the classroom but also look at the "difference differences make."[56] For Kohli, social studies can engage us in raising questions toward developing a more equitable and just society.

Kohli's political coming-of-age story exemplifies how one teacher came to rethink teaching social studies. In Chapter 3, E. Wayne Ross undertakes a philosophical and political critique of the traditional curriculum against which Kohli rebelled and provides a rationale for teaching critical, democratic social studies. Ross argues against traditional approaches to social studies for their legitimation of "spectator democracy in which a specialized class of experts identifies our common interests and then thinks and plans accordingly. The function of those outside the specialized class is to be 'spectators' rather than participants in action."[57] Ross calls for teachers to be "committed to helping students understand their own social situation and contribute to the redressing of social injustice; they must engage students in active inquiry and analysis that resists the status quo."[58]

William B. Stanley (Chapter 4), like Ross, develops a rationale for critical social studies but takes a cautious postmodern stance. Stanley explicitly responds to Counts' question, "Dare the schools build a new social order?" Reconstructionists like Counts, Stanley points out, accurately analyzed that U.S. society was characterized during the Depression by great inequality in wealth and power. Furthermore, they astutely noted that schools have typically been called on to "transmit the dominant culture and help to maintain social stability and status quo power relations"—often through indoctrination.[59]

But Counts and the other reconstructionists are wrong, writes Stanley, to assert that the indoctrination of the right should be countered by indoctrination from the left. Instead, Stanley, siding with the pragmatists, argues that we cannot know the truth but can focus only on developing the social and communal conditions that provide us with the knowledge to guide our social actions. Rather than attempting to impose solutions on students, we need to confront them

> with genuine problematic situations for which they must work out possible solutions. Education can play a critical role in the process by providing genuine experiences wherein students can acquire a thorough understanding of their society, the means to critique it from various perspectives, and the opportunity to propose alternative forms of social action and arrangements.[60]

Although this approach does not advocate indoctrinating students in some fixed democratic conception of society, it is not neutral. The aim is to promote democracy as "a way of life" and the centrality of "practical judgment."[61]

Whereas Stanley shifts from Counts' social reconstructionism to the pragmatism of his contemporary, Dewey, Susan E. Noffke (Chapter 5) connects Counts to the African American progressive educators of his time. Jessie Fauset and Helen Whiting, for example, are two African American educators writing in the 1930s who worked with K–12 students to undertake local studies of African American communities. Noffke also builds on the critical writing of W. E. B. Du Bois, Carter Woodson, and Horace Mann Bond to develop an outline of a critical social studies. The themes Noffke describes are extended by Gloria Ladson-Billings in her discussion of the teacher education program "Teach for Diversity" (Chapter 10).

Reenvisioning Democracy and Democratic Discourse in Education

The authors of subsequent chapters demonstrate the contribution that social studies can make to developing practical judgment and a democratic way of life. Henry A. Giroux (Chapter 6) helps us understand why social studies needs to be linked to the wider culture. Giroux urges us to examine current political and cultural debates and link them to our pedagogical practices. Critical pedagogues, writes Giroux, need to recognize "the relevance of popular culture as a pedagogical sphere and its importance in any discourse that links critical citizenship and pedagogy" and "address the ethical responsibilities of a cinematic public, including fundamental questions about the democratization of culture."[62]

Popular culture is central to students' own identities and is also a contested terrain on which conservatives critique the media as liberal and use the media as a way to alter the discourse regarding the purpose of schooling, social goals, and culture. The conservatives' success is reflected in the extent to which the dominant discourse of schooling has been shifted away from developing in students strong academic and social knowledge and toward producing technically trained, credentialed workers and consumers. Education has taken on primarily vocational and narrowly ideological considerations; concerns about poverty and racial discrimination have been replaced by an emphasis on testing and standardization.

Critical pedagogues, then, need to create an environment where teachers and students can raise questions about popular culture. Such endeavors make it possible to create social change. "The best way," writes

Giroux, "to reduce symbolic violence in the culture must be part of a larger discourse about educating people to change the social and economic conditions that produce and sustain such violence." Teachers can be central actors in "translating theory back into a constructive practice that transforms the everyday terrain of culture and political power."[63]

Joe L. Kincheloe (Chapter 7) and Shirley R. Steinberg (Chapter 8) broaden Giroux's analysis to situate popular culture and social studies within the changing nature of the economy, work, and culture. Throughout the twentieth century, corporations have always desired to influence citizens, not only as workers but as consumers—recall the examples given earlier regarding efforts by the Chamber of Commerce and the National Association of Manufacturers to ensure that schools instill reverence for the free enterprise system in students.

Under Fordist industrial approaches—in which workers assemble products designed by others—Henry Ford (the archetypal Fordist!) hired social workers to teach employees to be rational consumers. Kincheloe argues that corporations in the new post-Fordist era have greater control over politics, culture, and education. Such changes require educators to engage students in examining the ways in which the economy, politics, work, culture, and education are related, corporate attempts to shape them for corporate purposes, and education's role in a democratic society.

Kincheloe and Steinberg propose revitalized social studies that become central to the curriculum. Cultural studies have the potential to revolutionize the academic disciplines and to promote new conceptions of citizenship. Social studies, by incorporating cultural studies, have the potential to bring together various fields—sociology, history, literature, and others—to challenge the dominant assumptions of disciplinary knowledge and culture.

Educators, as students of pedagogy, can analyze knowledge production and transmission, the construction of values, and identity formation. We can examine the ways in which cultural texts struggle for a hegemonic form of consent.

Learning to Teach Democratically

The next chapters turn from urging us to link social studies with wider cultural studies to providing pedagogical approaches to accomplish those goals. Perry Marker (Chapter 9) helps us think through how we might raise the questions Kohli suggests in a social studies classroom. Marker uses the pedagogic practices of Paulo Freire to develop guidelines for a democratic social studies classroom. Following Freire, Marker critiques the traditional "banking" approach to teaching where the teacher is "the expert and authority who imparts knowledge to students and expects students to adopt the prescribed perspectives and practices. This approach essentially reduces students to the role of passive learners and places them at the mercy of the teacher's philosophy and ideas."[64]

Instead, Marker, like the other contributors to this book, argues that all education is political. What he adds is an outline for a teaching process. He suggests that we begin by asking students: What do we know about what we are studying? Just as significantly, we ask them: What don't we know? The former question helps students "find social meaning in their own experience." The latter allows students and teachers to explore the limits of their own expertise.

From those beginning questions, teachers and students can work together to consider what we want to find out about what we do not know, how we can find information, and what resources we have to find the information. Students gain practice in framing their own questions and answering them.

Finally, Marker looks at how we can present and share our findings and what specific proposals we can make to implement them. These questions keep us from being satisfied with merely answering our questions and push us on to figure out how to share learning in a way "that invites consideration, scrutiny, and questions."[65] Furthermore, attempting to implement the findings leads us to act on what we have learned as part of transforming the world. The point, to paraphrase Marker (and Marx), is not only to understand the world but also to change it. In his chapter, Marker elaborates on these points, plus provides specific examples of what a Freirien pedagogy might look like in the social studies classroom. The classroom becomes a place where students and teachers together ask questions, learn, share their knowledge, and change the world.

Gloria Ladson-Billings (Chapter 10) develops a critical theory that encompasses not only the work of Giroux and others described previously, but also that of African-American theorists Du Bois and Woodson (also described by Noffke) and practitioners Septima Clark and Esau Jenkins. She uses their work to design and implement a teacher education program, "Teach for Diversity."

After providing us with a description of the program, Ladson-Billings describes not so much its successes as the difficulties in developing critical pedagogues who ask questions about difference and inequity. Preservice teachers, she writes, find it difficult to translate their own good intentions into meaningful classroom practices. It takes time and dedication to develop the skills of classroom organization and lesson planning.

In the next chapter, Edward Buendia, Shuaib Meacham, and Susan E. Noffke (Chapter 11) also examine preparing social studies teachers, this time focusing less on preservice teachers and more on their own practices as teacher educators. The authors reflect on their efforts to practice what they preach by looking at the "theoretical conceptions as well as the practical aspects of a critical approach to preservice social studies education—one that emphasizes social critique as well as inquiry in teaching and learning to teach."[66] Their chapter provides us with a theoretical approach to developing a methods class, an approach that emphasizes developing a community of learners who continue to question their beliefs, questions, and practices. Their chapter also provides the reader with a wealth of resources for creating a curriculum.

Hursh, Goldstein, and Griffith (Chapter 12) have been active in creating and implementing curriculum in urban high schools. In their teaching, they have worked to develop

> schools where teachers and students raise questions of whose knowledge should be in the curriculum and of how power and inequality are maintained, and in the process they create new knowledge. Schools should become places where, as Michelle Fine suggests, students give voice to their own concerns and use history, political science, and other social sciences to make sense of their own lives.[67]

They describe their efforts to create such an environment in an eleventh-grade U.S. history course and a ninth-grade seminar on education. They often met resistance on the part of the students to engage in critical discussions because the students focused on gaining the information that would enable them to pass their state final exams. Further, students sometimes, as Herb Kohl[68] describes, choose to "not learn" in order to maintain their own identities in opposition to schools and schooling.

But Hursh, Goldstein, and Griffith were sometimes successful in opening "dangerous spaces," where students felt safe enough to raise difficult questions and make controversial comments. Students engaged in conversations regarding the Million Man March, acting and talking black or white, loving one's race as opposed to being racist (posed by a young black woman), and the difference between naming oneself black and naming oneself African American.

Wayne Ross (Chapter 12) returns to the politics of the social studies curriculum by examining "the current curriculum standards movement and" arguing "that it misleads us with a simple solution to a complex problem and, as a result, diverts us from attending to the conditions of schools and how they might be re-envisioned in more democratic ways."[69] He begins by surveying the current curriculum standards movement demonstrating the influence of neo-conservative groups and how such standards promote standardized school knowledge and teaching. His chapter then becomes a call for teachers to become involved in the necessary task of creating curriculum and teaching methods fully aware that knowledge is contested and teaching practices reflect particular notions, as Dewey wrote, of what kind of democratic society we desire.

In the final chapter, Sandra Mathison reminds us of the centrality of evaluation in developing a democratic social studies. Evaluation, like curriculum standards, greatly influences what and how we teach, but evaluation, unlike standards, rarely is explicitly analyzed and discussed. Mathison contends that we ignore evaluation at our own peril.

What and how we evaluate is every bit as political as what and how we teach. Mathison outlines a process through which parents, students, and teachers can participate in a collaborative evaluation process. By engaging in the process described, stakeholders in the educational outcome can deliberate different points of view, criteria, standards, and means of assessment for the social studies. Mathison's aim is to create Dewey's democratic communities, places where participants are obliged to "engage in careful consideration and discussion of alternatives, for the purpose of creating a better way of life."[70] This approach to evaluation fosters the democratic pedagogies the other authors describe.

It is appropriate that we conclude with a reference to Dewey, a comrade of Counts. In presenting the authors in this book, we intend to engage the reader in the process of considering alternatives for creating a better way of life. We hope that these chapters provide the reader with the rationale and resources for using social studies to develop critical democratic citizens and a new social order.

NOTES

[1]George Counts, *Dare the School Build a New Social Order?* (New York: John Day, 1932).

[2]See, for example, William Bennett, *The De-valuing of America: The Fight for Our Culture and Our Children* (New York: Summit Books, 1992), especially

Chapter 2, "What Works in American Education and Why," where he writes that a good curriculum would consist of the Bible, selected plays of Shakespeare, the founding and guiding documents of American political life, and the novel *The Adventures of Huckleberry Finn*. See Diane Ravitch and Abigail Thernstrom, *Democracy Reader: Classic and Modern Speeches, Essays, Poems, Declarations and Documents on Freedom and Human Rights Worldwide* (New York: Harper-Collins, 1992).

[3]See, for example, John Dewey, "Can Education Share in Social Reconstruction?" *The Social Frontier* 1 (1934): 11–12.

[4]Elizabeth Fones-Wolf, *Selling Free Enterprise: The Business Assault on Labor and Liberalism 1945–1960* (Urbana: University of Illinois, 1994), p. 190.

[5]Herbert Kliebard, *The Struggle for the American Curriculum: 1893–1958* (New York: Routledge, 1995).

[6]See, for example, Frederick Winslow Taylor, *The Principles of Scientific Management* (New York: Harper and Brothers, 1911).

[7]David Snedden, "Education for a World of Team Players and Team Workers," *School and Society* 20 (November 1924): 554–556.

[8]John Dewey, in *The New Republic* 3 (May 5, 1915): 40.

[9]Harold Rugg, *The Social Studies in the Elementary and Secondary School. Twenty-second Yearbook of the National Society for the Study of Education*, Part II, 1–27 (Bloomington, Ill: Public School Publishing Company, 1923). See also the inaugural issue of *The Social Frontier: A Journal of Educational Criticism and Reconstruction*, Oct. 1934 with George Counts as editor.

[10]Counts, pp. 261–262.

[11]Harold Rugg, *Man and His Changing Society. The Rugg Social Science Series of the Elementary School Course (Vols. 1–6)* (Boston: Ginn, 1929–1932).

[12]Fones-Wolf, *Selling Free Enterprise*, pp. 190–191.

[13]Ibid., p. 200, quoting businessman J. C. Yeomans.

[14]Ibid., p. 7.

[15]Marshall Smith and Brett Scoll, "The Clinton Human Capital Agenda," *Teachers College Record* 96 (Spring 1995): 389–404.

[16]*Education Week* (February 14, 1996): 17.

[17]East Irondequoit (New York) School District, *Preparing for the 21st Century* (1993), np.

[18]Rochester City (New York) School District, *Design Tasks/Goals* (1994).

[19]Kincheloe, this volume, p. 104.

[20]Ibid., p. 98.

[21]Ibid., p. 106.

[22]W. E. B. Du Bois, *The Philadelphia Negro: A Social Study* (Millwood, NY: Kraus-Thomson, 1973), original work published in 1899; and *Black Reconstruction in America: An Essay Toward a History of the Part Which Black Folk*

Played in the Attempt to Reconstruct Democracy in America: 1860–1880 (New York: Atheneum, 1962), original work published in 1935. Carter G. Woodson, *The Mis-education of the Negro* (New York: AMS Press, 1933/1977).
    [23]See Susan Noffke, this volume, p. 76.
    [24]See James Banks, "The African-American Roots of Multicultural Education," in *Multicultural Education, Transformative Knowledge, and Action: Historical and Contemporary Perspectives,* James Banks, ed. (New York: Teachers College Press, 1996), pp. 30–45.
    [25]See Ira Shor, *Culture Wars: School and Society in the Conservative Restoration, 1969–1984* (Boston: Routledge and Kegan Paul, 1986); and Gerald Graff, *Beyond the Culture Wars: How Teaching the Conflicts Can Revitalize American Education* (New York: W. W. Norton, 1992).
    [26]Diane Ravitch, "Multiculturalism: E Pluribus Plures," *The American Scholar* 59 (3) (1990): 340.
    [27]Arthur Schlesinger, Jr., *The Disuniting of America: Reflections on Multicultural Society* (New York: Norton, 1992).
    [28]E. D. Hirsch, "Cultural Literary," *The American Scholar* 52(2) (1983): 165.
    [29]E. D. Hirsch, *Cultural Literacy: What Every American Needs to Know* (New York: Vintage, 1988).
    [30]William Bennett, *The Book of Virtues: A Treasury of Great Moral Stories* (New York: Simon and Schuster, 1993).
    [31]Edward Wynne, "The Great Tradition in Education: Transmitting Moral Values," *Educational Leadership* 43(4) (1985/6): 9.
    [32]Edward Wynne, "Students and Schools," in *Character Development in Schools and Beyond,* edited by Kevin Ryan and George McLean (New York: Praeger, 1987).
    [33]Landon Beyer and Daniel Liston, *Curriculum in Conflict: Social Visions, Educational Agendas, and Progressive School Reform* (New York: Teachers College Press, 1996).
    [34]Angela Davis, "Gender, Class, and Multiculturalism: Rethinking 'Race' Politics," in *Mapping Multiculturalism,* edited by Avery Gordon and Christopher Newfield (Minneapolis: University of Minnesota, 1996), pp. 40–43.
    [35]Linda Mitchell, "Get Ready to Manage a Salad Bowl," *Kennedy Career Strategist* 5 (January 1990): 3, quoted in Angela Davis, "Gender, Class, and Multiculturalism."
    [36]Angela Davis, "Gender, Class and Multiculturalism."
    [37]Bennett, *The Book of Virtues.*
    [38]Herb Kohl, "The Politics of Children's Literature: What's Wrong with the Rosa Parks Myth," in *Rethinking Our Classrooms: Teaching for Equity and Justice,* edited by Bill Bigelow, Linda Christenen, Stan Karp, Barbara Miner, and Bob Peterson (Milwaukee, WI: Rethinking Schools, 1994), pp. 137–140.

[39]Ibid., p. 140.

[40]Ibid., p. 140.

[41]Susan Cahan and Zoya Kocur, *Contemporary Art and Multicultural Education* (New York: The New Press, 1996).

[42]Ibid., p. xvii–xviiii.

[43]Ibid., p. xviii.

[44]Ibid.

[45]Mary Ann Raywid, "The Discovery and Rejection of Indoctrination," *Educational Theory* 30 (1980), 1–10.

[46]Counts, *Dare the School . . .* , p. 9.

[47]Stanley, this volume, p. 72.

[48]Hursh, Goldstein, and Griffith, this volume, p. 192.

[49]James S. Leming, "Past as Prologue: A Defense of Traditional Patterns of Social Studies Instruction," in Murry Nelson, ed., *The Future of Social Studies* (Boulder, Colo.: Social Studies Science Consortium, 1994), cited in Ross, "Redrawing the Lines," this volume, p. 43–63.

[50]Ibid., p. 49.

[51]John Dewey, "Education and Social Change" (1937), cited in *John Dewey and American Democracy,* by Robert Westbrook (Ithaca: Cornell University Press, 1991), p. 507.

[52]John Marciano, *Civil Illiteracy and Education: The Battle for the Hearts and Minds of American Youth* (New York: Peter Lang, 1997).

[53]Ibid., p. 181.

[54]Ibid., p. 184.

[55]Kohli, this volume, p. 36.

[56]Ibid., p. 37.

[57]Ross, this volume, p. 57.

[58]Ibid., p. 59.

[59]Stanley, this volume, p. 65.

[60]Ibid., p. 72.

[61]Ibid.

[62]Giroux, this volume, p. 87 and 91.

[63]Ibid., p. 93.

[64]Marker, this volume, p. 137.

[65]Ibid., p. 140.

[66]Buendia, Meacham, Noffke, this volume, p. 165.

[67]Hursh, Goldstein, and Griffith, this volume, p. 192.

[68]Herb Kohl, *I Won't Learn from You: And Other Thoughts on Creative Maladjustment* (New York: New Press, 1994).

[69]Ross, "Diverting Democracy," this volume, p. 203.

[70]Mathison, this volume, p. 230.

CHAPTER 2

Teaching in the Danger Zone
Democracy and Difference

WENDY KOHLI

SITUATING MYSELF

Skating on Thin Ice[1]

My assignment, as someone who does not usually write for the social studies education audience, is to say something about democratic education. I accept the assignment with enthusiasm, not only because of my interest in the theme as a teacher educator and former social studies teacher but also because of the importance it holds at this historic moment, when the rhetoric of democracy is used by many for all sorts of contradictory ends.[2] We are living in a time when many citizens with divergent political views are doubting the viability of the democratic system in the United States. More and more people are expressing deep reservations about the legitimacy of the two-party system—a system in which very small portions of the eligible electorate continue to elect presidents, a system that all too often allows special interest lobbyists to have more say than the average citizen in who governs.

It is also a time when the purposes of education have come under considerable scrutiny as educators struggle to adapt to changing social, cultural, and economic conditions. The perennial tensions between the individual and the community that have shaped educational discourse for much of our history continue to challenge us as we educate for and in a multicultural society.

For many educators, the discourses of democracy and education go hand in hand. We believe that it is through education that we create

democratic culture and that it is within a democratic culture that education may flourish, carrying on the Enlightenment tradition of critical-
mindedness and even rebelliousness. It is with this legacy in mind that I
write this essay, for I wonder what has happened to the critical spirit that
education is supposed to nurture? How can educators reignite that spirit
in our students? How can we challenge ourselves and them to think anew
about the assumptions that inform our taken-for-granted views of democratic society? What gets in the way of that goal? What are we afraid of?

What Have You Learned in School Today,
Dear Little Girl of Mine?[3]

As a way into this essay, I want to recount some of my formative educational experiences that have had a profound effect on how I have come
to think about politics and history in general and about democracy and
education in particular. Like Benjamin Barber, I embrace a concept of
democracy that is a participatory process requiring the involvement of
individuals within community. I want a "strong democracy" that "revital-
izes citizenship . . . [through] a form of government in which all of the
people govern themselves in at least some public matters at least some of
the time."[4] I am no longer satisfied with conceptualizing democracy as an
abstract thing or product, defined and protected by constitutional law.
Nor can I be content with the way representative democracy has served
me and countless other U.S. citizens, particularly those of us from "the
margins."

     Growing up as the youngest daughter of a working-class family in a
small town in upstate New York during the 1950s, I could not see many
visions of a future that would look all that different from the lives of my
mother and older sisters. As much as I loved them, I did not want to get
married early, have several children, and work my fingers to the bone, especially as my mother had. So I made a decision in second grade that
school was going to be my "out." I began plotting my escape route
through college with the help of some women teachers who spotted my
talent and determination. My family was not thrilled with the direction I
was taking, insisting that there would be no money for me to go to college. But by the time I graduated from high school in 1967, the state university system, under the direction of the governor at that time, Nelson
Rockefeller, had expanded, as had government-subsidized loan programs for higher education. History was on my side.[5]

     With little guidance from my high school counselor and none from my parents, I chose the State University College at Cortland, ostensibly for its nationally known program in physical education; I had been an outstanding scholar-athlete. The more compelling reason for this choice was that it would alleviate my parents' anxiety: it was only a two-hour drive from home, it was "safe" because many classmates from my high school went there, and it would set me on a track to become a teacher, one of the only professions my parents thought "useful" for girls.[6] As excellent as the program was, however, my stint in physical education was short-lived. It was my course work in political theory, history, economics, and geography that ignited my desire to become a teacher. Up to that point, I had not been at all keen on that career direction but saw few other avenues for me that would also keep me connected to my family.

This academic direction also opened the way for me to think more about what it meant to be engaged in social change, expanding the concept of citizen to mean someone who took seriously his or her role as a maker of rather than a spectator of democratic society at the local and national levels. Until those critical political theory courses, the idea of citizen was an abstract entity, a dead concept that harked back to the Greek polls in most unfavorable ways, particularly as seen through the eyes of a young woman who could not "see" herself in the polis because she was not allowed in.

But most important of all, my new course of study let me know what I had not learned in high school. I found myself asking all too often, "Why haven't I heard this before?" I still remember my first undergraduate political science course in 1967. Reading Charles Beard's *An Economic Interpretation of the Constitution of the United States*,[7] I saw for the first time the underside[8] of our democratic tradition: the *constitution* was clearly not written for me, a girl from an unpropertied family. Nor was it written for black people. The Beard text startled me into challenging some of my unquestioned assumptions about liberal democracy in the United States. For example, I never really thought it possible that inequality was structured into our system. I just thought it was an accident that some people were better off than others and that, in time, all would be well for everyone, even me.

These challenges to my political understandings were bolstered by economic analyses that critiqued capitalism and the "leisure class"; by readings in the social history of the United States that filled in important gaps about the experiences of Native Americans, African Americans, working people, and women; and by participation in pedagogically innovative cultural and political geography courses that broadened my perspective on the global effects of imperialism. I was seeing a picture of the United States that was completely different from the one I had been shown in high school.

With all this to launch me, as well as the critical understanding of the educational system that I was getting from my educational foundations professors, I was on my way to becoming a critical pedagogue.[9] Naive or not, I was committed to teaching an inclusive truth about our history—a truth that encompassed the possibilities as well as the problems of our democratic tradition and documented our national successes along with the persistent effects of racism, classism, sexism, and imperialism.[10]

Teaching against the Grain

The first test of this commitment to speaking truth to power came in 1970, when the United States invaded Cambodia, an action that precipitated events at Kent State, Jackson State, and subsequent student strikes in universities all over the country. I was a student teacher during this volatile time and became acutely aware of how complex the duties and responsibilities of public school teachers were. I also had to take notice, in a much more self-interested way, of the power[11] that educational institutions could wield over those who did not conform to their political agendas, and there were political agendas. If I went out on strike with student colleagues on campus, I would most assuredly flunk student teaching. I decided, along with the rest of my cohort of student teachers in the program, to keep my commitment to classroom teaching and use it, where appropriate, as an opportunity to discuss Vietnam and U.S. involvement in Southeast Asia.

Even with this responsible—in our view—decision, I still almost failed because my particular college supervisor, once she learned of our political activism, thought all thirty-five of us were "inadequate" teachers. We were inadequate even though we had been "excelling" before then and were all leaders in an urban education project that had as its goal teacher-directed school-based reform. (This project was ahead of its time; it anticipated site-based management by a decade.) Only with the intervention of a sympathetic college administrator were we given a fair assessment. After another year as a senior intern in this innovative program, which sought to empower teachers to create better teaching and learning communities, I graduated with a K–12 certification in elementary and secondary social studies education. But attached to this hard-earned credential was a chastened view of just how democratic schools were, particularly for the professionals who practiced within them.

My first paid teaching job in a small, rural community in central New York was the second instance when the intersection of politics and teaching put my career in jeopardy. Even though I thought my teaching practices fell within the conservative norms of the school, I found myself called down to the principal's or superintendent's office more frequently than my students. It seems that my superiors thought I was "insubordinate" for not asking permission to make changes in the curriculum, changes that seemed quite modest to me. My offenses included encouraging a student newspaper as a way to foster reading and writing. The students had chosen *The Revolution* as the name for the paper. The name of the paper and not the paper itself seemed to be the real offense because it indicated more rebelliousness (albeit symbolic) than the administrators were willing to tolerate.

Another of my transgressions was inviting a member of the community who had built a geodesic dome on his property to speak on Earth Day about his views on solar energy and ecology. This speaker was considered a local hippie because of his ponytail. Again, I was done in by my association with symbolic rebelliousness; I would not be a good role model for students.

In retrospect, these acts seem rather harmless, but in 1972 they were too much for this particular school. *I* was too much. I was seen as a subversive. In their eyes, I was subverting the authority of the principal and superintendent. My professional discretion was not valued. Curriculum decision making rested in the hands of the administrators.

Just as important to this small-town school, I was perceived as undermining the common values of this community.[12] They did not want an outsider shaking up that consensus in any way, and "they" included many of my fellow teachers. Difference was not tolerated in this school system. The situation reminded me of the slogan antiwar demonstrators were taunted with in the late sixties: "Love it or leave it." In this first teaching job, I was supposed to love the way things were done or get out. I left before they had a chance to "leave" me.

The Shifting Terrain of the Social Studies Teacher

Things have changed some since my first years as a teacher. Many of the curricular gaps have been filled; the histories of women, people of color, and working people, for example, are more prominent in texts. But all too often they are given short shrift, trivialized, or relegated to the margins at the end of the chapter.[13]

At the same time, even as the rhetoric of educational reform sings the praises of "site-based management," teachers endure increasing constraints on real participation in curricular decisions. These constraints emanate from the school administration, as well as from local school boards that take their cues from an ever more volatile national political climate.[14]

Teaching social studies is challenging because of the nature of the subject matter taught, and it is complicated by the effects of professionalization, with its rhetoric of neutrality. In much of our professional socialization, teachers of all grades learn that we are supposed to remain neutral conveyors of information. Teachers who want to explore complex political and social issues, especially issues on which they have strong views, risk accusations of being too political, of indoctrinating students, or, in today's political parlance, of pushing political correctness. This is not to suggest that teachers should be unconcerned with possible abuses of their position as authorities. But what is lost in all of the accusations about indoctrination and correctness is the point that all positions have some ideological content, even those that appear most benign or neutral. What is defined as the moderate or mainstream position of most teachers often masks deep ideological investments that are transmitted as the "received" or "selective" traditions.[15]

The challenge facing teachers is to help students critically analyze the evidence and arguments before them and make available as much ammunition as possible. To do this, we need to challenge our own selective knowledge if we are going to enable students to become engaged and empowered learners and engaged and empowered citizens. We have to ask ourselves how, "from a whole possible area of past and present, certain meanings and practices are chosen for emphasis, certain other meanings and practices are neglected and excluded."[16] And we need to be prepared for the challenges that come our way as students investigate our role in perpetuating this "selective tradition." We will have to face the Wendy Kohlis in our classes who find out, somehow, that things are not the way they were taught, that there really is no Santa Claus.

BEING CRITICAL ABOUT DEMOCRACY AND OTHER RECEIVED TRADITIONS

Risky Business

What does taking a critical stance as a teacher have to do with democracy and education? What does critical pedagogy have to do with democratic education? To answer that, I want to return to what I call my "there is no Santa Claus" experience as a first-year college student. Why did I have to wait until I was finished with high school to read more complete (and critical) accounts of U.S. history and culture? Why was I denied access to my own history as a working-class girl? Why had I not been taught to be a more critical reader and interpreter of history?

Certainly there are many reasons for this, but based on all my years as a teacher and scholar, the one that I have come to believe is that school as a system is not designed to educate students, its future citizens, to be critical-minded, contrary to the rhetoric of our Jeffersonian heritage. Doris Lessing offers insight into this when she says:

> Ideally, what should be said to every child, repeatedly, throughout his or her school life is something like this: "You are in the process of becoming indoctrinated. We have not yet evolved a system of education that is not a system of indoctrination. We are sorry, but it is the best we can do. What you are being taught here is an amalgam of current prejudice and choices of this particular culture. The slightest look at history will show how impermanent these must be. You are being taught by people who have been able to accommodate a self-perpetuating system. Those of you who are more robust and individual than others will be encouraged to find ways of educating yourself—educating your own judgment. Those that stay must remember, always and all the time, that they are being molded and patterned to fit into the narrow and particular needs of this particular society."[17]

A considerable body of research supports the position that schooling is needed to reproduce the values and beliefs of the dominant culture and to track people into particular economic and social roles within a market economy.[18] Other theorists who go even further suggest that the way schools are organized and the kinds of processes used to examine, classify, and control students make the end goals of schooling normalization, conformity, and docility, not a critically engaged and informed citizenry.[19]

For those of us who see ourselves as extending the Deweyan tradition of progressive education, this vision of the current educational landscape is a bitter pill to swallow. Accepting even a mild version of these critiques poses a dilemma for educators who want to promote democracy. If we continue with our work, are we not implicated in the kind of cultural reproduction, domination, distortion, and normalization these critics identify? At the same time, to abandon our work would leave young people even more at the mercy of a destructive process.[20] What are we to do? Is there a way out?

I have no easy answers to these questions, but I am sure that we can no longer afford to ignore these criticisms. Nor can we ignore the evidence that seems to indict our democratic institutions and processes for their lack of vitality. Regardless of a person's political commitments, there seems to be just cause for taking a good hard look at the kind of society we have and how we can revitalize it.[21] The situation demands that we become radical in our thinking and acting and take the risks that are worth taking.

Just what are those risks and for whom? For many teachers, they are not all that different from risks I faced as a student teacher. With the resurgence of right-wing politics and propaganda and its emerging reactionary agenda, the United States of 2000 is in some ways far more repressive and regressive than it was when I came of age politically in the 1960s. Regardless of the humanist twist that is put on the role of teacher, and regardless of the individual commitment to young people that most good teachers have, the bottom line is that public school teachers are agents of the state. As such, they must carry out the policies of the state or risk losing their jobs. Administrators and even colleagues create a kind of surveillance[22] team to make sure the normative boundaries of schools remain intact. The surveillance occurs at many levels and in a variety of apparently harmless and even well-meaning forms, ranging from peer coaching and outcome-based education to the overall process of professionalization. This process ensures that no one strays too far from the acceptable, dominant discourse of teaching. The fear of being labeled unprofessional, which is instilled in teachers in subtle and not so subtle ways from the start of our professional education, is the coercive element. (Remember my fear as a student teacher?) If not for this fear, teachers would be far more willing to take risks than they are now.

As a corollary to risk taking, teachers must be more alert to the subtle disciplining practices exerted through educational curriculum and pedagogy.[23] We need to understand how even progressive pedagogy regulates the behavior of the student and of the teacher through the examination and classification of people. Drawing on Foucault's notion of governmentality, James Donald argues that the commonplace understandings of psychological development and socialization that inform educational discourse "are better understood as technologies of government."[24] These practices have as their aim "to turn children into good citizens whose competencies, tastes, and consciences would be attuned to broader socio-political objectives," objectives of the state.[25]

Teachers need to be reminded that surveillance occurs not only from those in traditional positions of power at the macro level within the system, such as superintendents, school boards, and state education departments, but also at the micro level from students, parents, and other colleagues. It is risky business putting out information that does not paint a rosy picture of our country, that does not support the cultural myths that many depend on to make sense of the world. Teachers who challenge the received knowledge, who teach against the grain, who give voice to "subjugated knowledges"[26] are not always popular messengers. Even teachers who do not lose their jobs could be viewed by students and other co-workers as weird or even dangerous. The times require us to have the courage to be dangerous, at the same time recognizing that there are differential dangers. Not all teachers are at equal risk; much depends on how you are positioned, on your identity(ies), on your particular situation.

DANGEROUS KNOWLEDGE

Democracy in the School and Classroom

What must we be prepared to share with our students if we want to keep our commitment to democratic education and to educating about democracy? One place to start is to look at the school itself. Progressive educators like John Dewey, Ella Flagg Young, and Jane Addams nearly a century ago argued that it was a contradiction to educate students for their future as citizens in a democracy in schools that were decidedly undemocratic institutions.[27] Even with various attempts, such as the progressive movement, to transform schools to be more child-centered or more democratic, schools persist in, with, and by their hierarchical, authoritarian structures.[28] Not only are they undemocratic for students but they are relatively undemocratic for teachers as well.

If we think of democracy in terms of the way decisions are made, schools are a far cry from the (racist, sexist, and classist) Athenian ideal of direct democracy. I do not think schools fare much better as democratic institutions when using the formal representative model that has become synonymous with contemporary life.[29] Most educational decisions are made in a top-down way, at the upper echelons of the educational bureaucracy. Teachers do have some say over certain decisions in their classrooms and generally have elected representatives to speak for them in their professional organizations. But the level of substantive democratic participation in schools has become increasingly limited for teachers and even more so for students.

Except for the ritualized participation of certain groups of students in student government, most schools are organized to minimize the student's role in decision making. Certainly, students have virtually no say over the content of the curriculum, over how their time is structured, and over how they are grouped or tracked to learn. In this arena, adults are complicit in what has come to be called "adultism," the systematic oppression of young people. Alice Miller has written powerfully on this subject. She laments that "all advice that pertains to raising children betrays more or less clearly the numerous, variously clothed needs of the *adult*. Fulfillment of these needs not only discourages the child's development but actually prevents it."[30]

Very few adults, including many well-meaning teachers, really take young people seriously and treat them with the respect that is their due. If we did, schools could no longer continue to function in their present form; we could no longer teach as we do. Taking young people seriously requires adults to listen to them in ways to which adults are not generally accustomed.[31]

Miller is not very hopeful that this can happen. From her "antipedagogic" perspective, she sees all pedagogy as "poisonous."[32] The poison affects upbringing to the depressing degree that

> When children are trained, they learn how to train others in turn. Children who are lectured to, learn how to lecture; if they are admonished, they learn how to admonish; if scolded, they learn how to scold; if ridiculed, they learn how to ridicule; if humiliated, they learn how to humiliate; if their psyche is killed, they will learn how to kill—the only question is who will be killed: oneself, others, or both.[33]

I think that this cycle can stop, but only if adults are committed to doing the kind of emotional work necessary to heal the wounds inflicted on children by the close (hurt) adults in their lives. We must also let young people speak for themselves. Adults need to stop speaking for them; adults need to allow them to create spaces to exercise their own voices in their own ways. But this is a dangerous pedagogical stance. As Giles Deleuze claims: "If the protests of children were heard in kindergartens, their questions were attended to, it would be enough to explode the entire education system."[34]

I think the educational system is already exploding right before our eyes, especially in urban areas, where it has been systematically abandoned as a result of classist and racist policies and practices. Many of our young people are trying desperately to get our attention.[35] Why not give it to them? What have we got to lose? I think we have a great deal to gain.

Different Forms of Democracy

Reconstructing school to be more democratic requires more than changing the structures and processes for decision making. It also requires us to teach about democracy in a more truthful, more complete way. Generally, even in the best classrooms, democratic theory and practice are represented by a "thin," liberal rendition, "one whose democratic values are prudential—and thus provisional, optional, and conditional—means to exclusively individualistic and private ends."[36] This orientation to democracy as a system that protects the rights of individuals is prevalent in contemporary high school social studies textbooks. Here is a typical example of how *democracy* is defined in one such text:

> Democracy is a philosophy of government that recognizes the right of the people to take part directly or indirectly in controlling their political institutions. The word *democratic* describes such a government. It also describes practices of society as a whole that enlarge opportunities for people and that place emphasis on the dignity of the individual.[37]

This definition may be good for openers, but just as a point of departure. Our students need to be encouraged to ask critical questions of this portrayal of our system. For example, why in the United States do we insist on separating political rights from economic rights in our democratic discourse? Why is democratic theory so embedded in the received liberal tradition that it becomes unnatural—even subversive and unpatriotic—to mention economic rights in the same breath as democracy? Why are our students not encouraged to ask about the rights and responsibilities of multinational corporations vis-à-vis communities? How democratic is it for corporations to make decisions as private entities when corporate decisions have significant public effects on the well-being of millions of citizens living in communities? Are these questions too dangerous to ask? Too dangerous for whom? For what?

Just what kind of democratic theory(ies) are our students reading? Do they even know about the many conflicting views on what democracy is within just the Western liberal tradition? Now that the Soviet Union can no longer be conveniently positioned as our political nemesis, is it not the time to forgo the dualisms of "democratic" and "totalitarian"? And what of the tendency to collapse socialism into totalitarianism, and capitalism into democracy? With this in mind, I was struck by an entry in another high school social studies textbook that attempted to distinguish socialism from totalitarianism.

> Many Americans equate socialism with the communism practiced in the closed societies of the Soviet Union and Eastern Europe. But there is a difference. Although communism in theory was supposed to result in a "withering away" of the state, communist governments in practice tend toward totalitarianism, controlling both political and social life through a dominant party organization. Some socialist governments, however, practice *democratic socialism.* They guarantee civil liberties (such as freedom of speech, freedom of religion) and allow their citizens to determine the extent of government activity through free elections and competitive political parties. *Outside the United States, socialism is not an inherently bad thing* [emphasis added]. In fact, the governments of Britain, Sweden, Germany, and France—among other democracies—have at times since World War II been avowedly "socialist." In the United States, however, socialism has such a bad connotation that Reverend Jesse Jackson initially asked the Democratic Socialists of America, who were preparing to support him for the presidency in 1988, not to support him. Ultimately the group did endorse Jackson for his position on economic issues, at the same time noting that he was *not* a Socialist.[38]

Do the authors mean to say that socialism is an inherently bad thing inside the United States? Why not use this section of the textbook to pose critical questions about why "many Americans equate socialism with communism" or why a presidential candidate would be so frightened of being labeled a socialist?

Perhaps the time has come to explore as well the taken-for-granted assumption in the United States that the United States is the most democratic democracy or best democracy in the world. Even if we bracket for a moment the uncomfortable question, "Can a capitalist system be democratic?" and just stick to mainstream political theory, we need to ask of ourselves and our students what other forms of government may offer "the people," as Henry Graff requires, more "direct and indirect" control over their political institutions. Certainly, proportional parliamentary systems can allow more minority voices than our flawed two-party system. Why is it so dangerous to let young people in on these other models? Are we still, indirectly, teaching them to love it or leave it?

What Is a Citizen?

Another aspect of our received tradition of liberal democratic humanism that needs critical attention is that of the abstract, generalized "citizen." As I learned the painful way in my first political science class, those protected by the Constitution did not include women and black people. Just as Marxist theory was able to subvert the notion of the citizen by a class analysis and its critique of bourgeois liberalism, certain feminists and postcolonial writers have extended or revised that critique of the concept by looking at its race- and gendered-based construction. As Anne Phillips makes clear:

> The feminist challenge to the abstract, degendered individual has combined with the earlier critique of those who took class as the only interesting divide to usher in a new politics based around heterogeneity and difference. Not just "the" sexual difference: the most innovative of contemporary feminist writing moves beyond a binary opposition between male and female towards a theory of multiple differences. The myth of homogeneity is then seen as sustaining a complex of unequal and oppressive relations.[39]

No longer can we continue to make mythic the individual or the citizen in democratic society through our disembodied, disembedded abstract language. Citizens have particular identities; they are female, male, black, white, poor, rich. And the ramifications of these different identities affect the experience of being a citizen.

Feminist theory has also challenged the public-private split that undergirds our perception of citizenship. Nel Noddings, for one, has argued that the concept of citizen should be expanded to include private activities like homemaking and that what are now considered activities and relationships in the private domain should be moved to center stage for public view.[40]

In the United States, a society that is profoundly affected by institutionalized racism, sexism, classism, adultism, and the oppression of gay and lesbian people must begin to investigate the concepts that permeate its political theory and practices. Anne Phillips reminds us that "democracy implies equality, but when it is superimposed on an unequal society, it allows some people to count for more than others."[41] It is time that we, along with our students, examine the underside of our democracy and look at the effects of oppression on and within it. I believe that by facing our history and our present squarely we will be able to create the kind of society that our people—all of our people—deserve. To do this, we need to begin in the classroom, one of the few places left in our malled-over communities where it is still possible for a public to participate within a public space, albeit in space often marked by segregation and division.

EDUCATING FOR A DIFFERENT DEMOCRACY: A DEMOCRACY OF DIFFERENCE

The Classroom as a Laboratory of and for Democracy

Social critic Manning Marable argues that people of color are radically redefining the nature of democracy. We assert that democratic government is empty and meaningless without active social justice and cultural diversity. Multicultural political democracy means that this country was not built by and for only one group, Western Europeans; that our country does not have only one language, English; or only one religion, Christianity; or only one economic philosophy, corporate capitalism. Multicultural democracy means that the leadership within our society should reflect the richness, colors, and diversity expressed in the lives of all our people. Multicultural democracy demands new types of power sharing and the reallocation of resources necessary to create economic and social development for those who have been systematically excluded and denied.[42]

Are public educators up to the challenge? Public schools provide both problems and possibilities for an emerging democracy of difference. Instead of the obsolete organizing metaphor of the melting pot that infused twentieth-century educational institutions with the values of Americanization (read "homogenization"), today's imagery must be able to refigure diversity and plurality in relation to oneness by stressing our differences in the midst of our commonalities. A liberal reading of difference gave us various forms of multicultural education that celebrate and manage differences. I want to suggest, along with other feminists like Elizabeth Ellsworth, Patti Lather, and Deborah Britzman, that the celebration may be premature.[43] We need to take a look at differences to see "what difference difference makes." And that may mean unleashing some unpleasant, even some unwanted, issues in our classrooms.

Taking differences seriously to see what difference they really make and to whom, we must look at the long-term effects of institutionalized oppression. We must see differences as cultural constructs that reflect social position and that contain powerful social meanings. Being "black" or "female" is not simply about being a different color or different gender. In a society of structured inequalities, being different in these ways means being less than. To challenge the underside of our liberal-democratic traditions and practices, we must look head-on at the systems of oppression that go hand in glove with them. And to look directly at them means we must be prepared to see, hear, and feel the emotions that accompany these forms of oppression, both institutionalized and internalized. The celebration may have to be delayed in some cases until some of the righteous indignation and buried pain can be aired. That is scary stuff for most people, even for those of us who do the airing. As bell hooks reminds us, "Many teachers are disturbed by the political implications of a multicultural education because they fear losing control."[44] She goes on to say that "the unwillingness to approach teaching from a standpoint that includes awareness of race, sex, and class is often rooted in the fear that classrooms will be uncontrollable, that emotions and passions will not be contained."[45]

Classrooms are not known for being places to air conflict and emotions safely, and teachers are not known for encouraging such airings. But if we are serious about educating for democracy, and about educating democratically, then we need to be serious about differences within our classrooms and be prepared for the consequences of taking those differences seriously. As I have said elsewhere, this

> is not just about *including* more voices or perspectives in the conversation. These newly included voices may be amplified by anger, even rage. They may be diminished by fear, embarrassment, or inadequacy. And they may be filled with grief and grievance.[46]

What is required are pedagogical strategies that move beyond the liberal and even critical traditions that have informed our teaching practices. I think here of the postcritical approaches that make problematic the emancipatory education of Freire, as well as certain critical-feminists.[47] Without rehearsing their characteristics, we know that most critical pedagogies rely heavily on dialogue and the presumption that if we all talk enough together, we will be able to come to understand each other. But much teaching involving dialogue obscures the multiple identities each person-in-dialogue holds. For example, I am not just a woman. I am a white woman raised working class with a particular sexual orientation. At any given moment in a dialogue, I have to ask myself, "Who is the I who is speaking?" Multiple identities or subjectivities dramatically complicate the process of dialogue. Another complication is the acknowledgment of the myth of the "rational individual in dialogue." We all bring many unexpressed hurts to any conversation, hurts that stem from systematic forms of oppression. Fear of expressing some of these hurts keeps us from really creating truly democratic spaces, spaces that recognize and validate differences. Elizabeth Ellsworth has suggested that, to do this, we need to move "from a concept of eventually unified dialogue to the construction of 'strategies in context' for dealing with the unsaid and unsayable present within classrooms."[48]

To engage in such a pedagogy of difference would require more than the validation of differences within a given classroom. It would also need to offer the processes necessary to overcome the emotional effects of oppressive conditioning that are generated by our differences, pedagogical strategies that would allow a plurality of voices—in a range of timbres— to emerge in a classroom, voices that may not be welcomed equally by everyone in the room. As Deborah Britzman has pointed out, it is both imperative and difficult to create classroom space to "say unpopular things."[49] These unpopular things include addressing racism head-on. Britzman offers direction from the cultural theorist Stuart Hall:

What I am talking about here are the problems of handling the racist time bomb and doing so adequately so that we can connect with our students' experience[s] and can therefore be sure of defusing it.[50]

After the O.J. Simpson case, certainly we can no longer deny the deep divisions over race that exist in the United States. And those divisions are present in our classrooms with our students. They are also present in us. I agree with Stuart Hall "that [racial] experience has to surface in the classroom even if it's pretty horrendous to hear: better to hear it than not, because what you don't hear you can't engage with."[51]

To address racism, teachers are going to have to prepare themselves. We are going to have to see ourselves as raced, classed, and gendered:

"teacher," like "citizen," is no longer a disembedded, disembodied category or position. Contrary to the rhetoric of professionalism, we are not neutral or neutered dispensers of knowledge and information. We have been on the receiving end of oppression ourselves. We cannot help having internalized some of this. And it shows in our teaching. How I have come to understand historical and political history has to be affected by my own identities, my own experiences, my own subjective responses to the world. We must acknowledge this and deal with our own racism, classism, and sexism if we are to create opportunities for our students to do so together. I still believe that

> if we are to create classrooms that are democratic, non-coercive spaces welcoming multicultural diversity—differences—we must have teachers who are imaginative and courageous. [We] must be able and willing to endure conflict and anger, tears and pain, unpredictable directions. [We] must be committed to [our] own "unlearning." And [we] must be well-informed enough about historical circumstances to help the children understand what's at stake in it all . . . for all of us.[52]

To do this, we will have to overcome fear, the fear that keeps us from "speaking truth to power" and the fear that prevents us from facing ourselves honestly.

NOTES

[1]I refer here to the trenchant critique about our "thin democracy" that Benjamin Barber makes in *Strong Democracy: Participatory Politics for a New Age* (Berkeley: University of California Press, 1984).

[2]I think here, for example, of the conservative agenda of the "Contract with America" that purports to have the rights of all individuals at heart, yet there has been an explicit lack of public debate on important policy decisions such as medical aid for the elderly and poor. I think of the much-publicized militia groups, who act undemocratically in the name of "giving government back to the people." At the other end of the political spectrum, I see advocacy groups such as Act Up demand urgent policy changes in AIDS research through an "in your face" confrontational political strategy.

[3]The name of a political folk song sung by Pete Seeger and others.

[4]Barber, *Strong Democracy,* p. xiv.

[5]When I reflect on the importance of low-interest student loans for working-class and poor students, I shudder at the impact current federal cuts are having on the lives of so many students today. I am afraid history is no longer on their side.

[6]Not only was teaching a "useful" vocation for girls, making a college education worth it, but to my family it meant that I would come home and teach in a local school.

[7]Charles Beard, *An Economic Interpretation of the Constitution of the United States* (New York: Macmillan, 1960).

[8]See Maxine Greene's *Dialectic of Freedom* (New York: Teachers College Press, 1988) for an eloquently developed account of the underside of freedom and democracy in the United States.

[9]At this point in my development, the work of Brazilian educator Paulo Freire, the author of *Pedagogy of the Oppressed* (New York: Herder and Herder, 1970) had not yet been taken up in full force in educational circles in the United States.

[10]James Loewen has written a marvelous book, *Lies My Teacher Told Me* (New York: New Press, 1995), which asks what has gone wrong in the teaching of history to our high school students. He dedicates it to "all American history teachers who teach against their textbooks."

[11]The power in this case was the educational establishment as I knew it at the time.

[12]This emphasis on core or common values anticipates the national debate of the 1980s, sparked by the publication of such books as E. D. Hirsch's *Cultural Literacy* (Boston: Houghton Mifflin, 1987).

[13]See, for example, Nel Noddings, "Social Studies and Feminism," *Theory and Research in Social Education* 20 (Summer 1992): 231.

[14]I think, for example, of the campaign waged by the Christian Coalition to elect right-wing ideologues to local school boards with the express purpose of imposing a conservative social and political agenda on the curriculum.

[15]See, for example, the work of Michael Apple, *Ideology and Curriculum* (New York: Routledge, 1990), who draws heavily on Raymond Williams, a British cultural theorist.

[16]Raymond Williams, as quoted in Apple, *Ideology and Curriculum,* p. 6.

[17]Doris Lessing, *The Golden Notebooks* (New York: McGraw Hill, 1962), pp. xxiii–xxiv.

[18]I will not restate all of the research on the social and cultural production and reproduction that occurs in schools, but I encourage reading it. See, for example, the work of Jean Anyon, Madeleine Arnot, Michael Apple, Henry Giroux, Peter McLaren, Joel Spring, and Kathleen Wciler, to name a few.

[19]See the incisive work of Michel Foucault, *Discipline and Punish* (New York: Vintage Press, 1979) for his "genealogical" research on institutions like schools and prisons.

[20]I want to make it clear that individual teachers in schools across the country have had success, in spite of professional and political constraints, at educating students to analyze critically and to become engaged, informed citizens. At

the same time, I think it is a limited kind of success, compared with what is at stake in the big picture.

[21]The many political theorists besides Benjamin Barber who are grappling with these questions include Robert Bellah, Seyla Benhabib, Ann Ferguson, Jane Mansbridge, Carole Pateman, Michael Sandel, Michael Walzer, and Iris Young.

[22]I think here of the analysis Michel Foucault makes of schools in his book *Discipline and Punish.* See his chapters "The Means of Correct Training" and "Panopticism" (pp. 170–228) for an excellent account.

[23]Once again, I refer you to Foucault's work on "disciplinary practices" in *Discipline and Punish,* as well as two contemporary theorists who have extended Foucault's work to educational theory: *Sentimental Education* by James Donald (London: Verso, 1992) and *Schoolgirl Fictions* by Valerie Walkerdine (London: Verso, 1990).

[24]Donald, *Sentimental Education,* p. 47.

[25]Ibid.

[26]That knowledge identified by Foucault and others as that which is excluded from dominant discourse.

[27]See, for example, John Dewey, *Democracy and Education* (New York: Macmillan, 1916/1944), and Jane Addams, *Democracy and Social Ethics* (New York: Macmillan, 1920).

[28]Some interesting research has analyzed the discursive practices of progressive education from a poststructuralist point of view that disputes our taken-for-granted notions of child-centeredness and progressive pedagogy. See the work of Valerie Walkerdine and James Donald.

[29]James Marshall, "Democracy and Education" in *What Is Education?* (New Zealand: Dunmore Press, 1981).

[30]Alice Miller, *For Your Own Good: Hidden Cruelty in Child-rearing and the Roots of Violence* (New York: Farrar, Straus, Giroux, 1983), p. 97.

[31]It is not our fault that we do not treat young people with dignity and respect. Most of us were never treated that way either. I think here once again of Alice Miller's powerful work in this area.

[32]Miller, *For Your Own Good,* p. 96.

[33]Ibid., p. 98.

[34]As quoted in James Marshall's unpublished manuscript, "Foucault's Technologies of Power: Implications for Education," 1989.

[35]They often do it by not giving us their attention. I think, for example, of Luann Johnson in the film and book *Dangerous Minds.* She needed to get her students' attention to show them she cared.

[36]Barber, *Strong Democracy,* p. 4.

[37]Henry Graff, *America: The Glorious Republic* (Boston: Houghton Mifflin, 1985), p. 264.

[38]Kenneth Janda, Jeffrey Berry, and Jerry Goldman, *The Challenge of Democracy: Government in America,* 2d ed. (Boston: Houghton, Mifflin, 1989), p. 24.

[39]See Anne Phillips, *Democracy and Difference* (University Park: Pennsylvania State University Press, 1993), p. 90.

[40]Noddings, "Social Studies and Feminism," pp. 234–235.

[41]Phillips, *Democracy and Difference,* p. 91.

[42]Manning Marable, *Black America: Multicultural Democracy in the Age of Clarence Thomas and David Duke* (New Jersey: Open Magazine Press, 1992), p. 13.

[43]See, for example, Deborah Britzman, Kelvin A. Santiago-Valles, Gladys M. Jiménez-Muños, and Laura M. Lamash, "Dusting Off the Erasures: Race, Gender and Pedagogy," *Education and Society* 9 (1991): 88–99; Elizabeth Ellsworth, "Why Doesn't This Feel Empowering? Working through the Repressive Myths of Critical Pedagogy," *Harvard Educational Review* 59 (1989): 297–324; or Patti Lather, "Post-Critical Pedagogics: A Feminist Reading," *Education and Society* 9 (1991): 100–111.

[44]bell hooks, *Teaching to Transgress* (New York: Routledge, 1994), p. 35.

[45]Ibid., p. 39.

[46]Wendy Kohli, "Educating for Emancipatory Rationality," in *Critical Conversations in Philosophy of Education,* ed. W. Kohli (New York: Routledge, 1995), p. 110.

[47]See, for example, Lather, "Post-Critical Pedagogics," pp. 100–111.

[48]As quoted by Lather, "Post-Critical Pedagogics," p. 102.

[49]Britzman, et al., "Dusting Off the Erasures," p. 98.

[50]Stuart Hall, as quoted in ibid.

[51]Ibid.

[52]Kohli, "Postmodernism, Critical Theory and the 'New' Pedagogics: What's at Stake in the Discourse?" *Education and Society* 9 (1991): 45.

CHAPTER 3

Redrawing the Lines
The Case against Traditional
Social Studies Instruction

E. WAYNE ROSS

There is a widely held belief in our society that activities that strengthen or maintain the status quo are neutral or at least nonpolitical, and activities that critique or challenge the status quo are "political" and many times inappropriate. For example, for a company to advertise its product as a good thing, something consumers should buy, is not viewed as a political act. If a consumer group takes out an advertisement to charge that the company's product is not good, perhaps even harmful, however, this is often understood as political action.

This type of thinking permeates our society, particularly when it comes to schooling, teaching, and social studies education. "Stick to the facts." "Guard against bias." "Maintain neutrality." These are admonitions or goals expressed by some social studies teachers when I ask them about keys to successful teaching. Many of these same teachers (and teacher educators) conceive of their role as designing and teaching courses to ensure that students are prepared to function non-disruptively in the society as it exists. This goal is thought to be desirable, in part because it strengthens the status quo and is seen as an unbiased or neutral position. Many of these same teachers view their work in school as apolitical, a matter of effectively covering the curriculum, imparting academic skills, and preparing students for whatever high-stakes tests they might face. Often these teachers have attended teacher education programs designed to ensure that teachers were prepared to adapt to the status quo in schools.

Anyone who has paid attention to recent debates on school reform efforts (particularly social studies curriculum reform) knows that schooling is a decidedly political enterprise.[1] The question in teaching (as well as in teacher education and school reform) is not whether to advocate but the nature and extent of one's advocacy: "The question is not whether to encourage a particular social vision in the classroom but what kind of social vision it will be."[2]

It is widely believed among educators that neutrality, objectivity, and absence of bias are largely the same thing and always good when it comes to teaching social studies. However, consider the following: Neutrality *is* a political category, that is, not supporting any factions in a dispute. Holding a neutral stance in a conflict is no more likely to ensure rightness or objectivity than any other stance, and often it is a sign of ignorance of the issues. Absence of bias in an area is not absence of convictions in an area; thus *neutrality is not objectivity.* To be objective is to be unbiased or unprejudiced. People are often misled to think that anyone who comes into a discussion with strong views about an issue cannot be unprejudiced. The key question is whether the views are justified.[3]

The ideology of neutrality that dominates current practices in social studies education (at the elementary and secondary levels, as well as in teacher education and research) is sustained by theories of knowledge and conceptions of democracy that constrain rather than widen civic participation in our society. In this chapter, I examine how the theory of knowledge and conceptions of democracy that support what has been called "traditional social studies instruction" function to obscure political-ideological consequences of mainstream social studies. These consequences include conceptions of the learner as passive, democratic citizenship as a spectator project, and, ultimately, the maintenance of status quo inequalities in society. Before venturing into an analysis of traditional social studies, we must explore the differences, even among progressive educators, over issues of education and indoctrination. The debates among the social reconstructionists in the 1930s, which are explored in the following section, can be instructive for us in understanding issues of advocacy in classrooms and schools today.

EDUCATION AS INDOCTRINATION?

The principal obstacle to achieving democratic education (and thus a democratic society), according to John Dewey, is the powerful alliance of class privilege with philosophies of education that sharply divide the mind and body, theory and practice, culture and utility.[4] In Dewey's day, and still today, prevailing educational practice is the actualization of the philosophy of profoundly antidemocratic thinkers. One of the major stumbling blocks in efforts to create democratic schools and society has been the tendency (even of progressive educators) to fall prey to the ideology of neutrality, that is, the belief that advocacy in teaching is to be avoided. Even preeminent progressive educators have become weak-kneed over teaching against the status quo, as can be seen in the debates from the 1930s over indoctrination and counterindoctrination.

In 1932 George S. Counts published *Dare the School Build a New Social Order?* In that pamphlet, Counts undertook three themes: (1) criticism of the child-centered approach of romantic progressive educators, (2) assigning to teachers a key role in both educational and social reform, and (3) the democratization of the American economy. Counts' views on the role of teachers and schools in the society were bold and optimistic but not naive: "He thought that the unique power the school possessed was its ability to formulate an ideal of a democratic society, to communicate that ideal to students, and to encourage them to use the ideas as a standard for judging their own and other societies."[5] Counts' views on shaping students' character and the moral and political agenda of schooling had much in common with Dewey's. As Westbrook, a biographer of Dewey, argues, the moral and political aspect of Dewey's educational theory was no less explicit and a good deal more radical than his curricular aims. For example, in his efforts to transform education, Dewey fought hard against the dualism of "culture and utility," which provided the basis for disparate types of education (e.g., academic and vocational) and segregation of students. Dewey described the distinction between culture and utility as a dualism embedded in a social dualism: the distinction between the working class and the leisure class."[6] At the Laboratory School at the University of Chicago, Dewey said, "the social phase of education was put first."[7]

In the 1930s, Dewey joined with Counts and other leading educators critical of the individualism of child-centered progressivism who were seeking to join educational reform to radical politics. These "social reconstructionists" battled for control of the Progressive Education Association; founded a journal that published a wide-ranging critique of capitalism, *The Social Frontier;* and urged American teachers to join the democratic left.

The issue of advocacy was divisive, even among the social reconstructionists. Dewey and Counts disagreed over whether radicals should "indoctrinate" students with beliefs adversarial to status quo ideology. This issue produced heated debate in *The Social Frontier* and elsewhere in the mid-1930s. Dewey and Counts agreed that much of the education in American schools was little more than indoctrination, "especially with reference to narrow nationalism under the name of patriotism, and with reference to the dominant economic regime."[8] Although Dewey did not advocate a "value-neutral" education, he was confident that if teachers cultivated democratic character and intelligent judgment in their students the existing social order would be scrutinized.[9] Counts argued that capitalism could not be reconstructed into a more humane social order unless conservative indoctrination to which students were subjected in schools (and elsewhere) was challenged by radical counterindoctrination. Counts urged teachers to be undeterred by the "bogies of imposition and indoctrination" and to seize the power they had to shape young minds.[10] Dewey believed that the threats to democracy that existed in schools did not justify the counterindoctrination proposed by Counts.

Counts argued, in *Dare the School,* that the essentialist view that maintains that education is some "pure and mystical essence that remains unchanged from everlasting to everlasting" is a dangerous fallacy. According to this view, "genuine education must be completely divorced from politics, live apart from the play of social forces, and pursue ends peculiar to itself."[11] The corollary of this fallacy is that schools should be impartial in emphases and that no bias should be given instruction. As Counts illustrates, complete impartiality is impossible because the whole of creation cannot be brought into schools. "This means that some selection must be made of teachers, curricula, architecture, and methods of teaching."[12] Counts argued that opponents of imposition, like Dewey, who advocated the "cultivation of democratic sentiments" in children or the promotion of child growth in the direction of a "better and richer life" were acquiescing to imposition. From Counts' point of view, to isolate education from politics (or schools from society) was to undermine the goal of achieving an education that strives to promote the fullest and most thorough understanding of the world possible. Imposition is inevitable and must be accepted because the failure to do so "involves clothing one's own deepest prejudices in the garb of universal truth and the introduction into the theory and practice of education of an element of obscurantism."[13]

While Dewey opposed Counts' strategy for countering the indoctrination rampant in schools, he was mindful of the necessity of *deciding* what ought to be in schools and society. *Democracy and Education* opens with a discussion of the way in which all societies use education as a means of social control by which adults consciously shape the dispositions of children.

Today Counts' arguments for radical counterindoctrination are given little heed by teachers and teacher educators. The bogies of imposition and indoctrination have deterred us from coming to grips with the ideological elements embedded in routine practices of teaching (and teacher education). And the fear of imposition and indoctrination has preempted, for many people, the conceptualization of schools as sites in the struggle for a more democratic society.

Critical examination of the discourses of teaching and schooling is the heart of progressive education. Discussion of educational aims, priorities, curricular sequence, instructional methods, student assessment, and so on is not merely about knowledge but also about values and power and thus cannot be understood outside the political and historical context. The institution of schooling and the conventions of teaching that exist in the present have a long history behind them. Attempts to prepare students to live in society simply on the basis of what is obvious in the present are bound to result in adoption of superficial practices that, in the end, will only make existing social and educational problems more acute and more difficult to solve.[14]

The following section illustrates how contemporary social studies education is justified in relation to the status quo.

TRADITIONAL SOCIAL STUDIES INSTRUCTION: ACCEPTING THE LINES AS DRAWN

The dominant pattern of classroom social studies pedagogy is characterized by text-oriented, whole-group, teacher-centered instruction, with an emphasis on memorization of factual information.[15] This approach, labeled "traditional social studies instruction" (TSSI) by Leming,[16] has persisted in social studies classrooms throughout the past century as a result of the pressure of the organizational setting and school culture and, despite widespread criticism and alternatives offered by some teachers, teacher educators, and researchers.[17]

As part of his argument defending TSSI, Leming presents a composite description of four Midwestern teachers via a fictional Mr. Jones in an effort to capture the common pattern of classroom practice. The following description of a typical day in Mr. Jones' class exemplifies TSSI.

> Lecture is the primary form of instruction; coverage of material in the textbook is the dominant factor in decisions about what to teach and how to teach it. The textbook is the primary source of assignments in

the course. Typically, curricular decisions are justified to students [on] the basis of: "We have to finish chapter 6 this week because we need to get one more chapter in before the end of the semester." Only rarely are controversial issues mentioned in class; when they are, it is usually in the form of a soliloquy by Mr. Jones. Students occasionally disagree with Mr. Jones, and he encourages and attentively listens to their perspectives. He appears reluctant to engage students in dialogue on such issues and quickly returns to the subject matter at hand.

Depth is clearly sacrificed for breadth in Mr. Jones' classroom; fostering higher order thinking skills is not an important objective in his classroom. This is reflected most obviously in his exams, which are focused entirely on low-level cognitive goals. When questioned about this Mr. Jones defends his teaching style in terms of developing students' understanding and appreciation of our nation's history, its form of government, and the values upon which our society is based. Mr. Jones considers himself a loyal and patriotic American and wants his students to share that orientation.

Students generally like Mr. Jones. . . . He believes deeply that his job is to teach content, and he tries to do so in the most interesting manner possible. He is an avid collector of historical memorabilia. The discharge of a flintlock rifle and a display of his extensive collection of Nazi Germany artifacts are highlights of the semester that students always remember.[18]

In the balance of Leming's description of Mr. Jones, we find that the part of his day that gives him the most satisfaction comes after school, when he sponsors activities such as the Youth in Government program and takes teams to the Mock United Nations, Civics Bee, and Geography Bee competitions. Mr. Jones is also actively involved in local politics, serving as mayor of his town.

Leming points out that Mr. Jones' classroom teaching would receive low marks if commonly held standards were applied, but he argues that this bifurcated approach to social studies education is a commonly held and carefully considered approach among social studies teachers. Leming goes on to argue that focusing on "mastery of social science content in the classroom" while reserving activities aimed at developing the attributes of citizenship for outside the classroom is the best possible approach for social studies teachers because: (1) "the reward structure in schools clearly focuses on the conventional pursuit of accepted education goals by teachers"; (2) a "realistic appraisal of teacher efficacy" illustrates that significant gains in higher-order thinking, attitude change, and active citizenship skills are objectives that are "difficult, if not impossible to achieve"; and (3) teachers are expected to demonstrate disciplinary expertise because the "dominant socially accepted purpose" of schools is to transmit knowledge.[19]

In his explication of TSSI, Leming mounts both a bold defense for the status quo in social studies classrooms and an assault on those who advocate goals and methods of social studies education that emphasize outcomes that would move beyond the "neutrality" of the status quo. For Leming's Mr. Jones, peace, world hunger, poverty, and multiculturalism are dismissed as possible organizing topics for social studies instruction because they represent "particular ideological perspective[s] . . . currently politically popular."[20] Leming argues that the conventional wisdom of Mr. Jones—TSSI—is supported by evidence that shows that social studies teachers are doing as well as their colleagues when it comes to achieving learning outcomes. The presumption is that the routine or "traditional" organization of topics for social studies instruction is objective, neutral, and apolitical. In TSSI, there is no place for self-consciousness or reflexivity regarding the politics and ethics of knowing the world and teaching about it. The ideological biases of TSSI go unquestioned. Mr. Jones most likely believes he is merely presented the world as it is. By definition, the conventional wisdom of the day is widely accepted, continually reiterated, and regarded not as ideological but as reality itself.[21]

Mr. Jones' beliefs reflect the ideology of neutrality that has been internalized in the consciousness of many members of the social studies education community (teachers, teacher educators, and researchers). The linkages between political agendas and pedagogy or research are blurred by the legitimation function of schooling and educational research. For example, many educational research studies accept the objectives of pedagogical programs and are organized to "explain" how the objectives were reached.[22] Research on "effective teaching" extols the value of direct instruction as opposed to teaching that promotes student-to-student interaction, democratic pedagogy, and a learning milieu that values caring and individual students' self-esteem. Many researchers (and practitioners) do not question the assumed conception of student achievement represented in this research—efficient mastery of content as represented by test scores. As a result, issues such as the criteria for content selection, the mystification and fragmentation of course content, linkages between improved test scores and national economic prosperity, and the ways in which the social conditions of schooling might unequally distribute knowledge remain unexamined.

Uncritical acceptance of "traditional" educational objectives as the basis for action (in research studies or classroom pedagogy) is no less ideological than proposing that social studies instruction should be multicultural, antiracist, and internationalist in its orientation. Resisting the status quo in education—rebelling against "reality"—is always difficult. A useful first step is to better understand the theories of knowledge and conceptions of citizenship that provide the foundation for the "reality" of TSSI.

A VIEW FROM THE SIDELINE: KNOWERS AND CITIZENS AS SPECTATORS

In his defense of TSSI, Leming argues that social studies educators should accept the "lines as drawn" as the inevitable nature of things and that any redrawing is ideological and to be avoided. If, however, one defines *ideology* as the frame in which people fit their understanding of how the world works, a view of one's mission is as ideological for what it leaves out as for what it includes.[23]

As represented by Leming's Mr. Jones, TSSI is based on a doctrine of inevitability, in which the status quo is accepted without serious examination. Current circumstances are understood as merely the way the world is and reflective of the general consent of the populace. In this way of thinking, conceptions of the roles of teachers and students in schools and the conventional goals of education must remain unchallenged.[24] Thus TSSI accepts the lines as drawn and deflects questions about how education is used as a means of social control and to what ends. It leaves no room to consider questions such as: What do we mean by democracy? What kind of democracy do we want?

Mr. Jones' bifurcation of the subject matter content of social studies education and "citizenship activities" is a manifestation of theories of knowledge and democracy that conceive of the model knower-citizen as a detached spectator.

Knower as Spectator

The ideal knower in TSSI is based on a spectatorial theory of knowledge in which the knower is "imaged as someone looking on disinterestedly from behind a plate-glass window."[25] Social studies content is treated as an object to be taken in with minimal subjective interference. This process of knowing is like the children's game of hidden pictures. The artifacts, animals, plants, and people to be espied are already in the picture. No changes need to be make in the picture. What is needed is a more concerted effort on the part of the viewer, until the appropriate object comes into focus.[26]

This theory of knowing is modeled after what takes place in the act of vision.

> The object refracts light to the eye and is seen; it makes a difference to the eye and to the person having an optical apparatus, but none to the thing seen. The real object is the object so fixed in its regal aloofness that it is a king to any beholding mind that may gaze upon it.[27]

This bipolar conception of a knowing situation does not work well in a world of interacting, mutually influencing affairs. There is a *subject* (the spectator-knower) confronting an *object* (that which is to be known, in this case the content of social studies education). The spectator-knower's primary task is construction of a mental image corresponding to an ordered and absolute external world. This theory of knowledge relies on absolute, singular, or unified premises, most often about "taking in the world out there" rather than "world making."[28]

Dewey's alternative to the bipolar knowing envisioned by modern epistemology (and embodied in TSSI) is a tridimensional paradigm: inquirer, subject matter, and objective.[29] In this framework, there are "subject-matters to be investigated. The 'objects' are the objectives aimed at in such investigations. Humans are 'inquirers who, as a result of some interest, are examining the subject-matters in light of a particular objective.' "[30] By referring to the material under investigation as subject matter rather than object, Dewey avoids the temptation to fasten onto a single meaning as ultimately determinative, as the content of social studies is treated in TSSI. Subject matters can be investigated from various perspectives, depending on the objective of the inquiry. As Boisvert points out in his analysis of Deweyan thought, "The primacy of any particular set of results can only be judged in relation to the purposes of inquiry. It is not a direct intuition of the single, 'really real' structure hidden behind appearances."[31]

In the bipolar model of knowing, for example,

> the human "subjects" trying to understand the "object" water may be said to have completed their task once the chemical composition H_2O has been identified. As Descartes put it in his *Discourse,* "since there is only one truth concerning any matter, whoever discovers this truth

knows as much as can be known." It is less likely, on the Deweyan
model, that subject-matter will be confused with a unidimensional
"object" to be attained once and for all.[32]

What, then, is the objective of Mr. Jones' TSSI? The answer is *control*, in two distinct but related senses of the term. In one sense, Mr.
Jones' pedagogy is shaped by the assumptions of modern epistemology
(with its characteristic dualisms of mind-body and subject-object),
whose aim is for students to develop a mental image corresponding to
"reality"—an internal mind attempting to capture external materiality.[33]
"The spectator's meaning involves a world in some sense ordered; independence of the world from the perceiving subject; the seeking of true
representations, designations, and depictions of the world; and the need
to control order . . . the aim is for control called knowledge."[34] In this
framework, the knower has a cognitive task, which is to perceive the "objects" that exist in the external world; knowledge is the adjustment between the thing and the intellect.

As mentioned earlier, Dewey argued that all societies use education
as a means of social control by which adults consciously shape the dispositions of children. When educators present the world that surrounds us
as one-dimensional and knowable by merely "looking on disinterestedly
from behind a plate-glass window," human understanding is constructed
as passive rather than active, there is no entry for multiple examinations
of the affairs of the world as represented (in textbooks, media, etc.) for
alternative perspectives on the world, and the objectives and interests of
those who constructed *the* representation of the external world are obscured. This circumstance allows for control in a second sense—that is,
social control via thought control. If, however, humans are understood as
inquirers who, as a result of some interest, are examining their world in
light of a particular objective, the single, determinative meanings of the
world found in many social studies texts and classrooms will be crashed
upon the rocks of what Dewey described as "intelligence in operation."

According to TSSI, the human "subjects" (i.e., students) in Mr. Jones'
class who are trying to understand the "object" history may be said to
have completed their task once the "facts" have been identified, committed to memory, and put to use on a test. When the content of social studies education is understood as a "subject matter," in the Deweyan sense,
and not as object, new emphases are introduced. The spectator theory of
knowledge underlying TSSI focuses on a single vision of the world,
whereas Dewey's "experimental" theory of knowledge allows for and

encourages multiple investigations—investigations that are driven by explicit and varied interests and objectives.

Students in Mr. Jones' class encounter history as a compendium of facts within a textbook. These "facts" are presented as *the* truth. Little or no attention is given to questions of how these particular representations of the past came to be or what objectives or interests might have motivated historians and textbook authors to write the history contained in a particular textbook. We can suppose that students in Mr. Jones' class encountered the study of the Holocaust, for example, as do most students in the United States—as an isolated event of genocide, sprung from the evil mind of Hitler and his Nazi cohorts. Can social studies teaching and curriculum that separates study of the Holocaust from the development of fascism be seen as neutral, objective, or unbiased? How do students understand fascism when it is lifted above the mass murders and resistance it engendered in the mid-twentieth century?

As Rich Gibson points out, education that treats the Holocaust and fascism separately cannot begin to foster comprehension of what created fascism and its attendant mass murders, nor can it create the kind of consciousness necessary to oppose it on ideological or material terms.[35] The film *Schindler's List,* which is now a major part of Holocaust studies in social studies classrooms, offers no understanding of how fascism came to power or of fascism's roots in capitalism and racist mystical ideology that seeks to have the masses adopt the mythology of their oppressors as reality. Neither the film nor mainstream textbook accounts of the Holocaust mention how fascism was resisted and ultimately defeated by working-class people of all religions and nationalities or the role communists played in leading the resistance.[36] Fascism did not fall from the sky, nor did the Holocaust, but TSSI, with its emphasis on presentation of the world as a one-dimensional object waiting to be viewed correctly and once and for all, does not allow interrogations that would uncover multiple meanings of the social world and the motivations and interests that drive certain representations. "The subject-matters that surround us . . . are not one-dimensional objects waiting to be viewed correctly and once and for all. They are subject-matters, repositories of multiple possibilities, many of which remain latent until the activities of inquirers help bring them out."[37] Teaching methods that are openly political and urge their own critique are pivotal in classroom practices that seek to work against the appearance of more modern forms of fascist ideology and practice.[38] Pedagogies that encourage one-dimensional understandings of the world, obscure the objectives and interests served by dominant forms of knowledge, and fail to foster active learning that explores multi-ple possibilities for understanding are no less ideological and clearly more deceptive.

The Deweyan conception of knowing upsets traditional views of the knower as spectator receiving data from the objective world. With its em-phasis on active inquiry into problematic situations, this outlook on learning (1) undermines a single privileged perspective of the world (which is promoted by TSSI and its focus textbook memorization), (2) affirms the importance of experimentation in learning (i.e., learners-inquirers use "intelligence in operation" or some form of doing, rather than passively absorbing facts), and (3) treats doubt, uncertainty, and puzzlement as not merely "subjective" conditions to be set right by ob-taining a clearer picture of the world but rather conceives of the everyday experience of humans as problematic situations that provide the impetus for thinking and doing. This last component of learning—the rejection of atemporal, acontextual starting points for knowing—presents particular problems for traditional social studies instruction.

Citizen as Spectator

Social studies education is consistently framed in relation to citizenship education and particularly the preparation of individuals to participate in a democratic society. "Since doubt, uncertainty, and confusion are not merely internal, subjective phenomena, the path of inquiry also cannot be merely mental or internal,"[39] and knowing involves some doing, ac-tive participation that alters existing conditions.

In 1992, Marker and Mehlinger's review of the social studies cur-riculum concluded that the apparent consensus that citizenship education is the primary purpose of social studies is "almost meaningless." Few so-cial studies educators disagree that the purpose of social studies is "to pre-pare youth so that they possess the knowledge, values, and skills needed for active participation in society."[40] Arguments have been made that stu-dents can develop "good citizenship" through the study of history; through the examination of contemporary social problems, public policy, social roles, or social taboos; or by becoming astute critics of society.[41] The question, of course, is whether social studies should promote a brand of citizenship that is adaptive to the status quo and interests of the socially powerful, as does TSSI, or whether it should promote citizenship aimed at transforming and reconstructing society—a question that has fueled debates since Thomas Jesse Jones first employed the term *social studies.*[42]

Marker and Mehlinger's conclusions about the meaning of "citizenship education" reflects, in part, a failure of social studies educators to interrogate the meaning of words such as *democracy, capitalism, freedom of speech,* and *equality.* This failure is not really surprising in light of the modernist conception of knowing that dominates the field and that promotes acceptance of preformulated knowledge rather than active inquiry into the problematic situations of everyday life. That spectator knowing leads to spectator citizenship is a predictable consequence.

What is democratic citizenship? Within the standard definition of democracy, citizens should have the opportunity to inform themselves; take part in inquiry, discussion, and policy formation; and advance their ideas through political action. In social studies education, however, democracy is much more narrowly conceived: the citizen is a consumer, an observer, but not a participant. Citizens have the right to ratify policies that originate elsewhere, but if these limits are exceeded, we have not democracy, but a "crisis of democracy."[43]

As illustrated before, TSSI promotes spectator citizenship by situating students outside the knowledge construction process as passive recipients of prepackaged information and by teaching a conception of democracy that is almost always equated with elections and voting. The procedure of allowing individuals to express a choice on a proposal, resolution, bill, or candidate is perhaps the most widely taught precept in the social studies curriculum. In this conception of citizenship, individual agency is construed primarily as one's vote, and voting procedures override all else with regard to what counts as democracy. Democracy, in this case, is not defined by outcomes but by application of procedures and autonomous action of individuals.

In social studies classes, "exercising your right to vote" is taught as the primary manifestation of good citizenship; this, along with understanding the procedural aspects of government (e.g., how a bill becomes a law, the branches of government, separation of powers, and strictly delimited "rights and responsibilities"), is the primary focus of citizenship education. Preparing youth so that they possess the knowledge, values, and skills needed for active participation in society, the consensus goal of social studies, is defined in relation to the "given" nature of capitalist democracy. Rarely are students asked to consider questions such as: What do we mean by democracy? What kind of democracy do we want? What are the functions of education and the communications media in a democratic society?

Teaching citizenship based on capitalist democracy and proceduralism leaves little room for individuals or groups to exercise direct political action, and the bounds of the expressible are limited.[44] Citizens can vote,

lobby, and exercise free speech and assembly rights, but as far as govern-
ing is concerned, they are primarily spectators. Traditional social studies
instruction preserves strict boundaries around the operative conceptions
of democracy and citizenship in our society. In this sense, TSSI is a critical element within an ideological system (perpetuated by the education
system writ large, as well as the media and the political system)
constructed to ensure that the population remains passive, ignorant, and
apathetic.[45]

The way TSSI accomplishes this goal is by teaching definitions and
principles of democracy in the abstract and parallel to the history of
events in the world and contemporary experiences of students. For the
most part, school history presents the United States in terms of its mag-
nificence and dedication to the highest moral values. There is room
within this history to highlight the errors and failures of the nation's
pursuit of its noble objectives, but what is missing is an effort to expose
the systematic patterns and to trace these "anomalies" to "the conscious
planning that regularly underlies them or to their roots in the pattern of
privilege and domination."[46] For example, common topics for study in
social studies include the enslavement of Africans in the United States
and the subsequent Civil War, the genocide of Native Americans, and the
civil rights movement. But the threads of capitalism, fascism, racism,
and class domination that tie these topics together are rarely woven together. Students study the role of the United States in world affairs and
its foreign policy doctrine of spreading American-style democracy, including the overthrow of governments or invasions of Iran (1953), Guate-
mala (1954), Cuba (1961), Grenada (1983), and Iraq (1991), to name but
a few, to protect the interests of American business. However, the first
principle of U.S. foreign policy—that is, to ensure a favorable global environment for U.S. industry, commerce, and finance[47]—is rarely articulated in social studies classrooms (or the media).

Perhaps most important, students in social studies education rarely
have the opportunity to examine the variant of democracy that is synonymous with most people's understanding of the term: capitalist democracy.
The Federalists expected "that the new American political institutions
would continue to function within the old assumptions about a politically
active elite and a deferential, compliant electorate."[48] As Noam Chomsky
points out, despite the Federalists' electoral defeat, their conception of
democracy prevailed, though in a different form as industrial capitalism
emerged. This view was most succinctly expressed by John Jay, president of the Continental Congress and first chief justice of the U.S.

Supreme Court: "The people who own the country ought to govern it."[49] Jay's maxim is the principle on which the United States was founded and is maintained.[50]

The bifurcation of knowing and doing in social studies allows narrow conceptions of democracy to survive and thrive. This is because the boundaries of the discourse on democracy and citizenship are nearly impenetrable to questions of how the lines are drawn. The democratic ideals most often taught in schools are premised on the philosophical prejudices of eighteenth-century social contract theorists like Locke, who posited that societies are composed of atomistic individuals bearing an uncanny resemblance to eighteenth-century theorists themselves: educated, articulate, propertied, and with clearly defined interests.[51] These premises, however, are rarely interrogated. In effect, TSSI gives students the instruments to trace the lines drawn by others, rather than opportunities to examine those lines and consider how they might be redrawn.

What, for example, might students find if they examined Jay's maxim in light of the historical record and their own experience in the contemporary world? Social studies students are rarely in a position to seriously consider questions such as: Why capitalist democracy and not socialist democracy? Why does big money control law making? Why does the average CEO make 419 times the wage of the average blue-collar worker? What motivates the physical and constitutional assaults on immigrants and poor people? These questions are not routinely a part of social studies classrooms because they are generally considered the roots, not of democracy, but of a "crisis of democracy." Leming argues that the dominant socially accepted purpose of schools is to transmit knowledge, which is a variant of James Mill's frank acknowledgment of the purpose of schooling: to "train the minds of the people to a virtuous attachment to their government" and, more generally, the arrangements of the social, economic, and political order.[52]

Throughout the twentieth century, progressive intellectuals, media figures, and educators (e.g., Walter Lippmann, George Kennan, Reinhold Niebuhr, and many Deweyites) have promulgated spectator democracy—in which a specialized class of experts identify what our common interests are and then think and plan accordingly. The function of those outside the specialized class is to be spectators rather than participants in action. This theory of democracy asserts that common interests elude the general public and can be understood and managed only by an elite group. According to Lippmann, in a properly running democracy the large majority of the population (whom Lippmann labeled "the bewildered herd") is protected from itself by the specialized class's management of the political, economic, and ideological systems and, in particular, by the manufacturing of consent—bringing about agreement on the part of the public for things that they do not want.

Traditional social studies instruction legitimates spectator democracy. In many ways, TSSI reflects Niebuhr's admonition that " 'cool observers' must create the 'necessary illusions' and 'emotionally potent oversimplifications' that keep the ignorant and stupid masses disciplined and content."[53] I do not doubt Leming's claim that the teachers upon which the composite Mr. Jones is based are thoughtful and professional. I do not believe that individual teachers (teacher educators and researchers) generally engage in conscious deceit. However, when practitioners readily adopt beliefs that serve institutional needs—needs defined by elites in service of their interests (e.g., test scores and standardized curriculum), rather than needs as defined by people themselves—they are likely to be contributing to the perpetuation of the status quo and all of its attendant inequities and injustices.

REDRAWING THE LINES

This examination of traditional social studies instruction illustrates how particular theories of knowledge and conceptions of democracy function to obscure the political and ideological consequences of mainstream social studies education. These consequences include conceptions of the learner as passive, democratic citizenship as a spectator project, and, ultimately, the maintenance of status quo inequalities in society. Often, social studies educators eschew openly political or ideological agendas for teaching and schooling as inappropriate or unprofessional; however, it should be clear in light of this analysis that the question is not whether to encourage particular social visions in the classroom but rather what kind of social visions there will be.

Defining the visions to be pursued in social studies education is not something that can be done once and for all, or separated from the experience of everyday life in a specific time and place. We can, however, identify pedagogical means that put teachers and students on track to discuss what the purpose of social studies education might be. Dewey's often quoted, seldom enacted definition of reflective thought is:

> Active, persistent, and careful consideration of any belief or supposed
> form of knowledge in the light of the grounds that support it and the
> further conclusions to which it tends constitutes reflective thought.[54]

Teaching from this standpoint means focusing on outcomes and consequences that matter (not merely results of standardized tests) and interrogating abstract concepts, such as democracy, for more meaningful understandings.

In this approach, learning is understood as synonymous with inquiry into problems faced by real people in their everyday lives. The goal of citizenship education, then, is not to inculcate students into capitalist democracy but rather to help students question, understand, and test the reality of the social world we inhabit. This objective can be achieved, for example, through local community studies, which provide concrete laboratories for reflection, analysis, skills building, and contributions to the community. In schools that operate in poor communities, it means directly confronting and responding to the social injustices that exist in our society. Remember that neutrality is not objectivity, and educators who are committed to helping students understand their own social situation and contribute to redressing social injustices must engage with students in active inquiry and analysis that resist the status quo.[55]

Redrawing the lines of social studies education also means understanding the nested contexts of the classroom and recognizing that the contexts that shape teachers' practices are, in turn, shaped by teachers themselves. This dialectical relationship between teachers' beliefs and actions and the contexts in which they work harbors a powerful and as yet untapped rejoinder to the top-down, centralized initiatives currently dominating school reform. Social studies teachers have traditionally understood their power to affect change as stopping at the classroom door, hence the bifurcation of knowing and doing as represented in Mr. Jones' work. True educational reform, however, includes engaging policy debates and other struggles in and beyond the classroom.

> If we recognized that effective education requires students to bring their real lives into the classrooms, and to take what they learn back to their homes and neighborhoods in the form of new understandings and new behavior, how can we not do the same? Critical teaching should not be merely an abstraction or academic formula for classroom "experimentation." It should be a strategy for educational organizing that changes lives, including our own.[56]

Many key educational issues are determined in the larger context of community, state, and national politics (e.g., curriculum standards, mandated high-stakes tests, voucher plans, and privatization schemes). Teachers' efforts in the classroom are inextricably tied to broader endeavors to transform our society. If social studies educators (and others) truly want to transform schools, we must recognize and act on connections between classrooms and society. If we can find ways to link work for democratic reforms in schools and society, both will be strengthened.[57]

Engaging in an attempt to redraw the lines of traditional social studies instruction is not without risks. To quote Chomsky,

> To ask serious questions about the nature and behavior of one's own society is often difficult and unpleasant; difficult because the answers are generally concealed, and unpleasant because the answers are often not only ugly . . . but also painful. To understand the truth about these matters is to be led to action that may not be easy to undertake and that may even carry significant personal cost. In contrast, the easy way is to succumb to the demands of the powerful, to avoid searching questions, and to accept the doctrine that is hammered home incessantly by the propaganda system. This is, no doubt, the main reason for the easy victory of dominant ideologies, for the general tendency to remain silent or to keep fairly close to the official doctrine with regard to the behavior of one's own state and its allies while lining up to condemn the real or alleged crimes of its enemies.[58]

For citizenship education to have meaning, we must give it one. Social studies educators can choose to stand behind a totem that celebrates the status quo and makes spectators of us all, or we can reject the lines as drawn as the inevitable nature of things and start to construct a new vision.

NOTES

[1]See, for example, the account of the development of statewide social studies frameworks in New York and California: Catherine Cornbleth and Dexter Waugh, *The Great Speckled Bird: Multicultural Politics and Educational Policymaking* (New York: St. Martin's Press, 1996); and the story of the development of the national history standards in Gary B. Nash, Charlotte Crabtree, and Ross E. Dunn, *History on Trial: Culture Wars and the Teaching of the Past* (New York: Knopf, 1997).

[2]Kenneth N. Teitelbaum, "Contestation and Curriculum," in Landon E. Beyer and Michael W. Apple, eds., *The Curriculum* (New York: Routledge, 1988), pp. 32–55.

[3]The explication of these terms is taken from Michael Scriven, *The Evaluation Thesaurus,* 4th ed. (Thousand Oaks, Calif.: Sage, 1994).

[4]See Robert B. Westbrook, *John Dewey and American Democracy* (Ithaca, N.Y.: Cornell University Press, 1991).

[5]Wayne J. Urban, "Preface," in George S. Counts, *Dare the School Build a New Social Order?* (Carbondale: Southern Illinois University Press, 1978), p. x.

[6]John Dewey, *Democracy and Education* (New York: Free Press, 1916), p. 341.

[7]Westbrook, p. 104.

[8]Ibid., p. 507.

[9]Ibid.

[10]Ibid., p. 506.

[11]Counts, p. 15.

[12]Ibid., p. 16.

[13]Ibid., p. 9.

[14]John Dewey, *Experience and Education* (New York: Collier, 1938), p. 77.

[15]Arthur Applebee, Judith Langer, and I. Mullis, *The Nation's Report Card: Literature and U.S. History* (Princeton, N.J.: Educational Testing Service, 1987); Robert E. Stake and J. A. Easley, *Case Studies in Science Education 2: Design, Overview and General Findings* (Urbana: Center for Instructional Research and Curriculum Evaluation, University of Illinois, 1978).

[16]James S. Leming, "Past as Prologue: A Defense of Traditional Patterns of Social Studies Instruction," in M. Nelson, ed., *The Future of Social Studies* (Boulder, Colo.: Social Science Education Consortium, 1994).

[17]Larry Cuban, "History of Teaching in Social Studies" in J. P. Shaver, Ed. *Handbook of Research on Social Studies Teaching and Learning* (New York: Macmillan, 1991), pp. 197–209; Linda M. McNeil, *Contradiction of Control: School Structure and School Knowledge* (New York: Routledge, 1988); Fred M. Newmann, "Classroom Thoughtfulness and Students' Higher Order Thinking: Common Indicators and Diverse Social Studies Courses," *Theory and Research in Social Education* 19 (1991): 410–433.

[18]Leming, pp. 17–18.

[19]Ibid., pp. 19–20.

[20]Ibid., p. 20.

[21]Ellen Willis, "We Need a Radical Left," *Nation* 266 (June 29, 1998): 18–21.

[22]Thomas S. Popkewitz, "Educational Research: Values and Visions of Social Order," *Theory and Research in Social Education* 6 (1978): 20–39.

[23]J. Wypijewski, "A Stirring in the Land," *Nation* 265 (September 8–15, 1997), 17–25.

[24]Leming has argued that social studies teacher educators are out of touch with the reality of classroom teaching and should abandon critiques of practice

and proposals for new curricula and focus instead on assisting teachers in solving the problems that arise for the current circumstances of their work. See his "Ideological Perspectives Within the Social Studies Profession: An Empirical Examination of the Two Culture Thesis," *Theory and Research in Social Education* 20 (1992): 293–312.

[25]Raymond D. Boisvert, *John Dewey: Rethinking Our Time* (Albany: State University of New York Press, 1998), p. 35.

[26]Ibid.

[27]John Dewey, *The Quest for Certainty* (New York: Minton, Blach, 1929), p. 23.

[28]Lynda Stone, "Philosophy, Meaning Constructs, and Teacher Theorizing," in E. Wayne Ross, J. W. Cornett, and G. McCutcheon, eds., *Teacher Personal Theorizing: Connecting Curriculum Practice, Theory and Research* (Albany: State University of New York Press, 1992), p. 29.

[29]Boisvert, p. 36.

[30]Ibid.

[31]Ibid.

[32]Ibid.

[33]Stone, p. 29.

[34]Ibid.

[35]Rich Gibson, *Teaching About the Holocaust in the Context of Fascism,* unpublished manuscript (Detroit: Wayne State University, 1998).

[36]Gibson, "Teaching About the Holocaust." http://www.pipeline.com/~rgibson/FASCSOC.htm (August 10, 1999).

[37]Boisvert, p. 37.

[38]Gibson, p. 1.

[39]Boisvert, p. 41.

[40]Gerald Marker and Howard L. Mehlinger, "Social Studies" in P. W. Jackson, Ed., *Handbook of Research on Curriculum* (New York: Macmillan), p. 832.

[41]See, for example: Michael Whelan, "History as the Core of Social Studies Curriculum," in E. Wayne Ross, ed., *The Social Studies Curriculum: Purposes, Problems, and Possibilities* (Albany: State University of New York Press, 1997), pp. 21–37; Ronald W. Evans and David Warren Saxe, eds., *Handbook on Teaching Social Issues* (Washington, D.C.: National Council for the Social Studies, 1996); Donald W. Oliver and James P. Shaver, *Teaching Public Issues in the High School* (Boston: Houghton Mifflin, 1966); D. P. Superka and S. Hawke, *Social Roles: A Focus for Social Studies in the 1980s* (Boulder, Colo: Social Science Education Consortium, 1982); Maurice P. Hunt and Lawrence E. Metcalf, *Teaching High School Social Studies: Problems in Reflective Teaching and Social Understanding* (New York: Harper, 1955); Shirley Engle and Anna Ochoa,

Education for Democratic Citizenship: Decision Making in the Social Studies (New York: Teachers College Press, 1988).

[42]E. Wayne Ross, "Social Studies" in D. A. Gabbard, *Knowledge and Power in the Global Economy: Politics and the Rhetoric of School Reform* (Mahwah, NJ: Lawrence Erlbaum, 2000), pp. 237–246.

[43]Noam Chomsky, *Necessary Illusions: Thought Control in Democratic Societies* (Boston: South End Press, 1989).

[44]Ibid.

[45]Noam Chomsky, *On Power and Ideology* (Boston: South End Press, 1987).

[46]Chomsky, *On Power and Ideology,* p. 12.

[47]Chomsky, *Necessary Illusions.*

[48]Joyce Appleby, *Capitalism and the New Social Order* (New York: New York University Press, 1984), p. 73.

[49]Chomsky, *Necessary Illusions,* p. 14.

[50]See Joshua Cohen and Joel Rogers, *On Democracy* (New York: Penguin, 1983).

[51]Boisvert.

[52]Quoted in Chomsky, *Necessary Illusions,* p. 13.

[53]Chomsky, Necessary Illusions, p. 19.

[54]John Dewey, *How We Think* (Lexington, MA: Heath, 1933), p. 8.

[55]Michael Peterson, Kim Beloin, and Rich Gibson, *Whole Schooling: Education for a Democratic Society.* http://www.uwsp.edu/acad/educ/specproj/wsc

[56]Stan Karp, "Beyond the Classroom," *Rethinking Schools 8* (1994): 24.

[57]E. Wayne Ross, "The Struggle for Democratic Community," *Theory and Research in Social Education* 24 (1996): pp. 234–236.

[58]Noam Chomsky, *Towards a New Cold War: Essays on the Current Crisis and How We Got There* (New York: Pantheon, 1982): pp. 9–10.

CHAPTER 4

Curriculum and the Social Order

WILLIAM B. STANLEY

What role should the schools play in the social order? This question has troubled our educational debates since the birth of the nation. Most often, schools have been used to help maintain the society they serve. In this sense, schools have been viewed as an institution well suited to building public support for our culture and social structures. Schools function to transmit the dominant culture and help to maintain social stability and status quo power relations.

Conversely, schools have also been called on to promote social change and social transformation. The promotion of civil rights and desegregation is one recent example of using the schools to bring about major social change. But, although schools have been pointed in both directions vis-à-vis social change, promotion of social stability has been the major role of schooling. In the current debate over schooling, we hear again calls for the schools to return to their primary task of cultural transmission, the emphasis on core values and the basic knowledge that all our citizens need.

In 1932, George S. Counts posed the question, "Dare the school build a new social order?" at a talk given at the annual meeting of the Progressive Education Association. Over the last two decades, there have been occasional appeals to revive the social reconstructionist approach to curriculum and educational reform.[1] When considering the relevance of social reconstructionism to the current educational debate, it is worth recalling the context in which George Counts first challenged educators to build a new social order in 1932.

First, keep in mind that Counts' question was asked in the depths of the worst depression our nation had yet experienced. The public faith in our major institutions had been undermined, and there was a growing sense of desperation among large sectors of the population. Arguing that desperate times called for desperate measures, Counts did not rule out the possible need for violence to bring about social change. He reasoned that those powerful groups that controlled the bulk of our national resources would not willingly give up such control. Theodore Brameld, a younger and more radical proponent of social reconstructionism, was also willing to support violent means, if required, to bring about necessary social change. Unlike Counts, Brameld was strongly influenced by Marxist thought and for a brief time accepted the possible need for a dictatorship of the proletariat as a necessary phase in the transition to a more radically democratic social order.

Both Counts and Brameld significantly moderated their views and shortly came to reject violence (and, in Brameld's case, a proletarian dictatorship) as reasonable political action. Indeed, Counts developed strong anticommunist feelings and helped lead the fight to drive communists from leadership positions in the American Federation of Teachers in New York. Brameld, over time, became a critic of orthodox Marxist thought but did retain elements of what we now refer to as neo-Marxism in his work. What these two scholars did not change was their strong feelings regarding the rightness of their cause and the importance of imposing reconstructionist views through schooling. We need to think more about the sense of certainty that orients the reconstructionist position.

A second important feature of the context in which Counts posed his reconstructionist challenge was a growing intellectual backlash against the pragmatic theory of John Dewey, William James, and C. S. Peirce. This backlash gained force in the 1920s but was neither uniform nor entirely successful. Dewey continued to be a leading intellectual figure in the United States, as well as a critic of the reconstructionist position. In addition, the pragmatist George Herbert Mead's work emerged during the same period, until his sudden death in 1931. Nevertheless, the growing critique of pragmatism eventually led to the demise and temporary eclipse of this philosophical movement in the first three decades after 1945.[2]

There are probably many complex reasons for the resistance to pragmatic theory. Dewey and Peirce were not always easy to read or understand. At times, James, Dewey, and Peirce each took significantly different approaches in their work. Consequently, it is difficult, at best, to summarize a coherent and simplified account of pragmatism. To make matters worse, the followers of Dewey, in particular, often distorted his ideas. Such problems notwithstanding, I would argue for at least two central and interrelated reasons for the reaction against pragmatism, reasons that remain a part of the current educational debates.

One concern raised by critics on both the political left and right was the alleged relativism inherent in pragmatic theory. Pragmatism was an antifoundationalist philosophy that did not accept objectivism or arguments for absolute truths. Truth, for the pragmatist, was understood as tentative and relative to what counted as reliable knowledge (methods, assumptions) in a given context. For critics on both right and left, such an instrumentalist and relativistic orientation worked to paralyze social progress by failing to provide clear guidelines for social action.

A second and related concern that influenced the critics of pragmatism was the growing influence of modern science oriented by a positivist view of knowledge. This view of science held that objective forms of knowledge could be derived from the use of specific scientific methods. The positivist approach to knowledge insisted on the separation of "fact" and "value" claims. Science was not, and should not be, concerned with value judgments. Scientists were concerned with empirical questions that could be explored and possibly explained via scientific methods of observation, induction, and experiment.

At first glance, pragmatic theory seems to be deeply rooted in the modern scientific tradition, and in many ways it is. But the pragmatists defined *science* differently than their more positivist counterparts. In particular, they believed that the tendency to separate fact and value questions was based on a false dichotomy. In the pragmatist's view, both kinds of questions required the same sort of analysis and reasoning, and it was never possible to eliminate interpretive and value-laden thinking from science.

The pragmatic arguments gradually lost support during the 1920s with the rise of the scientific curriculum movement inspired by Thorndike, Bobbit, Charters, Snedden, and others.[3] This educational movement appeared to offer the hope of scientific solutions to the problems faced by the schools. Perhaps more important was the negative reaction to the pragmatist's refusal to endorse the view that values exist as positive entities prior to, and apart from, their linguistic expression and application. The pragmatists appeared to have abandoned faith in the central values many believed to be the core of our democratic culture. The perceived relativism of the pragmatists was exacerbated by the tendency of many progressive educators, who claimed to follow Dewey, to promote an educational program based on the "child's interests." Perhaps the best example of this effect was the child-centered focus within the progressive education movement, promoted by Dewey disciples such as William H. Kilpatrick. Dewey spent a lifetime trying to distance himself from these distorted representations of his ideas. By distorting Dewey's ideas and pragmatic theory in general, the child-centered progressives contributed to the suspicion that pragmatism lacked the theoretical commitment required to guide social policy and change. Of course, this sort of relativism was a threat to any educators, radical, liberal, or conservative, who believed that core values should be inculcated to either preserve or transform the social order.

We can see, therefore, that the reconstructionist challenge posed by Counts and others was part of a more general reaction that would combine a commitment to core values with a rigorous, "scientific" approach to the analysis of education's role in society. What distinguished the reconstructionists from more conservative critics of pragmatism was their radical critique of our socioeconomic system and a commitment to a radical form of democracy.

The "scientific" element in reconstructionism is found in their emphasis on the use of social science knowledge and "experts" to guide the building of a new social order. In essence, what the reconstructionists were proposing was an educational program as a form of countersocialization. The superior democratic (our) values of the reconstructionists would be used to orient the curriculum in opposition to the inferior or evil (their) values of the dominant conservative groups. Imposition or indoctrination was seen as a necessary—indeed, inevitable—component of education. The reconstructionists argued that because education could never be neutral, that it always worked to the advantage of some group and against others, and that because a powerful minority typically dominated the curriculum, indoctrination was necessary to countersocialize students to accept the reconstructionist's more democratic cultural program.[4]

So we return to the question posed at the start of this discussion, "Is the reconstructionist approach to education still relevant in our current situation?" Although our economy is much stronger now than it was in 1932, enormous social and economic problems are still characteristic of our society. Poverty, while affecting a lower percentage of the population than during the Depression, still afflicts millions of Americans, and the poverty rates remain at Depression-era levels for African Americans, Latinos, and Native Americans. In addition, the gap between the well-off and the poor has grown steadily over the past two decades. Racism, sexism, ethnic bias, and homophobia still permeate large sectors of our society (although we should note that these kinds of social problems received little or no attention by reconstructionists in the 1930s). In addition, war, crime, ecological pollution, overpopulation, and disease remain as problems on national and global levels. Finally, it is clear that our democratic culture remains fragile and unstable. The impact of new media forms, computer technology, unequal income distribution, campaign financing techniques, and other political and structural problems threaten the very survival of our democratic institutions.

In the face of such widespread problems and threats to our democratic culture, the reconstructionist emphasis on incorporating social criticism into the school curriculum seems more relevant than ever. Students lacking the competence for critical analysis of our society would be unable to function as fully participating citizens. But this sort of emphasis on social criticism was also a central feature of Dewey's pragmatic theory as applied to education and democracy, so the reconstructionists did not offer anything significantly new in this regard. What reconstructionism did offer was a more thorough analysis of the role played by ideology and indoctrination in education and of how education was used by powerful forces to maintain their control over our major institutions. Of the major pragmatic theorists, only Dewey had dealt significantly with such issues, but it can be argued that the reconstructionists gave indoctrination a new, in-depth analysis. A major problem, however, lies in how the reconstructionists decided to respond to this problem. As Dewey explained in reference to the reconstructionist position:

> The upholders of indoctrination rest their adherence to the theory, in part, upon the fact that there is a great deal of indoctrination now going on in the schools, especially with reference to the dominant economic regime. These facts unfortunately *are* facts. But they do not prove that the right course is to seize upon the method of indoctrination and reverse its object.[5]

For Dewey, schools needed to cultivate what he referred to as the "method of intelligence" or a form of practical reasoning. We need to give up what Dewey called the "quest for certainty" and Foucault "the will to know." Intelligence in a world without certainty was

> associated with *judgment;* that is, with selection and arrangement of means to effect consequences and with choice of what we take as our ends. A man is intelligent not in virtue of having reason which grasps first and in demonstrable truth about fixed principles, in order to reason

deductively from them to the particulars which they govern, but in virtue of his capacity to estimate the possibilities of a situation and to act in accordance with his estimate.[6]

This was the sort of judgment elaborated in pragmatism and the sort of practical judgment required by citizens in a democratic society. When we give up our quest for certain foundations for knowledge, we can shift our focus to the social and communal conditions and practices necessary to acquire knowledge sufficient to guide our social actions. Within this context, democracy is not understood as a core value but as a regulative ideal or a way of life in which humans interact to determine what should be their ends and the best means to attain them. For the pragmatist, then, democracy is something that education can (and should) be good for.

In contrast, the reconstructionists and many recent proponents of critical pedagogy have opted for a curriculum based on countersocialization. But we can see that there are at least three fundamental problems with this approach. First, we have no access to the sort of foundational knowledge that would give us the blueprint for building a new social order. We certainly can and should help our students examine critically the current social order and consider possible alternative ways we might organize our society to better serve human interests. But on what philosophical, political, or professional basis could we claim the authority to use public education to indoctrinate students to support some specific vision of social or political organization?

Second, the very act of critical, pragmatic teaching is undercut by any attempt to impose a particular solution to social problems on our students. The human capacity to use practical judgment is enhanced to the extent that students are confronted with genuine problematic situations for which they must work out possible solutions. To base our curriculum around social solutions already worked out by teachers or other experts would amount to removing the very opportunity required for the students to engage the process of exercising practical judgment. Indeed, the reconstructionist's approach demonstrated a lack of confidence in the very method of intelligence that had led them to the convictions they now wished to impose on their students. In other words, what our students need most is the sort of critical competence the reconstructionists employed in their own analysis of historical and social conditions. Why should we not have faith that our students could acquire the same abilities we have via their educational experience? In other words, by resorting to countersocialization, we deprive students of the conditions necessary for the realization and enhancement of the practical judgment required to fully participate in a democratic culture.

Third, Dewey and others were also critical of the reconstructionist's exaggerated faith in the school's ability to bring about social change. Dewey realized it was unrealistic to assume that public education can play the central role in the cultural transformation required to bring about a significant change in the social order. Several studies of teachers have documented their generally mainstream or conservative views. In other words, teachers are an unlikely group to assume the revolutionary role thrust on them by the reconstructionists. Furthermore, it is increasingly evident that the schools are only one among a variety of powerful educational institutions including the media, family, peer groups, religious groups, and the workplace.

For Dewey, the school remained a necessary but not sufficient institution for contributing to the construction of a more democratic social order. Not only were the schools but one among many institutions involved in the process of socialization but also the schools themselves were in many ways an integral part of the existing social order. Surely the public schools were in need of social reconstruction before they would be in a position to play a major role in the transformation of the social order.

For the reasons previously noted, only a reconceptualized form of social reconstructionism would be relevant to the current debate over curriculum and schooling. We can accept the reconstructionist view that the schools can never be neutral and that all approaches to curriculum are politicized. We can also agree that the schools do play a role in maintaining or transforming the social order. As Dewey observed, "It is not whether the schools shall or shall not influence the course of future social life, but in what direction they shall do so and how."[7] Thus, educators cannot escape the responsibility for assisting in the task of social change (or maintenance) and should be aware of the orientation they bring to this project.

The sort of orientation argued for here seeks to realize the basic interest all humans have in developing their competence for practical reasoning. Practical judgment is a fundamental human interest because it is intrinsic to what it means to be human. This form of judgment is required in human action aimed at doing what is really good for people. But the "good" is not specified in advance in accord with some taken-for-granted set of values. Instead, practical judgment requires critical examination of both what our ends should be and how such ends can be best achieved.

To help students develop their competence for practical judgment is to help them develop the critical ability to determine whether we should work to transform the social order and, if so, how to go about this effort. Like Dewey, I have faith that a more enlightened generation would work for social change. Education can play a critical role in the process by providing genuine experiences wherein students can acquire a thorough understanding of their society, the means to critique it from various perspectives, and the opportunity to propose alternative forms of social action and arrangements.

This reconceptualized approach to social reconstruction would not be neutral or ambivalent. It would promote democracy as a way of life and the centrality of practical judgment, including the necessity of social criticism. This is not an approach to curriculum that would ever be comfortable with the status quo, but it would not be aimed at the realization of some fixed or final conception of society. As noted earlier, to attempt to impose some fixed view of a new social order is to short-circuit the very competence students require to create social change for human betterment. The approach to curriculum supported here does not abandon the reconstructionist hope for a better world but suggests another way to conceive this dream. We should embrace the reconstructionist's warning regarding the danger of complacency and the need to work toward human betterment through education. And we can turn to our own pragmatic tradition to inspire our imagination and the unlimited possibilities of human potential.

NOTES

[1]William B. Stanley, *Curriculum for Utopia: Social Reconstructionism and Critical Pedagogy in the Postmodern Era* (New York: State University of New York Press, 1992).

[2]Robert B. Westbrook, *John Dewey and American Democracy* (Ithaca, N.Y.: 1991).

[3]Herbert Kliebard, *The Struggle for American Curriculum, 1893–1958* (Boston: Routledge and Kegan Paul, 1986).

[4]Stanley, Chapter 3.

[5]John Dewey, "Education and Social Change," *The Social Frontier* 3 (1937): 37.

[6]Dewey, *The Quest for Certainty* (New York: Capricorn Books, 1929), p. 70.

[7]Dewey, "Education and Social Change," p. 36.

CHAPTER 5

Identity, Community, and Democracy in the "New Social Order"

SUSAN E. NOFFKE

In February of 1932, George S. Counts gave a series of three speeches later published as *Dare the School Build a New Social Order?* that have since become classics in curriculum studies.[1] Historical value notwithstanding, these speeches can provide substance as well as symbol for thinking about social education today. Counts focused on three issues that are the focus of this chapter: (1) that a "child-centered" approach free of social content serves the interests of existing social elites, (2) that teachers need to take the lead outside the classroom to implement the democratic ideals they develop and teach within the classroom, and (3) that there is a need to democratize the economy—that even during a depression, scarcity is no justification for gross inequities.[2] While Counts criticized economic inequality, as with many other documents from the social reconstructionist literature, he sidestepped issues of racial oppression.[3]

For most of this century, social studies curriculum in the United States has been conceptualized primarily in terms of "expanding horizons," at times also embodying the concept of spiraling in scope and sequence—that is, returning to issues in presumably greater complexity as children grow and develop. Recurrent controversies over the actual content of social studies education have often reflected tensions over the means and ends of socialization efforts.[4] In many cases, including the current "standards" efforts, curriculum frameworks are posited on several assumptions:

- There is a universal citizen, a unique individual, within a community or social order.

- The development of children is a "natural" phenomenon, and learning follows the logical sequences of particular groups of adults.
- Education for life in a "democracy," thus far imperfectly realized, is a suitable goal for the social studies.

The current context for debate over the social studies, unlike that of the 1930s, includes no widespread acknowledgment of the widening gap between the haves and the have-nots. As with Counts in the 1930s, the racialized and gendered patterns of privilege and oppression, which to a large degree form the basis of U.S. economic and cultural life, are also not addressed in contemporary proposals for reform.

What is described here is part of a search for alternative roots for social education, ones that highlight the possibilities of new understandings of fundamental social studies concepts such as citizenship and justice. Such a conceptual reframing may allow movement beyond dominant patterns for curricular frameworks, toward a version of curriculum conceptualized as a process of creating and nurturing instances both of understanding and of opportunities for action. In the historical threads that follow are instances when the curricular and pedagogical assumptions differ greatly from those of many contemporary reform efforts. These examples are not intended to refute contemporary assumptions but rather to highlight the current scene as merely one configuration of meanings, grounded in a particular unequal and unjust cultural and economic system and designed to ensure its persistence.[5] Although this form of curriculum—and the acquiescence to inequality it embodies—has dominated, it has not always been the only way of thinking about social education, especially the education of young children.

SITUATING THE CHILD WITHIN THE SOCIAL CONTEXT AND THE CURRICULUM WITHIN THE CHILD'S IDENTITY

Many of the educational journals of the early 1900s are rich records of both pedagogical and curricular alternatives. Teaching methods were varied, often showing a strong influence of such innovations as the "project method"; integrated units were developed across subject areas, and curriculum was related directly to children's interests. Yet distinguishing some of these efforts was also different content—content directly related to the culture and context of the child, and clearly different from that of the dominant group. Rather than a curriculum built for a "universal" child, it was a conception of curriculum in which cultural identity and social context played a greatly valued role.

Jessie Fauset and Helen Whiting are but two examples of the many African American educators who were clearly part of the general movement for progressive education.[6] Their projects integrated the arts with the social sciences and in many ways embodied the kinds of active engagement with learning advocated both by progressive educators of the time and by current researchers. Yet their work is distinctive in the way that curriculum was connected to the identity and context of children. Over her long career, Whiting worked in many different levels of teaching and teacher education. One project involved fourth- and fifth-graders in actively pursuing topics of their own choice, focusing on local African American community resources, on the geography and history of Africa, and on African American history.[7] Fauset's work, while clearly part of the overall growth of literature written for children, also sought to counter the predominantly racist images of African and African American people in the writings of the time.[8]

Similar efforts at creating social learning experiences for Native American peoples, grounded in their own culture, were noted in *Progressive Education,* the journal of the Progressive Education Association.[9] Such efforts paralleled changes in Native American education aimed directly at dismantling earlier, repressive policies such as the removal of children to boarding schools and the enforcement of language and cultural change.

The theme of education as cultural struggle is very evident in the issues of *Negro History Bulletin,* edited by Carter G. Woodson. Resources and ideas for teachers that reflect a cultural basis for curriculum can be found in the issues of that journal, for example, on the "Children's Page," a regular feature of the early volumes. Going back at least as far as the turn of the century, the children's issues of the National Association for the Advancement of Colored People's journal, *The Crisis,* edited by W. E. B. Du Bois, one can see how the struggle of African Americans for education embodied both curricular and pedagogical elements, often with a clear attempt to counteract the oppressive images present in many educational materials.[10]

It is important to see such efforts and their dissemination through journals as part of a social struggle in the face of repression.[11] The children's issues of *The Crisis,* for example, include beautiful illustrations of children. Yet these are set alongside ongoing reports of lynchings and other instances of racial oppression. The efforts by Fauset, Whiting, Du Bois, Woodson, and others were part of the "long and arduous campaign to introduce materials dealing with Negro life into the schools."[12] Coupled with cultural identity was a focus on children's responsibility for and initiative in their own learning, as well as a view of their community as a resource.

By looking at the early 1900s, we can see that the current efforts to provide alternatives to "received knowledge," especially that in textbooks, are not new initiatives. Yet alternative instructional methods with strong links to children's interests or assumed developmental stages are not in themselves enough. As Beverly Gordon argues so well, the study of African American (and other) sources for curriculum and pedagogy is not merely an added resource for educational thought but a necessity.[13] Children are not only individuals but also part of multiple social worlds, various communities. Identity is at once personal and collective.

The social world that shapes identity and community also influences the world of curriculum making in social education. Horace Mann Bond, a contemporary of Counts and a leading African American educator, critiqued the process of "scientific curriculum making," of which the current standards effort is but one manifestation. His comments have important implications for contemporary debates:

> the method of activity analysis in the construction of a curriculum presupposes an elastic, democratic social order in which there are no artificial barriers set against the social mobility of the individual.[14]

Whether in the "activity analysis" of the early curriculum makers, in the elaborate works of "scope and sequence" charts so firmly embedded in contemporary curriculum making, or in the whirlwind of efforts to set national standards and state goals, the presupposition of a permeable social order that offers rewards for individual achievement remains a common, albeit false, thread. Issues of racial justice in the United States involve not only concepts of culture but also the role of the economy in the continuing construction of racial boundaries.[15] The construction of social studies curriculum cannot, therefore, be accomplished by a focus on a universal, individual child alone.

TEACHERS, KNOWLEDGE, AND COMMUNITIES

For Counts, education inevitably involves imposition; failure to recognize it "involves the clothing of one's own deepest prejudices in the garb of universal truth."[16] He offered a scathing critique of those who see education as producing an individual "who sees all sides to every question and never commits himself to any, who delays action until all the facts are in, who knows that all the facts will never come in," and who waits "until the solutions to social problems are found, when as a matter of fact there are no solutions in the final sense."[17] This assertion of knowledge as partial (and partisan) and as of necessity linked to social action has been a persistent, although not always heard, voice in social education.

Yet what are the prospects for teachers who would shape democracy in their classrooms? Counts firmly believed that the prospects were bleak: "On all genuinely crucial matters the school follows the wishes of the groups or classes that actually rule society," while "on minor matters the school is sometimes allowed a certain measure of freedom." But he held out the hope that "the future may be unlike the past," a hope skeptically pinned on teachers' efforts.[18] Although he did anticipate that efforts by teachers' organizations would play a role, he did not relegate action to that arena alone, rather asserting: "In their own lives teachers must bridge the gap between school and society and play some part in the fashioning of those great common purposes which should bind the two together."[19] Teachers could, to begin with, participate in social movements, despite attempts at sanction and censure.

Further, teachers can exercise strong and meaningful political activity in their school community. A common focus for early elementary school social studies is the community—the neighbors and neighborhoods of children. Community, though, is clearly not only a geographical but also a social and ideological construction. Alongside studies of local resources and services could come an examination of the political and economic assumptions and practices that affect communities, as well as the cultural ties that bind.

An example for teachers to see how to politically engage in their community lies in the work of the Highlander Folk Center. The work of Myles Horton and a host of others in labor struggle, in the civil rights movement, and most recently in Appalachian redevelopment through participatory action research is well-documented.[20] For example, Hinsdale, Lewis, and Walker (1995), in *It Comes from the People,* report the efforts of community members to rebuild the economic base for their communities by linking social action and social research. Community members, rather than passively accepting economic inequality, worked under the assumption that industrial plant closings happened "not because people did something wrong" but because "the whole economic system is predicated on the position that profits are more important than people."[21] Resources produced by the center—for example, the book *A Very Popular Economic Education Sampler*—provide abundant material for social education curriculum in the schools.[22]

Such participatory action research projects help in surfacing a long-standing issue in social education: whether social study needs to be seen as not only an academic subject but also as a tool in the struggle for social and economic justice. The resolution of this issue implies seeing the process of building a new social order not merely as a task of creating a new pedagogy and curriculum for children. Instead, social study becomes a community (local or global) activity for adults as well. Responsibility for constructing the new social order does not rest in schools and on children; rather, the major responsibility must lie with adults working for and with children. Teachers can work at creating the social conditions that embody the "new social order" (antiracist, economically just, gender fair), not only in their classrooms and in traditional avenues of social action but also in the activities of reading, discussing, and thinking through issues with their colleagues in schools, in their day-to-day work with churches and civic groups, and even in the work of raising their own children. The kinds of social critique necessary for building democracy in schools and with children can then be seen as integral to teachers' lives, within and beyond schools.

The work of the Highlander Center is very useful in seeing social studies as a living part of communities and social movements. History and the social sciences are not just aspects of academic knowledge; they are also a vital part of the struggle to improve human life. Children need to observe and connect with challenges to dominant ideas of racial, economic, and gender equity in the lives of teachers, academics, and other adults. These are the sources for the social studies, as well as the sources for the leadership of teachers in the new social order.

DEMOCRACY AND ECONOMIC JUSTICE

My attempt thus far has been to draw on particular theoretical and concrete resources, ones that see the new social order in its economic, racial, gendered, and political dimensions. The works of Woodson, Du Bois, and the people at the Highlander Center lead us to the position that racial and economic justice are integral parts of any concept of democracy and therefore logical sources for the social studies.[23] Attempts to think outside dominant culture, as exemplified in the culturally referential curriculum works of Fauset and Whiting, and to work toward change, as evident in the Highlander Center's efforts toward "getting information, going back and teaching it," are but small parts of the long struggle over social education.[24] I hold these up here not as icons but as a way to use them to help think through contemporary issues in citizenship, which is often asserted to be a major goal of social education.

In broadening the issues embodied in the citizenship aspect of the social studies, I find it useful to remember some thoughts from Myles Horton, which echo the third part of Counts' speech, on how we are to understand democracy within the social studies:

> Democracy needs to be not only political but a part of the fabric of society as a whole. When I use the word "democracy," it is not limited to political decision making, to voting. It is a philosophical concept meaning that people are really free and empowered to make collectively the decisions that affect their lives.[25]

He added:

> To have democracy, you must have a society in which decision making is real, and that means replacing, transforming, and rebuilding society so as to allow for people to make decisions that affect their lives. These decisions shouldn't be counteracted by an economic structure in which maximizing profits overrides all other values. It's a growing concept that has to do with moving in a certain direction. All you can talk about is the direction and some of the elements you want to see built into the kind of society that you don't have now but would like to see in the future. But as you move toward it, you may notice lots of weaknesses and limitations in your concepts, so you change them.[26]

Rather than through the separated disciplines of economic and civic education, what is invoked in the work of the Highlander is a sense in which democracy is tightly bonded with economic justice. Rather than a fixed and definable "objective" for the social studies, it is a concept that must be continually constructed as it is lived.

WHAT'S LEFT (PUN INTENDED) IS WORK

This chapter has been but the beginning of a much-needed search for alternative ways of thinking about the purposes and processes of social education for school children, as well as the education of those who work with them in building a "new social order." Social educators have another history, one not directly connected to the emergence of social science disciplines and not launched by a series of committees. Rather than highlighting a vested interest in the emergence of a professional group, there are voices in our history which reflect the struggle for social justice in and through education, often focusing on citizens in the midst of social struggle. The work of Septima Clark with the people of John's Island and the work of the citizenship schools represent only two of many such resources.[27]

Especially in the social studies in schools and in teacher education, focus on issues of identity and community is essential. Yet also vital to curriculum and social reform is the process of critiquing the notion of democracy at the same time as we pursue its intended goals of economic and political justice. How do or can we capture in the assumptions of "universal," "natural" developmental progressions, in the language of scope and sequence, or in the political platforms embedded in "standards" the tentativeness as well as the possibilities of education for a new social order? Perhaps what is needed is not only the question of how but also Counts' original question of "dare." That is as much an issue of determination and hope as it is of means.

Yet framing the question as "dare" the social studies build a new social order assumes it is a choice, not an imperative. It is a choice only for those already privileged. For many folks, the choice is never possible. Continuing the critical tradition also means getting beyond its blind spots, for example, the minimal ways in which social reconstructionists addressed issues of race and gender, while still valuing their critique of a system that supports social inequalities. Many years ago, Carter G. Woodson, in the work too often neglected in curriculum studies, *The Mis-Education of the Negro,* reminded us:

> In the first place, we must bear in mind that the Negro has never been educated. He merely has been informed about other things which he has not been permitted to do.[28]

Our construction of social education must bear this in mind. Without the recognition of the role of social education in the maintenance of oppression, reform efforts will be subverted into the maintenance of privilege.

We must remember the critical response of Horace Mann Bond:

> Let us confess that the schools have never built a new social order, but have always in all times and in all lands been the instruments through which social forces were perpetuated. If our new curriculum revision is to do better, it must undertake an acceptance of the profound social and economic changes which are now taking place in the world.[29]

Whether we look at child-centered curriculum, at the role of the teacher in social change, or in the nature of the economic democracy to which our citizenship efforts are directed, the new social order still has much to formulate. Our task as social educators is no less daunting than that of prior eras; it is also no less imperative. As Carter G. Woodson urged:

> But can you expect teachers to revolutionize the social order for the good of the community? Indeed we must expect this very thing. The educational system of a country is worthless unless it accomplishes this task.[30]

Acknowledgment

I wish to thank my dear friends and comrades, David Hursh and John St. Julien, for their helpful comments on an earlier draft of this paper.

NOTES

[1]George S. Counts, *Dare the School Build a New Social Order?* (Carbondale: Southern Illinois University Press, 1932/1978); Herbert M. Kliebard, *The Struggle for the American Curriculum* (New York: Routledge, 1995).

[2]Wayne J. Urban, "Preface." In Counts, pp. v–xiv.

[3]Ronald K. Goodenow, "The Progressive Educator, Race and Ethnicity in the Depression Years: An Overview," *History of Education Quarterly* 15 (Winter, 1975): 365–394.

[4]David Warren Saxe, *Social Studies in Schools: A History of the Early Years* (Albany: State University of New York Press, 1991).

[5]Michael W. Apple, *Ideology and Curriculum* (New York: Routledge, 1979).

[6]Violet J. Harris, "Jessie Fauset's Transference of the 'New Negro' Philosophy to Children's Literature," *Langston Hughes Review* 6, no. 2 (Fall, 1987): 36–43; Violet J. Harris, "Helen Whiting and the Education of Colored Children, 1930–1960: Emancipatory Pedagogy in Action" (paper presented at the Annual Meeting of the American Educational Research Association, Chicago, 1991).

[7]Helen Adele Whiting, "Negro Children Study Race Culture," *Progressive Education* 12 (March, 1935): 172–181.

[8]Harris, "Jessie Fauset's transference . . ."; Dianne Johnson-Feelings, *The Best of The Brownies' Book* (New York: Oxford University Press, 1996).

[9]W. Carson Ryan, Jr., and Rose K. Brandt, "Indian Education Today," *Progressive Education* 9 (February, 1932): 81–179.

[10]Ronald E. Butchart, "Outthinking and Outflanking the Owners of the World: An Historiography of the African-American Struggle for Education," in *Too Much Schooling, Too Little Education: A Paradox of Black Life in White Societies*, ed. Mwalimu J. Shujaa (Trenton, N.J.: Africa World Press, 1994), pp. 85–122; Violet J. Harris, "Historic Readers for African-American Children (1868–1944): Uncovering and Reclaiming a Tradition of Opposition," in *Too Much Schooling, Too Little Education: A Paradox of Black Life in White Societies*, ed. Mwalimu J. Shujaa (Trenton, N.J.: Africa World Press, 1994), pp. 143–175.

[11]William H. Watkins, "Black Curriculum Orientations: A Preliminary Inquiry," *Harvard Educational Review* 63 (Fall 1993): 321–338.

[12]Horace Mann Bond, "The Curriculum and the Negro Child," *Journal of Negro Education* 4 (1935): 161.

[13]Beverly M. Gordon, "The Necessity of African-American Epistemology for Educational Theory and Practice," *Journal of Education* 172 (1990): 88–106.

[14]Bond, p. 167.

[15]Ronald Takaki, *A Different Mirror: A History of Multicultural America.* (Boston: Little, Brown, 1993); Howard Zinn, *A People's History of the United States: 1492–Present* (New York: Harper, 1995).

[16]Counts, p. 9.

[17]Ibid., p. 18.

[18]Ibid., p. 25.

[19]Ibid., p. 28.

[20]Frank Adams, *Unearthing the Seeds of Fire: The Idea of Highlander* (Winston-Salem, N.C.: John F. Blair, 1975); John Gaventa, "The Powerful, the Powerless, and the Experts: Knowledge Struggles in an Information Age," in *Voices of Change: Participatory Research in the United States and Canada,* ed. Peter Park, Mary Brydon-Hall, Budd Hall, and Ted Jackson (Westport, Conn.: Bergin & Garvey, 1993), pp. 21–40; Myles Horton, *The Long Haul* (New York: Anchor/Doubleday, 1990).

[21]Mary Ann Hinsdale, Helen M. Lewis, and S. Maxine Waller, *It Comes from the People: Community Development and Local Theology* (Philadelphia: Temple University Press, 1995).

[22]Highlander Research and Education Center, *A Very Popular Economic Education Sampler* (New Market, Tenn.: Highlander Research and Education Center, 1997).

[23]Beverly Gordon, "Toward Emancipation in Citizenship Education: The Case of African-American Cultural Knowledge," *Theory and Research in Social Education* 12 (1985): 1–23.

[24]James Baldwin, "A Talk to Teachers," in *Multicultural Literacy: The Opening of the American Mind, The Graywolf Annual Five,* ed. R. Simonson and S. Walker (St. Paul: Graywolf Press, 1988), pp. 3–12.

[25]Horton, *The Long Haul,* p. 169.

[26]Ibid., p. 174.

[27]Cynthia Stokes Brown, ed., *Ready from Within, a First Person Narrative: Septima Clark and the Civil Rights Movement* (Trenton, N.J.: Africa World Press, 1990); George W. Chilcoat and Jerry A. Ligon, "Developing Democratic Citizens: The Mississippi Freedom Schools as a Model for Social Studies Instruction," *Theory and Research in Social Education* 22 (Spring, 1994): 128–175. See also John R. Rachal, "We'll Never Turn Back: Adult Education and the Struggle for Citizenship in Mississippi's Freedom Summer," *American Educational Research Journal* 35 (Summer 1998): 167–198.

[28]Carter G. Woodson, *The Mis-Education of the Negro* (New York: AMS Press 1933/1977), p. 144.

[29]Bond, p. 168.

[30]Woodson, p. 145

CHAPTER 6

Democratic Education
and Popular Culture

HENRY A. GIROUX

Educational reform has fallen on hard times. The traditional assumption
that schooling is fundamentally tied to the imperatives of citizenship designed to educate students to exercise leadership and public service has
been eclipsed. Schooling is now the key institution for producing professional, technically trained, credentialized workers for whom the demands of citizenship are subject to the vicissitudes of the marketplace
and the commercial public sphere. During the Reagan and Bush era in
the United States, the deeper issues that framed the meaning, purpose,
and use to which education might aspire were displaced by more vocational and narrowly ideological considerations.

The legacy of neoconservatism continues into the present in spite of
the election in 1992 of a moderate Democrat, Bill Clinton, to the presi-
dency. Under the leadership of a Congress controlled by a Republican
majority, financial retrenchment and downsizing overshadow questions
of social justice, equality, and community. Testing and standardization
replace considerations of poverty, racial discrimination, and class inequalities and how they are reproduced by and have an impact on the
schools. Schooling and the language of educational reform have increasingly become more supportive of goals designed to train students for administrative jobs, produce new knowledge for business and the military,
and reduce the art and politics of teaching to managerial and technical
considerations.

In the popular press, the nearly hysterical media point to political
correctness and the violations accorded the foundations of Western culture waged by multiculturalists and academic progressives. At the same

85

time, the guardians of Western civilization see no contradiction in their claim that public education be predicated on the virtues of a common culture rooted in the precepts of the Enlightenment while simultaneously arguing that language spoken at home by the children of immigrants, people of color, and subordinate groups is either illegal or un-American.

Of course, the war waged against the possibilities of an education wedded to the precepts of a real democracy is not merely ideological. Against the backdrop of reduced funding for public schooling, the call for privatization, vouchers, cultural uniformity, and choice, there are the often ignored larger social realities of material power and oppression. On the national level, there has been a vast resurgence of racism, evident in the passing of anti-immigration laws such as Proposition 187 in California; the remarkable attention given in the pubic press to *The Bell Curve,* a right-wing apology for racism; and the demonization of black youth in the popular media.

Similarly, poverty is on the rise among children in the United States, with 20 percent of all children under the age of eighteen living below the poverty line. Unemployment is growing at an alarming rate for youth, especially in the urban centers. Most disturbing about these social problems is that they have a decidedly racial overtone. Nearly half of all black children live below the poverty line; the unemployment rate among black males is nearly double that of their white counterparts. While black bodies are policed and disciplined in and out of the nation's schools, conservative and liberal educators define education through the ethically limp discourse of achievement, standards, and global competitiveness. In the world of policy making and talk show politics, it has become increasingly clear that imperializing power goes hand in hand with monoculturalism, racism, class inequality, and censorship. June Jordan has argued that she sees "every root argument about public education turning upon definitions of sanity and insanity." She goes on to ask, "Shall we submit to ceaseless lies, fantastic misinformation, and fantastic omissions? Shall we agree to the erasure of our beleaguered, heterogeneous truth? Shall we embrace traditions of insanity and lose ourselves and the whole real world? . . . What does public education in a democratic state require?"[1]

Of course, many writers in the traditions of critical education have attempted to challenge the right-wing fundamentalism behind educational reform in the United States while simultaneously providing theoretical signposts for a public discourse about education that is both prophetic and transformative. Eschewing traditional categories used by radicals, liberals, and conservatives, radical educators such as Donaldo

Macedo, Jonathan Kozol, and Bill Ayers have successfully exposed the political and ethical implications of the cynicism and despair that has become endemic to the discourse of schooling. In its place, such educators often provide a language of hope that inextricably links the struggle over schooling to understanding and transforming our present social and cultural dangers. Approaching their task historically, contextually, and ethically, such writers provide new insights in analyzing the shift to the ideological right that public discourse has taken in the last decade and how such a discourse has contributed to a new authoritarianism and a sustained attack on both the welfare state and the foundations of democratic leadership and life. Equally important is the authors' willingness to analyze the challenges that teachers will have to face around redefining a new mission for education, a mission that is linked to honoring the experiences, concerns, and diverse histories and languages that give expression to the multiple narratives that engage and challenge the legacy of democracy in the United States.

An equally significant insight of recent critical educational work is the emphasis on connecting the politics of difference with concrete strategies for addressing the relationship between schooling and the economy, citizenship and the politics of meaning, community and the reality of the heterogeneous student bodies and identities that increasingly inhabit our multicultural, multiracial, and multilingual schools. In this instance, the politics of educational reform becomes part of a politics of pragmatic possibility, attentive to both the reduction of injustices and suffering and the need for new alliances, a new politics of connectedness in which the production of knowledge, social identities, and social relations incorporates as a defining principle such categories as justice, equality, struggle, and democracy. In what follows, I want to extend this work by taking up the relevance of popular culture as a pedagogical sphere and its importance in any discourse that links critical citizenship and pedagogy. I especially want to engage the public debate about cinematic violence and the implications such a debate has for educators actively engaged in linking the imperatives of education and democracy.

CINEMATIC VIOLENCE AND THE QUESTION OF PEDAGOGY

There appears to be an enormous deadlock in developing a critical debate over cinematic and media representations of violence. It was evident in the public furor that emerged when Bob Dole, as the Senate majority leader, appearing at a fund-raising event in Los Angeles, condemned certain Hollywood filmmakers for debasing U.S. culture with images of graphic violence and "the mainstreaming of deviancy." Dole specifically condemned films such as *Natural Born Killers* and *True Romance* as "nightmares of depravity," drenched in grotesque violence and sex. Speaking for a Republican party that has increasingly moved to the extreme right, Dole issued a warning to Hollywood: "A line has been crossed—not just of taste, but of human dignity and decency. . . . It is crossed every time sexual violence is given a catchy tune. When teen suicide is set to an appealing beat. When Hollywood's dream factories turn out nightmares of depravity."[2] Dole's remarks were less an insightful indictment of the culture of violence than a shrewd attempt to win the hearts and minds of Christian conservatives and those in the general public who are fed up with the culture of violence but feel helpless in the face of its looming pervasiveness. Although Dole's stand regarding the relationship between Hollywood representations of violence and its impact on society is commendable, he failed to address a number of issues necessary to critically engage the culture of violence in this country.

First, political opportunism aside, Dole's remarks do not constitute a thoughtful and sincere analysis of the culture of violence. On the surface, Dole's comments about the orgy of violence and misogyny flooding American popular culture resonate with a deeply felt anxiety about the alleged innocence of commercial entertainment. But Dole is no spokesperson for criticizing or analyzing the violence in this country. Not only had he not viewed the films he criticized but also he argued that Arnold Schwarzenegger's killfest film, *True Lies,* represented the kind of film that Hollywood should be producing for family entertainment. Dole also refused to criticize the exploitive, bloody films made by Bruce Willis and Sylvester Stallone, both prominent Republicans. Second, Dole's refusal to address the culture of violence in broader terms, coupled with his role in actually reproducing such a culture, reveals a grave theoretical omission and unfortunate disingenuousness in his criticisms. At a time when "an estimated 100,000 children carry guns to school in the United States [and] gunfire kills on average 15 children a day,"[3] Dole drew no connection between the gun culture and the violence in our nation's streets, schools, and homes. As Ellen Goodman points out, "Anybody who is against violence in the movies and in favor of assault weapons in real life leaves himself open to all sorts of charges, the least of which is hypocrisy."[4] It is hard to believe that, following the Oklahoma City bombing, Dole refused to include in his critique of the culture of violence the rise of right-wing militia groups, the hate talk emanating from right-wing talk show hosts such as G. Gordon Liddy, or the gun culture supported by the National Rifle Association, which published a fund-raising letter in which federal law-enforcement agents were referred to as "Jackbooted Thugs." This letter prompted former president George Bush to resign from the NRA; Dole, however, remained silent on the issue.

What is the significance of Bob Dole's attack on Hollywood films he had not viewed and his refusal to address corporate interests aligned with the Republican party that have a big economic stake in the culture of violence? It may be that Dole's attack signals less of a concern with how the culture of violence is represented in this country than with the more central issue of who is going to control those cultural spheres that contain the possibility for creating complex forms of interaction, dialogue, and public interaction. Maybe it is the threat of popular culture as a site of critical dialogue that explains how Dole can criticize the vulgarity of popular films and rap music and at the same time advocate the defunding of the Public Broadcasting Systems, the National Endowment for the Arts, and other government support for the arts. The attack being waged on the arts, popular culture, and mass media suggests that conservatives want to homogenize culture rather than diversify it. To diversify culture would demand supporting those institutions or public spheres in which critical knowledge, debate, and dialogue would be necessary for people to make choices about how power works through culture and what it means to identify with, challenge, and rewrite the representations that circulate in popular and mass-mediated cultures.

The relevance of this debate for educators lies in the implication that the best way to reduce symbolic violence in the culture must be part of a larger discourse about educating people to change the social and economic conditions that produce and sustain such violence. This further suggests addressing how questions of pedagogy and commitment can mutually interact to challenge institutional structures of power that trade in oppressive forms of symbolic imagery and simultaneously refuse to address the limits of the media's potential for error and harm. Social justice is not part of the message that underwrites Dole's concern with media culture and its relationship with the public good. On the contrary, Dole represents an ideological position that advocates abolishing the Department of Education, privatizing public schools, and limiting funding for poor students who want higher education. But Dole's moral indignation is fueled not merely by political opportunism but also by a political project that engages the cultural public sphere in order to wage control over it rather than democratize it.

Unfortunately, Hollywood executives, directors, and celebrities responded to Dole's remarks primarily by focusing on his hypocrisy rather than by providing a forum for critically analyzing Hollywood's complicity with and responsibility for addressing the growing culture of violence in the United States. Oliver Stone, the director of *Natural Born Killers,* labeled Dole's attack "a 90s form of McCarthyism," and actor James Wood compared Dole's actions to the morality crusades that inspired censors of a previous era to attempt to ban *Catcher in the Rye* and *Ulysses.* Such remarks are defensive in the extreme and exhibit little self-consciousness of what Hollywood's role or responsibility might be in shaping popular culture and providing a pedagogical climate in which knowledge, values, desires, and identities are marketed on a daily basis to children and young adults, among others. The relationship between greed and the marketing of violence might inspire Hollywood executives and celebrities to be more attentive to the ravages committed in the name of the free market or to address their own ethical responsibility as cultural workers who actively circulate ideas and values for popular consumption. Claiming that the film, music, and television industries simply reflect what the public wants is more than disinguousness; it suggests political and ethical cowardice. Neither Dole's one-sided criticism nor Hollywood's defensive posture provides a helpful model for dealing with the culture of violence.

In the coming new information age, cultural workers and educators must raise important questions about what kind of teacher we want cinema to be, with special concern for how the representation of violence works to pose a threat "not only to our national health but to our potential for ever becoming a true participatory democracy."[5] To simply blame filmmakers and television executives for causing violence in the United States shifts critical attention away from the poisonous roots of violence at the heart of social and economic life in America. Blaming the media also absolves educators, community activists, politicians, and other cultural workers from assuming roles as critical citizens who need to address the complex relationships between the violence we absorb through the media and the reality of violence we experience in everyday life.

Cinematic violence, whether productively instructive or merely sensational, is not innocent; such violence offers viewers brutal and grotesque images that serve to pollute and undermine how children and adults relate, care, and respond to others. At stake here is not whether cinematic violence directly causes crime or is the determining force in the wider culture of violence. The causes of violence lie in historically rooted, complex economic and social issues that are the heart of American society. To blame Hollywood exclusively for the violence in American society would be a subterfuge for addressing the complex causes of violence at work in the larger social order. In a world demeaned by pointless violence, the question that must be raised concerns what responsibilities educators, filmmakers, other cultural workers, and their respective publics have for developing a cultural policy that addresses the limits and responsibilities for violence in cinema. Such a policy must address how the mass media and the film community can be held responsible for educating children and others about how to discriminate among different forms of violence, how to prevent it in real life when necessary, and how to engage its root social causes in the larger social and cultural landscape.

Violence is not merely a function of power. It is also deeply related to how forms of self and social agency are produced within a variety of public spheres. Cinema exercises enormous pedagogical authority and influence, and the reach, limits, and possibilities of its influence, especially on young children, can be addressed only through a coordinated effort in cultural spheres—schools, religious institutions, business corporations, popular culture, local communities, and the home. Such institutions need to develop a cultural policy that addresses the ethical responsibilities of a cinematic public sphere, including fundamental questions about the democratization of culture. Such questions provide a common ground for various organizations and publics to raise questions regarding ownership, power, and control over media culture. Cinema is neither a site of innocence nor a site of depravity. As a site that both respects the imagination and provides pedagogical possibilities for engaging audiences in complex representations of everyday life, cinema becomes a site where pedagogy and entertainment can merge to both educate and produce critical forms of engagement. The importance of such a pedagogical role for cinema demands that cultural workers raise important questions about who has access to the means of cultural representation and who does not and about the possibilities for democracy when gross financial inequalities and structures of power gain control over the apparatuses that produce popular and media culture.[6] Questions about culture are always pedagogical because culture in its symbolic and material forms cannot escape the issues of how meaning is negotiated, translated, and invested within different sites through complex layers of history, experience, and desire. But cultural issues also demand another register of inquiry regarding ownership, power, and control. Dole raises some questions about representations of violence but ignores entirely issues of control, ownership, and power.

Violence is not simply emanating from the movie theaters of America. Rooted in everyday institutional structures and social relations, violence has become a toxic glue that bonds Americans together while preventing them from expanding and building a multiracial and multicultural democracy. Once the brutality of degrading forms of representational violence are understood as threats to democracy itself, it might become possible to address it politically and pedagogically, as we would other issues concerning our national identity, public well-being, and social consciousness. In the end, Dole's political opportunism is a poor substitute for challenging the institutional structures of power that produce violence at every level of daily life, and his attacks against popular films, rap music, and other aspects of media culture offer little in the way of recovering media and popular culture as a site of democratic renewal, critical agency, and the nurturing of personal and political imagination. More productively, Dole's remarks do provide a challenge for educators to rethink not only how popular culture serves as a teaching machine that is central to how children learn and how their culture is shaped but also what it means for educators to take up the challenge of popular culture pedagogically as part of the broader challenge facing educators concerned about the crisis of democracy itself.

PEDAGOGY AND THE CHALLENGE OF DEMOCRACY

I want to argue that pedagogy as a critical cultural and political practice must become a defining principle for making popular culture relevant to the discourse of schooling and democracy. Pedagogy as a conceptual category offers new theoretical horizons for educators to understand how sites of learning outside schooling offer young people different forms of identification and subject positions and how such sites generate different pedagogical practices. Crucial to the notion of linking schooling with democracy is the need to create alliances among teachers and other cultural workers, such as artists, media workers, and social workers, who work in diverse sites and public spheres. Cultural workers who teach in diverse sites of learning often engage and address a shared set of assumptions regarding how knowledge is produced, skills are learned meaningfully, identities are shaped, desires are mobilized, and critical dialogue becomes a central form of public interaction. Around such pedagogical practices, teachers and other cultural workers can find a common ground in developing a public discourse and a set of alliances designed to further develop the role of educators as public intellectuals and teaching as a central dynamic of expanding democratic social relations within and across national and transnational terrains.[7] I want to expand on this issue by addressing three considerations crucial, though far from complete, for rethinking the role of the educator as a public intellectual and the importance of education as a critical, democratic practice that takes place in diverse sites of learning.

First, to understand more clearly how power works through the popular and the everyday to produce knowledge, social identities, and maps of desire, educators need to redefine what constitutes legitimate objects of social knowledge. Crucial here is the ongoing pedagogical work of understanding how social practices that deploy images, sounds, and other representational practices are redefining the production of knowledge, reason, and new forms of global culture. Cultural workers in most sites are now facing the task of interrogating how technology and science are combining to produce new information systems that transcend local-global and high-low culture dichotomies. Virtual reality systems and the new digital technologies that are revolutionizing media culture will increasingly come under the influence of an instrumental rationality that relegates their use to the forces of the market and passive consumption. Popular culture must be addressed not merely for the opportunities it provides to revolutionize how people learn or become cultural producers but for the role it will play in guaranteeing human rights and social justice. This point suggests the need for a new debate around reason, Enlightenment rationality, technology, and authority.

Second, educators and other cultural workers need to take seriously Walter Benjamin's call for intellectuals to assume responsibility for the task of translating theory back into a constructive practice that transforms the everyday terrain of cultural and political power. Beyond expanding the range of traditional and nontraditional media as part of the realm of public art, there is also the need to produce pedagogies that address the crisis of cultural identity that has emerged with the collapse of a public discourse forged in the binaristic determinations and fears of the Cold War. Transformative pedagogy should always be suspicious of its own politics while simultaneously demanding political and cultural projects tempered by humility, a moral focus on suffering, and commitment to moving beyond the inside-outside divide that separates forms of cultural work. On one level, this call suggests rejecting both the notion of the educator who speaks as the "universal intellectual" and the specific intellectual who speaks exclusively within the sometimes essentializing claims of identity politics. Radical pedagogical work needs to create spaces where educators and other cultural workers function as border intellectuals.[8] If the universal intellectual speaks for everyone and the specific intellectual is wedded to serving the narrow interests of distinct cultural and social formations, the border intellectual travels within and across communities of difference, collaborates with diverse groups, and occupies many sites of resistance while defying the specialized, parochial knowledge of the individual specialist, sage, or master ideologue. As border intellectuals, educators can articulate and negotiate different struggles as part of a broader effort to secure social justice, economic equality, and human rights within and across regional, national, and broader areas. What is at stake here is the possibility for educators to work collectively and find ways to make knowledge relevant to broad-based democratic change in an effort to transform the undemocratic institutional conditions that produce human suffering.

Third, despite the multiple languages, histories, and founding moments of the politics of identity and multiculturalism, its underlying commitment to political work has not been adequately developed as part of a wider project for social reconstruction and progressive educational change. Although issues of racism, class, gender, textuality, national identity, subjectivity, and media culture must remain central elements in defining a transformative pedagogical practice, the issue of radical democracy must be located at the center of such a pedagogy. Radical democracy in this instance favors the restructuring of political and economic institutions in ways that permit broad popular control over them. It means creating forms of self-management in all major political, economic, and cultural spheres of society. It also means restructuring social relations so that power flows from the base of society and not from the top.[9]

Needless to say, the politics of difference has broadened our understanding of how politics and power work through institutions, language, representations, culture, and across diverse economies of desire, time, and space. But in enabling this vast reconceptualization of power and resistance, it has failed to provide a clear sense of what these sites have in common. By addressing radical democracy as a political, social, and ethical referent for rethinking how citizens can be educated to deal with a world made up of different, multiple, and fractured public cultures, educators must construct a new ethical and political language to map the problems and challenges of citizenship in a newly constituted global public.

At issue is the necessity for progressive educators to develop a collective vision in which traditional binarisms of margin-center, unity-difference, local-national, and public-private can be reconstituted through more complex representations of identification, belonging, and community. As Paul Gilroy has argued, cultural workers need a discourse of ruptures, shifts, flows, and unsettlement, one that functions less as a politics of transgression than as part of a concerted effort to construct a broader vision of political commitment and democratic struggle.[10] He suggests a fundamental redefinition of the meaning of the educator as a public intellectual and of how, as educators, we view the sites where we address our work. As public intellectuals, we must define ourselves not merely as marginal, avant-garde figures, professionals, or academics acting alone, but as critical citizens whose collective knowledge and actions presuppose specific visions of public life, community, and moral accountability.

Critical educators in an age of insurgent differences need an expanded notion of the public, solidarity, and democratic struggle. What is crucial is a conception of the political that is open yet committed, respects specificity without erasing global considerations, and provides new spaces for collaborative work engaged in productive social change. The time has come for educators to develop a political project in which power, history, and human agency can play active roles in constructing the multiple and shifting political relations and cultural practices necessary for connecting the construction of diverse political subjects to the revitalization of democratic public life. Under these conditions, pedagogy would be unsettling without being terroristic, and politics would not mean, as Edward Said has pointed out, that the educator had fully arrived, but that one could never go home again.[11]

NOTES

[1] June Jordan, *Technical Difficulties: African-American Notes on the State of the Union* (New York: Pantheon, 1992), pp. 198–199.

[2] As quoted by John M. Broder, "Dole Blasts 'Deviancy' in Hollywood, Films, and Music," *Boston Globe* (June 1, 1995).

[3] Derrick Z. Jackson, "Sen. Dole's Amazon of Hypocrisy," *Boston Globe* (June 9, 1995), p. 23.

⁴Ellen Goodman, "A New Cast, Same Script," *Boston Globe* (June 8, 1995), p.18. On the sheer hypocrisy of Dole's remarks, see Jackson.

⁵Michael Roth, "Violence and the De-Meaning of America," *Tikkun* 9 (1994): 87.

⁶Herbert I. Schiller, *Culture Inc.* (New York: Oxford University Press, 1989).

⁷For an informative discussion on the relationship between radical democracy and transnational agencies and forms of resistance, see Gayatri Chakravorty Spivak and David Plotke, "A Dialogue on Democracy," *Socialist Review* 24 (1995): 1–22.

⁸For an exemplary essay on the border intellectual, see Abdul R. Jan-Mohamed, "Worldliness-Without-World, Homelessness-as-Home: Toward a Definition of the Specular Border Intellectual," in Michael Sprinker, ed., *Edward Said: A Reader* (Cambridge, Mass.: Basil Blackwell, 1992), pp. 97–123. I take up this issue in great detail in Henry Giroux, *Fugitive Cultures: Race, Violence, and Youth* (New York: Routledge, 1996).

⁹The concept of democracy that I am referring to can be found in the work of Stanley Aronowitz, Chantal Mouffe, Noam Chomsky, and Ernesto Laclau.

¹⁰Paul Gilroy, *The Black Atlantic* (Cambridge, Mass.: Harvard University Press, 1994).

¹¹Edward Said, *Representations of the Intellectual* (New York: Pantheon, 1994).

CHAPTER 7

Cultural Studies and Democratically Aware Teacher Education

Post-Fordism, Civics, and the Worker-Citizen

JOE L. KINCHELOE

The movement of cultural studies into the study of pedagogy constitutes one of the most significant academic developments of the last decade. Bringing together the various academicians who study cultural phenomena—anthropologists, students of communications, sociologists, historians, political scientists, students of literature, and more—cultural studies subverts the tendency toward specialization and disciplinary isolation. Thus, the point of cultural studies is not only to synthesize the work that takes place in a variety of disciplines but also to expose their silences, erasures, and modes of producing and legitimating knowledge. In this context, cultural studies plays the role of the perpetual outsider as it challenges the dominant assumption that disciplinary knowledge and culture itself have already been formed. Refusing to consider academic study as a series of deposits in Freire's "knowledge bank," cultural studies resists the canonization of knowledge. Because cultural studies proponents position culture as a lived activity, experienced within unequal power relations, that is still in the process of formation, culture can be democratically transformed.

With their tendency to view teaching as a technical act, along with their isolation from other colleges within the university, colleges of education can significantly profit from encounters with cultural studies. Focusing as it does on the production and legitimation of knowledge, cultural studies in a college of education opens new conversations about and understandings of the tacit assumptions embedded in the education subdisciplines. Cultural studies asks: What are the origins of the ways we construct the curriculum of educational leadership? How do culture and power relations affect the criteria for assessment in special education student placement? What are the political implications of the definitions of intelligence employed by educational psychologists? What cultural narratives ground the way methods courses teach students how to teach? What types of worker-citizens do we expect to produce in the schools where our teachers teach?

In this context, cultural studies brings new perspectives to the cultural conversation about democracy, citizenship, and their relationship to pedagogical issues. In particular, students of democracy can draw on the work of cultural studies in their attempt to understand how power works through social institutions, discourse, media representations, and the colonization of desire. At the same time it provides such political insight, cultural studies helps us rethink resistance in a global society made up of power-saturated public cultures. Our notion of transformative cultural studies is grounded in the effort to reshape power relations in a more democratic manner, to produce knowledge that provides individuals with insight into how to democratize social relations, and to provide contextual understandings that help us formulate emancipatory strategies in specific situations. In this context, students of pedagogy, with their emphases on the analysis of knowledge production and transmission, the construction of values, and the formation of identity, can make use of cultural studies to understand the interaction of pedagogy, power, democratic values, and social justice. At this conceptual juncture, teacher education can engage teachers in a critical pedagogy dedicated to the revitalization of civics. Such a civics would focus its attention on the appreciation of the diverse ways economic, political, and social forces shape lives and structure unequal power relations.

A critical civics education is sensitive to the way power colonizes subjectivity. Power in this process works in subtle ways, rarely imposing itself but more commonly engaging subjectivity in a process of negotiation and struggle for a hegemonic form of consent. Such consent is never fixed, as it constantly shifts within the specificity of historical conditions. This shifting struggle involves the meaning of language and texts that contain at some valence the interests of the dominant groups that produced them—interests involved with commodification, free market capitalism, and patriarchy. Whether the cultural text is Disney's *Lion King,* celebrating antidemocratic social relations; Mighty Morphin Power Rangers, privileging violent androcentric modes of conflict resolution;[1] or professional wrestling, with its racial encoding of white as victim for working-class white audiences,[2] subtle dynamics of power are at work. Such dynamics connect textual producers from an ever-shifting power bloc that at times unites corporate economic interests, patriarchy, and white supremacy to the shaping of our subjectivities and self-identities.

With these understandings in mind, I will provide an example of how cultural studies can be used to inform a democratically aware teacher education. As teacher educators and their students begin to see teaching and citizenship from the vantage point of cultural studies, I begin to understand the ways that the concepts are shaped by cultural forces. Such understandings can revolutionize the work of colleges of education, produce students capable of cultural analysis and sophisticated modes of civic thinking, and move teacher education into the scholarly conversation of the university. Our example involves the ways that the socioeconomic dynamics of post-Fordism are reshaping power relations, the nature of work, and democratic citizenship in the twenty-first century and the implications of this cultural process for teaching and teacher education.

FORDISM'S NEW MODE OF LIVING AND THINKING AND FEELING LIFE

The economic foundations of twentieth-century life were established in its second decade, when Henry Ford introduced his five-dollar, eight-hour day at his automobile assembly line in Dearborn, Michigan.[3] Drawing on the rationalism of modernism, Fordist production procedures became the highest expression of modernism and the lowest expression of worker dignity. Ford's four production principles were (1) the standardization of products, (2) the development of special-purpose machinery to be used in the construction of each separate model, (3) the fragmentation of tasks into their component parts and task assignments developed around the time-motion principles developed by Frederick W. Taylor, and (4) the flowline replaced static model assembly, in that instead of workers working around the static product, the product (the car) flowed past the workers on a flowline. Ford, of course, was not the originator of mass production and assembly lines. There are examples of such methods in use as early as the eighteenth century, but Ford was the first to bring the forms of modern industrial organization together at once with higher wages for workers.[4]

What made Ford's project unique was the totality of his scheme. Ford wanted to create a new type of worker and *human*—not just the human as efficient worker but also the human as efficient consumer. *Homo economicus/consumerus* would live, work, and consume in a new society, a modern, rationalized world. Writing from one of Mussolini's prisons, Antonio Gramsci recognized Fordism as a new "mode of living and thinking and feeling life."[5] So total was Ford's system that in 1916, concerned that workers would not learn how to consume properly, Ford sent a division of social workers into the homes of his workers to teach them morality, proper family life, and the characteristics of *rational shopping.* Fordism became synonymous with scientific forms of regulation associated with modernism.[6] Thus, Fordism became not only a mode of economic production but also a means of social and political regulation of the American population. In other words, Fordism represented a grand compromise: though labor maintained some say in collective bargaining, social security benefits, and the minimum wage, it held on to these rights in return for acceptance of Fordist production strategies and corporate schemes to boost productivity and work discipline. The grand compromise was grounded on the faith that if wage increases were linked to increased productivity, profits were sure to increase. Business and labor were partners in a common economic struggle. Government would serve as a bow-tied referee to protect in theory each institution from the excessive power and the low blows of the other.

It is not hard to see how schools were involved in the grand compromise. The spirit of the Fordist view of humans as efficient workers and efficient consumers is quite apparent in the history of twentieth-century American education. Only three years after the opening of Ford's Dearborn, Michigan, plant in 1914, David Snedden and Charles Prosser (education's efficiency proponents) helped Congress pass the Smith-Hughes Vocational Education Act—the highest expression of educational efficiency or educational Fordism. The study of teaching and teacher education after 1914 reflects this Fordist spirit, as students and lessons were reduced to standardized units, teacher methodology became a special-purpose technology designed to efficiently facilitate the education production process, knowledge was fragmented into discrete parts, learning was reduced to a technical problem, and students flowed by the teacher in an assembly line sort of process, with teachers dispensing knowledge here and measuring it there, making sure each child met the "quality standards" dictated by the "production managers" in developmental psychology.

THE BREAKDOWN OF FORDISM

As the Fordist compromise began to break down, observers saw not simply an economic decline but a decline of a way of life as well. Fordism as the economic expression of modernism carried the torch of Western civilization, as it reflected the modernist faith in progress, technological development, and rationality. These very elements and the arrangements of the Fordist economy based on them undermined the supremacy of the American economy.[7] The decline of Fordism signaled a decline in the post-Enlightenment faith in rationality as a panacea. As American products became shoddier and shoddier, as profits from planned obsolescence rose, and as students emerged from schools seeming to understand less and less about the world, the evidence of decline mounted.[8]

As the recession of 1973 destroyed the stable environment for corporate profits established by Fordism, the transition to a new regime of production and mode of social regulation began. Many economists locate the beginnings of the end of Fordism in the mid-1960s, with the rise of the Western European and Japanese economies, the displacement of American workers as a result of the success of Fordist rationalization and automation strategies, the decline in corporate productivity and profitability, and the beginning of an inflationary trend.[9] Fordism's ability to contain the contradictions of capitalism weakened during this period, as the inflexibility of American economic arrangements became more apparent. In long-term, large-scale, fixed-capital investments in systems of mass production, inflexibility undermined attempts to adjust to new designs necessary in changing consumer markets. In labor markets and contracts, inflexibility subverted attempts to reform workplaces with new forms of worker deployment. As Social Security, pension rights, and other entitlements expanded, government revenue collection was thwarted by a stagnant economy. The only avenue of flexibility led to a change in monetary policy that involved printing money at an accelerated rate to keep the economy stable. Thus began the inflationary spiral that ended the postwar boom. All of these specific rigidities were fastened to a configuration of political power that united big labor, big capital, and big government in the embrace of a set of narrow vested interests that undermined the productive capacity of the national economy.

As the oil crisis exacerbated the serious recession of 1973, the ability of American capitalism to extend the consumerist dream to a citizenry with sky-high aspirations was thwarted. No longer did even middle-class Americans believe that their economic lives were destined to improve.

The 1970s and 1980s witnessed a series of attempts at economic restructuring in an effort to respond to the collapse of Fordism. These restructuring efforts represented the first manifestations of an emerging
economic paradigm shift. Even with the evidence of an economic crisis,
the American middle class did not perceive any dramatic economic
change until the 1980s. Indeed, even in the mid-1980s, a majority of
Americans saw the changes as a moral breakdown and loss of American
economic, political, and military hegemony in the world. The "American
decline" was framed as a question of will that could be addressed by a renewal of nationalism and military preparedness.

This conservative response to the decline set the tone for policy
making on a variety of fronts—political, military, educational, and economic. Committed to economic policy with faith in the "wisdom of the
market," the conservatives attacked the liberal Fordist compromise, with
its embrace of the welfare state. As they attempted to dismantle the welfare state's safety net for the disadvantaged, conservatives in the 1970s,
1980s, and 1990s redefined freedom in economic terms. Freedom, they
argued, implies the right to compete and fail, more an entrepreneurial
liberty than a civil liberty. With the conservatives in power, the state
abandoned its Fordist role as the "Great Mediator" of the competing interest groups and unabashedly embraced corporate interests and need for
profits. At the same time conservatives were winning their political vic-
tories, many businesses were desperately seeking to escape the confines
of Fordist inflexibility in the workplace. This work would lay the foundation for post-Fordism.

POST-FORDISM: THE NEW ECONOMIC PARADIGM

Moving from assembly line production to flexible accumulation, post-
Fordist business and industry began to rethink their methods of economic production and social and political regulation. Increasing their
rates of innovation, centralizing ownership, and advancing the autonomy
of banks and financial agencies, the flexible specialists of the new economy have changed the face of consumption.[10] Business and industry in
this new paradigm are shaped to respond to markets rather than regulate
them. Innovative managers speak of their companies as a cadre of learners who monitor the market, research patterns of taste, and dissect the nature of style.[11] Management builds economic SWAT teams rather than a
bulky police force, as they think of economies of scope rather than

economies of scale. Production is based on limited runs, reducing costly reliance on large inventories. Such a strategy requires high-tech, flexible machinery and workers as learners who change duties with each alteration in consumer demand.[12] Business time is permanently altered, as the period between design, manufacture, and sales is contracted. The media-saturated hyperreality of the late twentieth century demands the hyper-adaptability of procedure.

This emerging post-Fordist regime of economic production is one dimension of a larger postmodern condition of hyperreality. New structures of cultural space and time generated by bombarding electronic images from local, national, and international locations shake our personal sense of place. Electronic transmissions move us in and out of different geographical and cultural locales instantaneously, juxtaposing nonlinear images of the world with comfortable personalities who have won our trust. Contact with hyperreality diminishes our ability to find meaning, to engender the passion for commitment. With so much information bombarding our senses, we lose our faith that we can make sense of anything.[13]

As we confront this information saturation of hyperreality, we enter into a postmodern identity—a postmodern sense of self. Although we appear to one another as single, bounded entities, we are socially superabsorbent, hiding beneath the surface a maze of personality fragments. Thus, the boundaries of individualism begin to fade like the chalk lines of a late-inning batter's box. As they fade, cultural studies helps us understand more clearly the relationship between social, political, and economic dynamics and the construction of individual consciousness. Our view of our roles as citizens, students, teachers, teacher educators, and educational leaders are tied up in this dynamic process of social construction. Obviously, such cultural issues can inform the purposes and the curriculum of teacher education.

POST-FORDIST CONSENT

In this post-Fordist era of dynamic flexibility of the workplace or, as Doug Kellner puts it, techno-capitalism, traditional forms of industrial and corporate power are magnified.[14] Faced by increasing pressure to compete internationally, corporate leaders seek new ways to maximize profits, including organizational and technological change to sophisticated procedures for labor control. Indeed, the post-Fordist discourse of

America's international economic competition constructs a justification for manipulation and the winning of Gramscian consent of students and workers. If America is not to be economically surpassed by the developing economies of disciplined and authoritarian Asia, the justification goes, we must cultivate more social obedience and commonness of purpose and less democracy and liberty. Uncritical education becomes one more aspect of the attempt to win the consent of workers in accepting their tenuous role in the post-Fordist global economy of the New World Order. Academic and vocational education, workplace training, the mobilization of worker affect involving at least with men the cultivation of a masculine work ethic, macho identification with the image of the "hard-workin' man," company loyalty, and work as a patriotic act—all combine to produce worker cooperation with corporate interest. These forms of regulation of students and laborers, when supplemented by the pronouncements of mass media, religious fundamentalism, and various branches of government, make for powerful forms of worker hegemony.[15]

The post-Fordist shaping of a consenting student and worker identity, of course, can be found in many venues. In a feminine context, the work of Linda Valli has been helpful in uncovering the nature of the regulation of young women students and workers in business education experiences. The students she observed were being trained for clerical jobs in offices, in the process learning about the technology of the contemporary office and its relation to the production of goods and services. Because office education students are almost always young women, Valli found significant information related to identity production vis-à-vis gender relations. Students were convinced that they already possessed the simplistic abilities the office needed, as no class time was used to improve office-related skills. The office was presented as a naturally low-skill workplace that is impervious to change. Working-class women, the course implied, must simply adjust their lives to these necessary realities, for contestation and resistance would be senseless and futile. Valli concludes that such educational experience contributes to the extension of these young women's identity as subordinate and dependent individuals.

Valli's girls were being conditioned to passivity—an act with profound but hidden political implications. Rewarded for uncritical acceptance of the unjust arrangements of the status quo, the students came to realize that critical thought and analysis have no place in work education. "Thinking" in Valli's office education program is compensated for the degree to which it reflects the ideology of mainstream courtesy, marked by a conception of resistance as distasteful and "unladylike." Thus, a form of politically passive conformity is cultivated that views good work education students and teachers as obedient to externally imposed ways of thinking and rules that demand the construction of "safe" female identities. Unless they are able to develop oppositional readings to the patriarchal ideology of the office education program or the hidden curriculum of the workplace (which some of the young women are able to do), these students will not be the type of employees who challenge the nature of corporate control.[16]

Contrary to the celebratory pronouncements of Newt Gingrich and other prophets of technocracy of a better day a'coming in a techno-capitalist, post-Fordist economy, the status of workers is more precarious than ever. The dawn of the post-Fordist age has been marked by a blatant redistribution of wealth, offensives against labor unions, caps on the minimum wage, adoption of exploitative labor practices such as the utilization of part-time and third world labor (usually women and minorities), the reestablishment of patriarchal sweatshops and domestic piecework, and the extensive use of subcontracting. Such policies have undermined the stability of the middle class, as an ever-increasing percentage of new jobs are low wage. A growing number of people are marginal to the workforce, as they accept "contingent employment" in jobs with few benefits and no assurance of security.[17] As post-Fordist changes have moved workers from industrial and agricultural jobs to service and information employment, many men and women have watched their middle-class status disappear. Workers with jobs in the industrial sector have been displaced by new technologies, computerization, and automation. These "deindustrialization" strategies affected middle-level and semiskilled jobs (nine- to twelve-dollar-an-hour jobs, in particular), resulting in further economic bipolarization.[18]

Despite these realities, most of the public conversation about post-Fordist changes are couched in very positive terms. Skill upgrading of work is the order of the day, many economists and educators write. Although skill upgrading is no doubt occurring in some industries, the total economic picture cannot be framed so positively, given the widening disparity of wealth and opportunity. School leaders call for an education to prepare future workers for the high-tech workplace, but research reveals that only a small core of workers will need such skills. Indeed, the way present workplaces are arranged in America, only about one of ten positions has been arranged to require high-skill workers. Deskilling is still the order of the day.

TECHNO-POWER, HIGH-TECH, AND THE SUBVERSION OF DEMOCRACY

Any teacher education that pretends to be concerned with issues of citizenship, social justice, and democracy cannot ignore the power dynamics of the post-Fordist global economy and their impact on civic life. Teachers need to be exposed to these issues to begin developing pedagogies dedicated to the creation of democratic spaces within schools and the larger social order. Make no mistake, the development of new technologies in post-Fordist corporate enterprises has not created a new era of power sharing. Indeed, corporate power in America has never been more entrenched than it is now. In this context, maybe the term *techno-power* can be used to describe the expansion of corporate influence through the use of post-Fordist technological development. Using techno-power, corporations have increased their ability to maximize capital accumulation. Businesses and industries via techno-power are better equipped to produce steady growth and, thus, higher profits, no matter what the social or ecological consequences. Via techno-power, firms are better equipped to control and exploit workers. Indeed, corporate growth is grounded on the ability to widen the gap between labor benefits and labor production. This situation is not exactly conducive to the prospect of power sharing in the workplace.

Understanding this techno-power, critical educators need to expose students to the dynamics of how it works. Liberal educators, carried away by the promise of techtopia, sometimes fail to address the web of corporate power students will confront in the workplace, the schools, and society at large. Some educators have happily proclaimed that "the interests of business and education are beginning to converge," ignoring the fact that corporations still operate on the basis of their private interests, even when they conflict with the public needs. With corporate public relations people leading the crusade, Americans have retreated from their commitment to the maintenance of a "public space." The needs of low-salaried workers, the poor, the environment—the needs of the public space—have diminished in importance to Americans. Freedom has been redefined as the right of corporations to desecrate this public space in the pursuit of private gain.[19] Technological development has undoubtedly changed what educators and students must know, but the dynamics of techno-power are rarely considered a part of that knowledge.

Despite conservative politicians and fundamentalist ministers' claims to the contrary, American commitments to the "private space" remain very strong. What have diminished over the last quarter of the century are commitments to the public space—community activities, political organizations, volunteer agencies, and the like. Most high school seniors, for example, say they do not think that a company going out of business has any moral obligation to pay its outstanding debts. In the name of profit maximization, American companies have shut down thousands of factories, moved entire operations to locations abroad, and migrated from state to state in search of cheaper labor and lower taxes. In 1991, in Tarrytown, New York, General Motors embarked on a campaign to lower its taxes by one million dollars a year. Announcing that it would close the Tarrytown plant unless workers made benefit and wage concessions and the city lowered its corporate taxes, GM held the city hostage. Because of the subsequent decline of tax revenues, the Tarrytown schools were forced to lay off personnel, eliminate new orders for books and school supplies, and delay needed repairs of school buildings.[20] Given technological advances enabling them to move operations from one state or country to another quickly, corporations have found themselves bestowed with new power. This is the nature of techno-power and its subversion of democracy.

TECHNO-POWER, KNOWLEDGE CONTROL, AND SUBJECTIVITY

Any analysis that involves cultural studies and pedagogy must address knowledge production and transmission and power relations. As corporate techno-power has expanded in the last quarter of the twentieth century, technology has come to play a more and more important role in organizing and regulating both economic life and knowledge production. Indeed, with a few exceptions, technology has been deployed as a tool of corporate leadership in its attempt to maximize profits and extend its power. Data banks, radio and TV transmissions, and transnational communications systems all contribute to a global network that allows corporate leaders to regulate markets all over the world. As these communications systems filter into cities, villages, and rural areas throughout the world, corporations present a view of the world (knowledge production and transmission) that promotes their interests. The process takes place in a quiet and subtle way, as values such as competitive individualism, the superiority of an unregulated market economy (neoclassical economics), and the necessity of consumption are implicitly promoted. People's subjectivities and their sense of who they are begin to be formed not interpersonally in their communities as much as by their radios, televisions, and CDs. The popularity of video compilations of old 1950s and 1960s TV commercials and the emotions they trigger within those of us who grew up in that era is evidence of this media-based identity formation.[21]

This corporate control of the media and the control of knowledge that accompanies it dramatically affect an individual's perception of the world in general and the nature of work in particular. In this chapter, I am calling attention to the cultural study of this pedagogical dynamic of techno-power. Colleges of education should be concerned with education, no matter what the venue; both institutional and cultural pedagogy fall into their domain of interest. Such pedagogies of techno-power are especially important when their implications for the survival of democracy are considered. The corporate ability, for example, to deploy its techno-power to portray American workers as lazy and unproductive dramatically affects the politics of labor-management relations. Managers can rally the public to support their denial of higher wages and more power on the shop floor to workers; after all, they do not deserve such rewards. These understandings of techno-power are essential to the education of young workers who are citizens in a *democratic* society. Empowerment of these worker-citizens can take place only when they are able to see through the myth that technological developments in media have served to produce a better-informed community. Indeed, students engaged in a critical democratic education begin to understand that private interests are building information monopolies; the public nature of information is quickly mutating into information as a private commodity. As fewer and fewer large corporations control the flow of information (2 percent of publishers, for example, now control 75 percent of the books published in the United States), public access to information contracts. In the process, techno-power expands and democracy retreats.

PENETRATING (UN)CONSCIOUSNESS: HAPPINESS IS HORSES

It is important for educators to understand that this attempted regulation of public opinion by way of media power is never simplistic. Many times, efforts to manipulate opinion backfire, as men and women perceive what is happening to them and rebel. Also, technologies such as computer links and information highways can be used to convey alternative messages that challenge corporate control. Still, however, many

Americans are unable to comprehend the degree of influence corporate leaders attain as they control TV and other media that bypass reason and focus directly on the management of human feelings and emotions. Media presentations that are not obviously political play to our emotions on a level that engages our political perspectives. Media images of exuberant children as they open gifts on Christmas morning have no overt political message. At a deeper level, however, such images tell us that happiness in our children can be evoked only by consumption of goods and services. If we truly love our children and want to see them happy, then we must support the interests of the corporations who produce these valuable products. The process of political opinion formation is not a linear, rational procedure, but grounded on our unconscious hopes and fears. Thus, when Mattel calls for lower corporate taxes and a better business climate in which to produce its toys, accede to its wishes. After all, this company allows us to make our children happy.[22]

It is not much of a conceptual stretch to argue that the development of late-twentieth-century information technology has not served simply to promote communication in a democratic society. On the contrary, the primary use of these technological innovations has been to sell and to create consumer markets for particular goods and services. Technopower becomes a medieval alchemist that, instead of turning base metals into gold, transforms "truth" into "what sells." Valuable information in this context becomes not that which explains or empowers but that which creates a cooperative community, a culture of consumption. Communication media do not exist to help ordinary citizens improve their lives or understand the demands of democratic citizenship. The need to capture the attention and the emotions of consumers transcends all other uses. In the process of improving ratings, TV reduces everything to the same level—everything that happens must be reconstituted to capture viewer interest. In terms of traditional notions of importance, all events and messages are equally trivial—death, destruction, war, famine, unemployment, beer, feminine hygiene products, weight loss programs, acne medications. CNN presents War in the Gulf and the Mission in Bosnia, both brought to you by Depends Undergarments.

The ethic of market values penetrates into our consciousness, into our everyday political observations. Reporters do not ask about Bob Dole's or Newt Gingrich's perspectives on information control in a democratic society; they ask who has best sold himself to the Republican party constituency or who has best manipulated media coverage with his sound bites. Questions of power sharing and social justice give way to the market value of short term profit making. The short term becomes the only future worth planning, as fashions, political opinions, personalities (your fifteen minutes of fame just ended), and even labor markets come and go in the life span of a mayfly. Academic institutions sacrifice their most cherished values as producers of knowledge and promoters of truth to these short-term market values. The promise of corporate capital quiets proponents of academic integrity, as universities produce data that extend the corporate power to open new markets. The famous Stanford Silicon Valley and the MIT-Boston Route 128 corporate-academic alliances illustrate higher education's co-optation. Many of the industrial relations that determine the curriculum of vocational programs illustrate secondary education's accommodation.[23]

As technology has extended government's surveillance capacities, the need for coercion has decreased.[24] Factory owners no longer need to bring in Pinkerton guards to control labor as they did in 1892 at Homestead Steel. In the 1990s, labor regulation methods attempt to induce workers to consent to control by management. Ben Hamper, a former rivethead at GM's Flint, Michigan, auto plant, described one of the more unsophisticated efforts to win worker consent. After introducing a giant cat named Howie Makem to promote worker morale in the plant, GM personnel managers installed a huge electronic message board that flashed "motivational" dispatches to the line workers. Alongside Howie Makem's face, managers sent messages such as "Quality is the Backbone of Good Workmanship," "A Winner Never Quits and a Quitter Never Wins," "Safety is Safe," "Squeezing Rivets Is Fun," and "Happiness Is Horses."[25] Some expressions of techno-power, we have to suppose, are more successful than others.

Throughout the era of TV, power wielders have become increasingly adept at the use of the media. Ronald Reagan's handlers in the 1980s set new standards for governmental manipulation of the electorate via TV and other technologies. To win mass consent, these media experts had to constantly provide TV with a "positive spin" on daily events; that is, they had to present a version of reality that portrayed Reagan and his policies positively. Over and over, like TV commercials, the administration fed the media this reconstituted and pasteurized version of events. Because news is a commodity that seeks to increase ratings, just like the entertainment sector of TV, networks never have enough information on the president. Knowing this, the handlers provided sound bites and visuals of Reagan that carefully presented the desired picture of reality. The corporate-driven worldview of the Reagan administration fit quite neatly with the corporate-run media.

Many students of power and media are amused by the common question: "Does big business control the media?" The only response to such an inquiry is that the media are big business. The corporate owners of the four major U.S. commercial networks are media monopolies. Squashing or absorbing any competition that might appear, these corporate conglomerates are above public accountability. The prospect of any serious competition in the future is undermined by the prohibitively high cost of establishing a media enterprise. The Reagan administration was extremely cozy with corporate leaders, so cozy, in fact, that General Electric (the owner of NBC) made ten billion dollars in profits during the first Reagan term (1981–1985) and paid not one cent in taxes. In these circumstances, the idea of democracy and the power of democratic institutions fade under the domination of corporate techno-power. Accountable to no one, such power continues to shape the nature of post-Fordist production and consumption.[26]

DAYS OF WINE AND ROSES VIS-À-VIS DAYS OF RAGE AND APATHY: THE ANTIDEMOCRATIC POLITICS OF CORPORATISM

All educators need to appreciate the economic and political impact of post-Fordist techno-power. Because of its subtle and hard-to-identify workings, few Americans have understood the process. Post-Fordist techno-power has produced a new political orientation in 1980s and 1990s America—a *politics of corporatism* that works to create a "good business climate." This neoconservative politics of corporatism has induced broad segments of the population to accept the existing economic and political inequalities and concurrently renew vile discrimination against various racial and ethnic groups. This antidemocratic politics of corporatism redefines equality in terms of the right to form a business and compete in the marketplace; it rejects discussion of economic and political alternatives to such beliefs. In this context, corporatism portrays worker empowerment as contrary to our "national values," characterizing it as an attack on the free enterprise system.[27]

We all can understand why the politics of corporatism works to establish good business climates: good business climates are marked by lower taxes, government-financed infrastructures, land grants, and the like. The complex workings of techno-power involve the attempt to win public support for this politics of corporatism, and this hegemonic process is never easy to understand. The workings of techno-power cannot be understood outside this consent-winning hegemonic context. Add one more factor to this hegemonic process: the politics of corporatism has not been accepted by the American public through a rational public political debate. No widely observed debate has discussed questions such as: How do we distribute income among classes? Should we regulate industry? Does the creation of good business climates serve the public good? In an age dominated by the media, information explosions, computerization, and information superhighways, politics is boring, and few people pay attention to it. At the same time, however, culture is fascinating, and most everyone attends to it. How many of us do not know something about O. J. Simpson, the royal divorce, Tonya and Nancy, Amy Fischer and Joey Buttafuco, the Menendez brothers, or the cola wars? What is extremely difficult for Americans to understand is that culture is the location where consent is won. Controlling the government may no longer even be necessary for corporate leaders to win political battles.[28] On many levels, such a statement may not make sense—which is the point. This statement does not mean that the politics of corporatism does not want governmental power, but it does mean that the world of the late twentieth century has changed. Corporatism, in other words, does not attain power by making the most persuasive political argument; it attains power by restructuring our private lives and our feelings and emotions at the level of our lived experience.

Here rests the secret of techno-power. With its access to people's private, everyday lives, techno-power is able to help shape our identities and, consequently, the ways we make sense of our experiences. Our consent is structured not only through political messages but also through pleasure and feeling derived by way of popular forms of television, music, dance, and movies. For example, when individuals experience self-expression through consumption and consumption-related practices, TV commercials may structure political meanings and dispositions through the pleasure they provide. As a consumer invests pleasure into the car he or she owns and the image such a purchase projects to the world, the effect of a Corvette commercial may take place on many levels. The ability of corporate advertisers to create imagery that connects and extends the consumer's pleasure holds a variety of effects. Consumers may identify the present economic arrangement as the one best designed to provide them with the pleasure the Corvette accords. They may have to adjust their lives within the boundaries of particular social conventions to make the money required to purchase the Corvette and the pleasures it provides. Engaging in such practices privileges certain political orientations, making, in this case, for a conservative identification with the maintenance of the status quo. It is important to note at this point that similar circumstances may produce very different effects in different individuals.

Students of corporate power and democracy have traditionally failed to understand that men and women make sense of reality both from the mind and from the heart and body. Corporate leaders, however, understood this notion long ago, as they designed their commercial advertisements not around a logical appeal to the buyer's rationality but around the regulation and reshaping of desire. Critical educators, in their attempt to uncover the workings of techno-power and the politics of corporatism, must understand what people know, how they come to know it, and how such knowledge and the process of obtaining it shape their consent to the powerful—that is, the workings of cultural pedagogy. In such an analytical process, democratic educators begin to understand the hegemony of techno-power, the ways popular culture undermines human potential, as well as the ways it helps construct human possibilities for self-direction and empowerment.

This potential for self-direction and empowerment, however, is undermined by the collapse of politics in America. Until we look at the political conversation taking place among workers and other citizens in Poland, the Czech Republic, Slovakia, Hungary, and other former communist countries, it is hard to realize the degree of the American lack of interest in the political. This absence of interest in politics does not mean that Americans are not outraged by workplace realities and inequities in schools and other institutions—they are. Every term I teach, my students express their moral indignation and outrage over modernist forms of stupefaction. Like *Network*'s Howard Beale they are "mad as hell and not gonna take it any more." But despite all of this anger and outrage, Americans remain for the most part politically inactive. American citizens have one of the lowest levels of voter participation of any industrialized democratic society. Participatory democracy is steadily weakening in the United States, as fewer and fewer people are involved in formulating civic agendas. We have lost our faith in the possibility of changing things. The American conservatism that has developed since the advent of post-Fordism in the 1970s reflects not satisfaction with the status quo but pessimism grounded on the belief that reform is impossible. The conservative resurgence of this era is grounded on a politics of pessimism.[29]

In such a circumstance, politicians can avoid dealing with political issues and question instead the others' character, family values, Americanism, military records, and so on.[30] These nonpolitical politicians win consent from voters with images of themselves as family men (picture slow-motion campaign videos of the candidate playing in the backyard with his dogs and his grandchildren). The complex aspect of this story of the workings of power and American depoliticization is that the same audience that understands many of David Letterman's subtle parodies of TV forms and formats also understands the less-than-subtle manipulative intent of the political commercials. In other words, growing numbers of Americans are sophisticated observers of the media who can identify the hegemonic practices of politicians. In a bizarre sense, the ability to regulate effectively becomes an art form, as some politicos are judged as more adept in the art form than others. The press often perpetuates such perspectives, as reports analyze elections not on the basis of issues or substance but on the basis of how well candidates exploit the media. Whose images were more successful? Who "came across" most sincerely? Whose political commercials were better produced? Such coverage exacerbates pessimism.

RUMBLE IN THE JUSTICE: CHALLENGING COMPETITIVE INDIVIDUALISM

As political activism is undermined, this neoconservatism is expressed by inactivity on a number of fronts. After the stock market crash of 1929 and the resulting economic depression, thousands of unemployed Americans marched on Washington. The return of massive unemployment to America in the 1980s elicited no such response, not even on a limited scale. The hopelessness of the politics of pessimism had undermined any form of political action. The success of neoconservativism in the 1980s and 1990s cannot be attributed to its economic success, as unemployment, low economic growth rates, and high growth of indebtedness persisted for a decade. Many analysts have argued that neoconservatism and its politics of corporatism have been nurtured by a shift from the collective values of the Fordist working class to a new embrace of competitive individualism. The celebration of the entrepreneur is a key feature of this competitive individualism; such an orientation has encouraged thousands of Americans to take the risk of going into business for themselves.[31] Despite the many success stories, there are far more failures. This rise of competitive individualism, with its neoconservative politics and its entrepreneurial culture, has helped induce a substantial redistribution of wealth to those who were already wealthy.

The return of competitive individualism has provided the camouflage for the politics of corporatism, corporate self-determination. Competitive individualism harks back to a nineteenth-century conception of social Darwinism, as it reignites the flame of classical economics. In many education programs, the impact of these political and economic positions on working men and women are not discussed. As techno-power broadcasts the corporate message throughout society, students find that they have never been presented with political or economic viewpoints that challenge competitive individualism and the politics of corporatism. Understanding that techno-power grants corporate leaders control of a photocentric, aural, and television-directed culture in which electronic images produce knowledge, political perspectives, and identity, critical democratic educators devise a curriculum that confronts techno-power. Such a curriculum is based on three principles: (1) it examines the historical context of particular assumptions techno-power makes about the role of workers, the nature of the workplace, and the needs of business; (2) it devises new ways of analyzing the pronouncements of techno-power, as it refuses to passively accept corporate representations of the world; and (3) it grounds its examinations of the worldviews presented by techno-power on the question: Whose interests are being served by the portrayals in question?

CIVICS EDUCATION INVOLVES ECONOMIC CITIZENSHIP

No critical civics curriculum can ignore the need for an analysis of economic citizenship. Economic citizenship grants workers a bill of economic rights that promises authentic participation in the affairs of public corporations, not a cosmetic form of worker participation that *allows* workers to choose the location of watercoolers.

An education for economic citizenship explores the causes of poverty and the forces that oppress and disempower people. At the same time, it provides insight into the ways that teachers and workers can act both individually and collectively to change work conditions. Economic citizens in a democratic society understand the demise of a public sphere and the ways that a politics of corporatism bias successfully redefined public concerns as private matters. The effect of such redefining is very important to the consolidation of power, as it removes from public discussion issues that affect all members of society. To argue that corporate pollution is a private matter that the corporation has a right to deal with on its own terms, free from public interference, is an antidemocratic proposition. To maintain that TV and print media are private interests opens a yellow brick road to domination by political and economic elites. In such contexts, the notion of public opinion carries less and less weight. Perverting the concept of freedom to mean "freedom from public interference" is a distortion of the American democratic imperative.

Economic citizens in a democracy understand the purposes of schooling and the ways that it can be used for both democratic and hegemonic purposes. Citizenship education in this context develops the intellect, ingenuity, and initiative to understand the connections among power, school experience, and an individual's future. The role of technology is an important feature in the analysis of these relations. A critical education for democratic citizenship promotes both understanding of and the ability to use contemporary technologies; at the same time, it encourages an appreciation of the social and political side effects of technology, as it focuses attention on issues such as toxic wastes and technological disemployment of workers. As education is often arranged at the beginning of the twentieth-first century, students leave school with little meaning-making experience; indeed, the idea of economic citizenship sounds alien and unrelated to the purposes of education. Questions such as: How do economic citizens help the society provide a meaningful role in the economy for all workers? and How does education prepare us for those meaningful roles? are not part of everyday school experience.

Meaning making is central to a critical pedagogy for economic citizenship. Economic citizens realize that much of the political talk of elections in the United States has little to do with the larger concerns of economic citizenship and sociopolitical meaning making. Economic citizens understand that the American political conversation should be concerned with the right of workers to shape production decisions and the arrangement of the workplace. Political debates should revolve around which strategies are best equipped to bring about such a democratic goal. In light of the post-Fordist changes occurring in the contemporary American economy, educational and public debate should be concerned with the growing numbers of peripheral workers and with strategies designed to undermine such growth. An education for economic citizenship analyzes this problem and diverse international responses to it—for example, Sweden's attempt to widen access to the core through a policy of full employment as opposed to Japan's exclusive preoccupation with core workers and their well-being.[32]

A key objective of an education for economic citizenship is the understanding that meaning is produced; it is not something that simply exists. All meaning is inseparable from meaning makers. In this context, democratic educators informed by cultural studies' concern with power, pedagogy, discourse, and desire understand that people who control technology, hold the power to provide moneys for investment, and manage the communication and transportation infrastructures of the society exert more power to make meaning (to make *our* meaning) than does the average person. Indeed, Henry Giroux points out that the production of meaning has become as important to the acquisition of political power as the production of consumer commodities.[33] Understanding this disconcerting aspect of contemporary society, economic citizens begin to design strategies to resist this techno-power. They make use of computers, for example, to disseminate information and to exchange ideas about worker empowerment and alternative forms of industrial ownership. Critical teachers and their students study these forms of political and economic organization in the hope of interrupting the control of techno-power.

FOR THE SAKE OF DEMOCRACY: A POWERFUL TEACHER EDUCATION

A cultural studies–driven teacher education examines the relationship between schooling and these democratic issues. A teacher education conceptualized vis-à-vis cultural studies conceives of pedagogy as a cultural act, in this post-Fordist context engaging students in the analysis of information production. As critical educators expose the relationship between a society's conception of work and its understanding of educational purpose, prospective teachers begin to conceptualize the complexity of the teaching act and understand that preparation for the field should consist of more than technical strategies to enhance the efficiency of delivering certified information to students. As teacher education students engage with cultural studies and the role of education in a democratic society, they begin to draw connections between the educational concept of tracking and the bifurcated workforce of the post-Fordist economy. When the relationship between work and school is examined in light of the tenets of an economic democracy, students begin to consider the nature of an education conceived in a culture devoted to promoting the dignity of every worker, a culture that believes that workers and consumers, as well as corporations, are citizens of the economic and political spheres of society, with the accompanying responsibilities of citizenship.

As a cultural studies–based teacher education exposes power relations in the connection between schools and work, it begins to uncover race, class, and gender components of the interplay. Put very simply, such a teacher education begins to help teachers make meaning in their lives and their professional understandings. As they begin to understand their identities as venues of ambiguity and struggle, male teachers may come to understand that the same masculinity that can ground an individual's desire to be a responsible and productive worker can create a consciousness that accepts the workplace as a natural and unchangeable fact of life. In this case, for example, a cultural studies–grounded teacher education interrogates the dynamics of masculine ways of seeing and draws connections between masculinity and oppression. It allows male students to understand that in mainstream culture male opposition to the cruel reality of work or the social Darwinian nature of the "free market" is viewed as an effeminate position. Such understandings are the first step in the life-long process of figuring and refiguring identity along the lines of the democratic values of connectedness, equality, justice, and freedom. What a powerful teacher education this could be.

NOTES

[1]Peter McLaren and Janet Morris, "Mighty Morphin Power Rangers: The Aesthetics of Macho-Militaristic Justice," in *Kinderculture: The Corporate Construction of Childhood*, ed. Shirley Steinberg and Joe L. Kincheloe (Boulder, Colo.: Westview, 1996).

[2]Aaron Gresson, "Professional Wrestling and Youth Culture: Teasing, Taunting, and the Containment of Civility," in *Kinderculture: The Corporate Construction of Childhood*, ed. Shirley Steinberg and Joe L. Kincheloe (Boulder, Colo.: Westview, 1996).

[3]David Harvey, *The Condition of Postmodernity* (Cambridge, Mass.: Basil Blackwell, 1989).

[4]R. Murray, "Fordish and Post-Fordism," in *The Post-Modern Reader*, ed. Christopher Jencks (New York: St. Martin's Press, 1992).

[5]Harvey, p. 126.

[6]Lawrence Grossberg, *Gotta Get Out of This Place* (New York: Routledge, 1992).

[7]Albert Borgmann, *Crossing the Postmodern Divide* (Chicago: University of Chicago Press, 1992).

[8]Robert Bellah, et al., *The Good Society* (New York: Vintage Books, 1991).

[9]Harvey.

[10]Patti Lather, *Getting Smart: Feminist Research and Pedagogy with/in the Postmodern* (New York: Routledge, 1991).

[11]Murray.

[12]Lawrence Grossberg, "What's in a Name," in *Occupied Reading: Critical Foundations for an Ecological Theory,* ed. Alan Block (New York: Garland, 1990).

[13]Timothy Luke, "Touring Hyperreality: Critical Theory Confronts Informational Society," in *Critical Theory Now,* ed. Philip Wexler (New York: Falmer, 1991); Peter McLaren, "Decentering Culture: Postmodernism, Resistance, and Critical Pedagogy," in *Current Perspectives on the Culture of Schools,* ed. Nancy B. Wyner (Boston: Brookline Books, 1991).

[14]Doug Kellner, "Reading Images Critically: Toward a Postmodern Pedagogy," in *Postmodernism, Feminism, and Cultural Politics: Redrawing Educational Boundaries,* ed. Henry A. Giroux (Albany: State University of New York Press, 1991).

[15]Roger Simon, Don Dippo, and Arleen Schenke, *Learning Work: A Critical Pedagogy of Work Education* (Westport, Conn.: Bergin and Garvey, 1991); Harvey.

[16]Linda Valli, "Gender Identity and the Technology of Office Education," in *Class, Race, and Gender in American Education,* ed. Lois Weis (Albany: State University of New York Press, 1989).

[17]Grossberg.

[18]Kellner; Russell Rumburger, "The Growing Imbalance Between Education and Work," *Phi Delta Kappan* 65 (January 1984): 342–346.

[19]Borgmann.

[20]S. Coontz, *The Way We Never Were: American Families and the Nostalgia Trap* (New York: Basic Books, 1992).

[21]Barry Smart, *Modern Conditions, Postmodern Controversies* (New York: Routledge, 1992); Henry A. Giroux, *Border Crossings: Cultural Workers and the Politics of Education* (New York: Routledge, 1992); Richard Brosio, *The Radical Democratic Critique of Capitalist Education* (New York: Peter Lang, 1994); Peter McLaren, R. Hammer, S. Reilly, and D. Shoole, *Rethinking Media Literacy: A Critical Pedgogy of Representation* (New York: Peter Lang, 1995).

[22]McLaren, Hammer, Reilly, and Shoole.

[23]John Goodlad, "Beyond Half an Education," *Education Week* 11 (February 19, 1992): 34, 44.

[24]Smart.

[25]Ben Hamper, *Rivethead* (New York: Warner, 1992).

[26]Brosio; McLaren, Hammer, Reilly, and Sholle.

[27]Grossberg.

[28]Giroux.

[29]Grossberg; Brosio.

[30]Coontz.

[31]Harvey.

[32]Murray.

[33]Henry A. Giroux, *Living Dangerously: Multiculturalism and the Politics of Difference* (New York: Peter Lang, 1993).

CHAPTER 8

The New Civics
Teaching for Critical Empowerment

SHIRLEY R. STEINBERG

It would be no revelation for educators to speak of the crisis of democracy in America. Hundreds of books and political science articles have documented diminishing American participation in the political process, the decline of voting, and the cynical withdrawal of men and women from political activism.[1] Scandal after scandal clouds legislative, judicial, and executive chambers, yet reforms rarely follow in the wake. The American public has come to the conclusion, unimaginable to citizens of previous generations, that the political arena is run by a few power interests unconcerned with the public good. What is the point of political participation? we as Americans ask. Nothing ever changes. Elected state and national officials assumed power in the last years of the twentieth century with as much as 33 percent and as little as 15 percent of the electorate's vote. I contend that such realities reflect the fact that Americans have been politically deskilled over the last generation by a constellation of social, political, and cultural events. In this context, we find ourselves in the eleventh hour of civics, and we must redefine civics, citizenship education, and social studies with a pedagogy of democratic citizenship that is taught not simply in the schools but in the society at large—in its workplaces, its media, and its government.

The global impetus for democratic discourse has shifted away from the modern birthplace of democracy, the venue of the great democratic experiment, to places such as Hungary, the Czech Republic, Latvia, and Estonia. The creeping powerlessness that afflicts the American electorate exacerbates the political illiteracy that, in turn, allows for the insipid public conversation about democracy. This vicious circle spins faster and faster in these times and destroys in its wake the hope traditionally identified with it. If power has something to do with the ability to act on our own belief, then the emerging powerlessness of the common person portends new manifestations of hopelessness. Such hopelessness may involve forms of social chaos unlike anything Americans have experienced before.[2]

THE POSTMODERN CONDITION

This social chaos has its origin within our modern age. Beginning with the industrial revolution, spinning through Fordism, we are now in a post-Fordist age that has redefined the world. Setting forth this condition (some call it postmodern, some call it late modernism) are certain distinct points that should be addressed to propose a critique and implement a new civics.

1. I contend that we are living in an age that is in a perpetual state of change. We notice a loss of touch with the past, not the good ole days as Reagan would have it, but a loss of connectedness with family, community, and democracy in general.

2. Media has induced an epistemological tear along the fabric of the modernist era. Far beyond McLuhan's global village, we find ourselves in a frenzied world, directed and produced by media. As Chomsky spoke of the filtering of the media, we have lived in a decade that brought us hyperfiltering: the Gulf War, compliments of Ted Turner, a year-long trial of an ex-football hero, Larry King's coronation of new kings, accusations of illicit affairs with a president and presidential candidates, and redefinitions of history itself—for example, the controversy over the Enola Gay, Rodney King and the Los Angeles riots, and the reality of the Holocaust. Media ask us questions and then answer them.

I can think of no better example than the *New York Times'* famous claim to print "all the news that is fit to print." Fit for whom? How do we define news? How does Ted Turner define news? Larry King? *A Current Affair*? We are living in an age that touted the launching of the first teacher in space and, within that same PR spin, watched seconds later as the entire shuttle exploded. Live. What is reality? What is embellished by the media? Past has been brought to present, the distant to near. We see the visual so completely that we are unable to see beyond its literalness.[3]

3. Our age is an age of commodification. Ways of seeing, vis-à-vis a virtual gaze, are commodified. Everything is for sale. Advertisements tap into love, hate, death, and patriotism to sell cologne, tires, Benetton

sweaters, and McDonald's hamburgers to the public. Advertising defines who we are by what we use. Disney describes to us what a family should be.

Along with this commodification of ownership, large corporations assist us in a new historical revisionism. Mattel redefines history by producing dolls that tell stories about when they existed during the Civil War, the first Thanksgiving, the westward expansion. Film revises history to the point that there is no question as to the reality and the virtual reality. Anthony Hopkins has now redefined Richard Nixon. John Hughes defined youth culture. Spike Lee speaks for African Americans. Film can erase even our recollections and replace them with the celluloid definition that fits the agenda of the director or production company. We remember with horror D. W. Griffith's *Birth of a Nation,* which in 1915 celebrated the bravery of the confederacy and the innate stupidity and laziness of the freed slaves. Images through Hollywood replace images of history. What is real? What is not real?

4. Culture has now become the primary terrain on which political sensibilities are constructed. High culture used to be defined in essential terms against the popular culture of the everyday. In this age, the age Baudrillard refers to as hyperreality, popular culture now must become an object for serious study and scholarship.[4]

5. The conditions of knowledge production have changed. Electronically produced information systems, computer engineering, and cyberspace now produce knowledge. New power relations have developed because of the cyberization of our society. Techno-power is created by those who control technology. Power and domination can now take place through the control of signs, symbols, and images. This domination includes the power to make meaning and to ascribe meaning to commodities and current events.

6. These conditions seriously challenge the hegemonic notion that Eurocentric culture is superior to other cultures. We must rethink the logocentrism, the androcentrism of the modernist era.[5]

7. Capitalism is undergoing reorganization on a global scale. The decline in the numbers of blue-collar workers, directly linked to technology, produces an employment nightmare. Corporate downsizing terrorizes office floors with larger numbers of part-time workers, lower pay, and few or no benefits. The inner city is financially collapsing, and economic growth is found in the suburbs, the "white flight" areas, and rural areas. The closing of American factories is constant; global expansion to exploit third world workers allows corporate profit margins to flourish

as Americans find themselves in the second and third generation of welfare.

8. The notion of hyperreality introduces an infinite proliferation of meanings. We are no longer in search of an epistemology that presents a larger notion of Truth. Meaning is undermined in a society saturated in images that have little connection with a rational notion of reality—advertising, public relations, spin doctors, publicity ploys. Information is passively consumed by the masses. This undermining of meaning undermines our ability to act politically; consequently, we are a nation of political illiterates, confused about the way the world operates.

9. Previous discourses and methods of analysis are unable to name and understand the changes of this condition. We must develop new discourses to critically deal with the instilled chaos I have described. The old stuff just will not work.[6]

ANSWERING THE UNANSWERABLE

How do we deal with this social chaos? How do we confront forms of race, socioeconomic class, and gender differences that threaten to shred the fabric of democracy? How do we identify power and how it works? I argue that a new civics must be problem centered in the sense that it is designed to raise awareness of the forces that work to undermine self-government and self-direction in general. Given the plethora of differences that fragment us, how can Americans develop a sense of solidarity, around which a new form of democracy can be developed? Prevailing ways of viewing the notion of solidarity tend to frame it as a form of consensus; a group organized on a sense of solidarity is a close-knit community with a common set of precepts. A new civics challenges such a perception, arguing that heterogeneous communities with differing belief structures can also achieve democratic solidarity. Indeed, such a group may be better equipped to cultivate democracy than those wedded to the old homogeneous model. The type of democratic logic emerging from a heterogeneous community often empowers participants to criticize more thoughtfully the injustice and exclusionary practices that afflict a social system. Criticism and reform of cultural pathology often come from a recognition of difference—from interaction with individuals and groups who do not suffer from the same injustices or who have dealt with them in different ways. Human beings always profit in some way from a confrontation with another system of defining what is important. Indeed, consciousness itself is spurred by difference in that we gain our first awareness of who we are when we learn that we exist independent of another or another's ways.

Democracy based on the concept of difference and solidarity is more inclusive and sustainable than democracy based on consensus. When we redefine the concept of solidarity as a notion grounded on the celebration of difference, the following characteristics emerge: first, solidarity grants different social groups in a democracy enough respect to listen to their ideas and to use them to consider existing social values; second, solidarity realizes that the lives of individuals in differing groups are interconnected to the point that everyone is accountable to everyone else. No assumption of uniformity exists here—just the commitment to work together to bring about mutually beneficial social change. In public political conversation, the ethic of solidarity grounded on difference elicits a dialogical sharing of perspective. In this process, a discourse of civics encourages democratic participants to see their personal viewpoints as particular sociohistorically constructed ways of seeing. As public discourse develops, citizens are exposed to more and more diverse voices. Such exposures facilitate the expansion of their social and political imagination, their vision of what could be. In such a process, democratic citizens are liberated from the limiting dualism of dominant expressions of liberalism and conservatism.[7]

Such efforts to reconceptualize democracy rarely exerted much of an impact in the last years of the twentieth century. Americans are unable to either perceive or articulate a crisis in democracy with the form and facade of self-government remaining elaborately in place. The technique and the mechanics of electoral democracy are more sophisticated now than ever before. Such realities lull the electorate into a frightening slumber; individuals fall into a democratic sleep that allows monied interests to dominate national, state, and local governments, while more humane interests are excluded. These new power relations have covertly changed the nature of American politics so profoundly that reincarnated citizens from only a generation ago would find them unrecognizable. A new civics, an expansion of social studies, would identify and describe the underlying patterns of these political dynamics—structures that tacitly work to undermine American faith in the workability of the nation's political institutions.

A new civics advocates not only a reconceptualization of democracy but a *prodemocracy* movement in America. Understanding that there is no correct way of defining or strategizing such a movement, as social studies educators, we avoid a blueprint for change. At the same time, however, we refuse to engage in vague proclamations that avoid formulating specific strategies for democratic renewal. Power wielders in the final analysis must be confronted; the power inequity of the status quo must be challenged. Political conflict may be a necessary first step in this prodemocracy movement, but the more difficult ultimate step involves some form of reconciliation. How this reconciliation is conceptualized is not something to be put off, such a reconciliation must begin with the conflicts necessitated by the disparity of power—issues of race, class, and gender.

A new civics, a renewed social studies is about politics and pedagogy. Pedagogy, as I define it, refers to a process that occurs not only in schools but also in the everyday practices of all social institutions. Pedagogy is central to any political practice because it refers to the ways people learn, knowledge is produced, and individual consciousness is constructed. For example, TV coverage of the American political scene produces a pedagogy that shapes a viewer's consciousness in relation to civic participation and ideological identification. By converting political spokespeople into celebrities, TV undermines the discussion of the issues of democracy and turns what passes as politics into discussions of personality and popularity. A more issues-focused democratic pedagogy becomes so unusual in the everyday life of a media-saturated polity that to some it appears subversive. In this context, some right-wing groups have issued warnings about individuals who "talk about democracy too much." Democratic pedagogy studies the production of our identities in relation to the way the world is represented and certain forms of knowledge are legitimated. If we are what we know, the forms of pedagogy that dominant groups employ do more than inform; they shape who we are. In this context, civics and social studies need to analyze what exactly is going on "here." What are we being molded into? What is the process of the molding? Is *molding* the right word? Is the process subtler and more interactive than "molding" connotes?[8]

Using the insights within social studies—sociology, political science, economics, media studies, philosophy, history, and geography—a new civics is truly an interdisciplinary course of study. Co-opting the cultural studies notion of methodological bricolage, I draw upon critical hermeneutics, textual analysis, ethnography, semiotics, deconstruction, content analysis, psychoanalysis, and phenomenology, combined with quantitative and historical data, to examine what civics might mean on the contemporary political-cultural landscape. Bricolage respects the complexity of the sociopolitical world by viewing such a context from as many differing frames of reference as practically possible.[9]

By facilitating our teacher education students in a teacher-as-researcher environment, a new civics can be constructed through negotiated curriculum and critical discourse. Students are not indoctrinated; rather, they are empowered to resist indoctrination by an empowering curriculum that is always self-conscious and elastic—never static.

TO INCLUDE IN A NEW CIVICS: DISTASTEFUL POLITICS

For generations, educators like Paulo Freire have demanded that we recognize teaching as a political act.[10] Yet within the study of the social studies, *politics* is often considered a nasty word, a topic unsuitable for polite conversation. I am speaking of politics within the metasense. For example, when a high-status position is filled by an individual with "friends in high places," often the word *politics* is whispered as the answer as to how he or she obtained the position. Such discussion implies several things: (1) the individual hired is not sufficiently qualified, (2) the process of the job search is contaminated, and (3) the political domain is an unseemly jungle where civilized activity is undermined by power struggles and crass deal making. A new civics examines the discourse of politics and the meaning of *political* in everyday life. We teach our students to include an analysis that sets the stage for a phenomenology of the political in the consciousness of Americans.

POLITICAL ILLITERACY

Democratic talk at the turn of the twentieth century is illusory because the media-dominated political landscape only simulates political reality. Often, TV creates an independent reality that people defer to and that ultimately removes them from real political life—that arena where political decisions are made. Whatever enthusiasm the pedagogy of media politics engenders, it fails to address the distancing qualities embedded in the medium itself. By no means is this meant to imply that TV cannot be a democratic tool. I do not buy into Neil Postman's notion that TV is a one-dimensional desocializing influence in contemporary American life. I contend that a media-saturated landscape does pose special problems not previously encountered in the American struggle for democracy. Although the media play extremely important roles in understanding political illiteracy, there are other social dynamics to address in the new civics and social studies education. Political illiteracy cannot be separated from particular power relationships in the larger American culture; extant forms of citizenship pedagogy in schools, media, churches, and other institutions often paint a safe civics that takes citizens through the motions but leaves them passive in the face of structural impediments to democratization. The deskilling nature of these pedagogies must be examined in detail.

POWER AND CRITICISM

Contemporary American democracy has been undermined by an epidemic of cynicism. Middle-class Americans have developed the perspective that political participation is a senseless and futile enterprise. Removed from the domain of power, they develop a crippling cynicism that subverts the will to self-governance. In the lower socioeconomic classes, men and women watch cynicism mutate to hopelessness and anger. The violence of the city signals a hopeless underclass so consumed with anger that it turns upon itself. As educators, we must engage our students in examining these conditions and exploring the definition and workings of power at the end of the twentieth century.[11] Power is something Americans talk about but something that is rarely understood. What is power? How does it work? What is its relationship to the demands of democracy? What does a pedagogy of citizenship need to say about power? Grounding its understanding of power at both the macrolevel of its production and the microlevel of its negotiation in everyday life, a new civics hopes to open a more sophisticated conversation about power and democracy.[12]

HYPERREALITY AND THE COLLAPSE OF MEANING

As the ability to make sense of and invest emotionally in the contemporary information-saturated society (hyperreality) has declined, the American spirit has been wounded. Hence, a crisis of motivation affects the political sphere directly.[13] For example, studying students of the contemporary era, we discern an omnipresent lack of interest in school, public affairs, and politics and at the same time a sometimes frenetic excitement with the cultural domain that surrounds them. Fashion, friends, cars, TV, rap music, skateboarding, and computer games do not bore the youth of hyperreality. A new civics studies these dynamics and, in the process, uncovers the forces at work in this context. Students study what constructs their consciousness and why. Education and politics have lost sight of a clearly articulated compelling sense of purpose. Who can invest in that which evokes no passion, no connection to the visceral features of everyday life. Thus, we must develop a system of meaning, a way of making sense of the world and our relation to it.[14]

THE PUBLIC SPACE: THE PRIVATIZATION OF DEMOCRACY

The idea of a public space is central to a new civics and social studies. The public space of a democracy is akin to a theater in which political participation is enacted through the medium of conversation. It is the sphere in which citizens deliberate about their common needs and concerns. A variety of factors have undermined the public sphere, not the least of which involves the power of capital to privatize spaces previously public—for example, the corporate attempt to "de-publicize" the schools. As an important aspect of democratic pedagogy, I propose that teachers employ a variety of strategies for opening new public spaces as opposed to one monolithic public space. The notion of public space should be examined as self-managed institutions. For example, the social studies classroom becomes a venue of both opinion formation and decision making. The new public space envisioned here refuses to exclude groups and organizations previously thought to be private or "special interest"—groups like those that work against racism, for ecological preservation, and in support of an economic democracy. Once again, invoking an understanding of power relations, we must focus on the patterns of exclusion that have rendered previous delineations of what constitutes a public space a mere facade of democracy.[15]

This new public space—a social studies classroom—becomes a place where students study ideas and thoughts from the viewpoints of those who have suffered. History is no longer taught from the victor's point of view, but with equity and consideration to all who were in power or subjugated within the era.

THE INADEQUACY OF TRADITIONAL CIVICS

As teacher educators, we must explore the history of civics and social studies in a larger attempt to disclose its presuppositions and assumptions. We employ historiography within teacher education to empower teachers in articulating what the previous mission of the American public school social studies curriculum was in relation to the larger society's effort to shape the prevailing notion of citizenship. The assumptions underlying the old pedagogy are contrasted with the presuppositions of the new civics. In this process, the philosophical infrastructure of a new pedagogy of citizenship and of social studies is delineated.

A PEDAGOGY OF CITIZENSHIP

The new civics and social studies are dedicated to an empowerment of students that results in their improved capacity to shape their own lives. Right-wing ideology speaks the language of self-direction but fails to specify the sociopolitical forces that undermine such efforts. The civics pedagogy discussed here grounds itself on the removal of such barriers and the nature of the struggle such a goal requires. At this point, a notion of democratic citizens as knowledge producers is offered for consideration. Included in this effort are confrontations with history that result in conversations about what should be considered a valued tradition and what falls short. Discussions about the ethical basis of democracy are important to the reconceptualization of civics. What ethical referents should structure the citizen's relationship to the body politic? Is the Western definition of reason adequate to the task of building a reason-based political pedagogy? If not, how might we reformulate a civics based on a reconceptualized notion of reason and a concern with feeling and emotion? To answer such questions, students need a highly creative form of thinking that is able to crash through the roadblocks of Western rationality. A new civics demands such a form of political cognition.[16]

THE NEW CIVICS AND THE REINVENTION OF ECONOMIC, POLITICAL, AND EDUCATIONAL INSTITUTIONS

I assume that a nation is democratic to the degree that it encourages self-criticism and uses the principles of democracy in the formulation and operation of its most important institutions. We must use examples in our teaching from the economic, political, and educational realms to concretize what the new democracy might look like. At the economic level, the idea of an economic democracy and what it might mean for workplaces exemplifies the prototype of democracy taken seriously. A reconceptualized notion of the political realm with its revitalized public sphere(s) must be delineated. Reconceptualized educational institutions, with their decentralized formats and emphasis on information access, research, student and teacher knowledge production, and interpretation, are described. A key characteristic of all three reformed institutions is that each operates on the assumption that students and citizens are not passive consumers but active participants in the everyday affairs of the sphere.

AN AMERICAN PRODEMOCRACY MOVEMENT

Last, as teacher educators, we must discover strategies for implementing the democratic pedagogy described. In many ways, we must design "how to" organize a politically literate group of students within our classrooms of hyperreality. The core of this curriculum development centers around the formulation of pedagogical strategies that assume that the manipulation of human beings is a vice and that individuals should have an important voice in democratic government.

IN CONCLUSION

Social studies is the interdisciplinary tool with which we are able to create democratic and cultural citizenship. In negotiation with the hyperreality of our world and in negotiation with the agendas and needs of our students, I argue for a rethinking of social studies, a new civics, committed to assisting our students in taking their places within the new century—in choosing their places within the new century—and with an awareness of the forces that shape them—a knowledge of who they are.

NOTES

[1]Jean Baudrillard, *Simulations* (New York: Semiotext(e), 1983); Richard Brosio, *The Radical Democratic Critique of Capitalist Education* (New York: Peter Lang, 1994); Noam Chomsky, *Necessary Illusions: Thought Control in Democratic Societies* (Boston: South End Press, 1989); E. Dionne Jr., *Why Americans Hate Politics* (New York: Simon and Schuster, 1991); Jean Elshtain, *Democracy on Trial* (New York: HarperCollins, 1995); Oscar Gandy, *The Panoptic Sort: A Political Economy of Personal Information* (Boulder, Colo.: Westview, 1993); Elizabeth Kelly, *Education, Democracy, and Public Knowledge* (Boulder, Colo.: Westview, 1995).

[2]Ulrich Beck, *Risk Society: Towards a New Modernity,* trans. Mark Ritter (London: Sage, 1992); Steven Best and Douglas Kellner, *Postmodern Theory:*

Critical Interrogations (New York: Guilford, 1991); Fred Block, *Postindustrial Possibilities: A Critique of Economic Discourse* (Berkeley: University of California, 1990); Stephanie Coontz, *The Way We Never Were: American Families and the Nostalgia Trap* (New York: Basic Books, 1992); Dennis Fehr, *Dogs Playing Cards: Powerbrokers of Prejudice in Education, Art, and Culture* (New York: Peter Lang, 1993); Kenneth Gergen, *The Saturated Self: Dilemmas of Identity in Contemporary Life* (New York: Basic Books, 1991); Henry Giroux, *Disturbing Pleasures: Learning Popular Culture* (New York: Routledge, 1994); William Greider, *Who Will Tell the People? The Betrayal of American Democracy* (New York: Touchstone, 1992); Lawrence Grossberg, *We Gotta Get Out of This Place* (New York: Routledge, 1992); David Harvey, *The Condition of Postmodernity* (Cambridge, Mass.: Basil Blackwell, 1989); Russel Jacoby, *Social Amnesia* (Boston: Beacon Press, 1975); Christopher Lasch, *The Revolt of the Elites and the Betrayal of Democracy* (New York: W. W. Norton, 1995).

[3]David Buckingham, "Television Literacy: A Critique," *Radical Philosophy* 51 (1989): 12–25; Henry Giroux, "Are Disney Movies Good for Your Kids?" in Shirley Steinberg and Joe Kincheloe, eds., *Kinderculture: The Corporate Construction of Childhood* (Boulder, Colo.: Westview, 1996); Robert Goldman, *Reading Ads Socially* (New York: Routledge, 1992); Douglas Kellner, *Television and the Crisis of Democracy* (Boulder, Colo.: Westview, 1990); Timothy Luke, "Touring Hyperreality: Critical Theory Confronts Informational Society," in Philip Wexler, *Critical Theory Now* (New York: Falmer, 1991); Jean Lyotard, *The Postmodern Condition* (Minneapolis: University of Minnesota Press, 1984); J. Tomlinson, *Cultural Imperialism* (Baltimore: Johns Hopkins University Press, 1991).

[4]Baudrillard.

[5]Joe Kincheloe, *Toil and Good Work, Smart Workers, and the Integration of Academic and Vocational Education* (New York: Peter Lang, 1995).

[6]William Doll, *A Post-modern Perspective on Curriculum* (New York: Teachers College Press, 1993); J. Fiske, *Power Plays, Power Works* (New York: Verso, 1993); Henry Giroux, *Living Dangerously: Multiculturalism and the Politics of Difference* (New York: Peter Lang, 1993); Maxine Greene, *The Dialectic of Freedom* (New York: Teachers College Press, 1988); bell hooks, *Outlaw Culture: Resisting Representations* (New York: Routledge, 1994); Linda Hutcheon, *The Politics of Postmodernism* (New York: Routledge, 1989); Harvey Kaye, "Education and Democracy: Should the Fact That We Live in a Democratic Society Make a Difference in What Our Schools Are Like?" in Shirley Steinberg and Joe Kincheloe, *Thirteen Questions: Reframing Education's Conversation* (New York: Peter Lang, 1994); Donaldo Macedo, *Literacies of Power: What Americans Are Not Allowed to Know* (Boulder, Colo.: Westview, 1994); Richard Slaughter,

"Cultural Reconstruction in the Post-modern World," *Journal of Curriculum Studies* 3 (1989): 255–270; K. Weiler, *Women Teaching for Change* (South Hadley, Mass.: Bergin and Garvey, 1988).

[7]Susan Welch, "An Ethic of Solidarity and Difference," in Henry Giroux, ed., *Postmodernism, Feminism, and Cultural Politics: Redrawing Educational Boundaries* (Albany: SUNY Press, 1991).

[8]Susan Adler, "Forming a Critical Pedagogy in the Social Studies Methods Class: The Use of Imaginative Literature," in Bob Tabuchnick and Kenneth Zeichner, eds., *Issues and Practices in Inquiry-oriented Teacher Education* (New York: Falmer, 1991); Robert Bellah, et al., *The Good Society* (New York: Vintage, 1991); Doug Kellner, "Popular Culture and the Construction of Postmodern Identities," in Scott Lash and Jonathan Friedman, eds., *Modernity and Identity* (Cambridge, Mass.: Basil Blackwell, 1992).

[9]Norm Denzin, and Yvonne Lincoln, "Introduction: Entering the Field of Qualitative Research," in Norm Denzin and Yvonne Lincoln, eds., *Handbook of Qualitative Research* (Thousand Oaks, Calif.: Sage, 1994).

[10]Ira Shor, *Empowering Education: Critical Teaching for Social Change* (Chicago: University of Chicago Press, 1992); Ira Shor and Paulo Freire, *A Pedagogy for Liberation: Dialogues on Transforming Education* (South Hadley, Mass.: Bergin and Garvey, 1987).

[11]Jonathan Kozol, *Savage Inequalities: Children in America's Schools* (New York: Crown, 1991).

[12]Grossberg.

[13]Kincheloe, *Toil and Trouble.*

[14]Bellah, et al.

[15]Giroux, *Living Dangerously;* Peter McLaren, *Critical Pedagogy and Predatory Culture: Oppositional Politics in a Postmodern Culture* (New York: Routledge, 1995).

[16]Deborah Britzman, *Practice Makes Practice: A Critical Study of Learning to Teach* (Albany: State University of New York Press, 1991); John Dewey, *Democracy and Education* (New York: Free Press, 1916); Macedo, *Literacies of Power;* T. Miller, *The Well-Tempered Self: Citizenship, Culture, and the Postmodern Subject* (Baltimore: Johns Hopkins University Press, 1993); Joanne Pagano, *Exiles and Communities* (Albany: State University of New York Press, 1990); William Pinar, William Reynolds, Patrick Slattery, and Peter Taubman, *Understanding Curriculum* (New York: Peter Lang, 1995); Philip Wexler, *Becoming Somebody: Toward a Social Psychology of School* (London: Falmer, 1992).

CHAPTER 9

Not Only by Our Words
Connecting the Pedagogy of Paulo Freire with the Social Studies Classroom

PERRY MARKER

*Any situation in which humans prevent others
from engaging in the process of inquiry is one of
violence. The means used are not important; to
alienate humans from their own decision making is to change them into objects.*[1]

In a democratic society, if social institutions are to successfully serve the
people for whom they were created, they need to be redefined, reimag-
ined, and transformed on an ongoing basis. The purpose of this chapter is
to discuss goals and strategies that provide a direct application for teaching toward democracy and transformation in social studies classrooms. It
is based heavily on Paulo Freire's idea that learning is based on a genuine
dialogue between teachers and students, who work as partners for a humane transformation rather than in passive accommodation to the world.
This chapter pays specific attention to students and teachers planning
their curriculum, the importance of student critique in the social studies
classroom, and teaching for transformation in the social studies classroom.

A BANKING EDUCATION

Paulo Freire refers to traditional education as "banking education"; education is an act of depositing, in which the students are the depositories
and the teacher is the depositor.[2] The teacher fills these depositories with
ideas that students obediently receive, memorize, and regurgitate. Freire
maintains that this concept of teaching involves attitudes and practices
such as the teacher who knows everything and the students who know

nothing; the teacher who chooses the curriculum content and the students, with no consultation, who adapt to it; and the teacher who enforces the choice and the students who comply with the choices of the teacher.[3] In comparing the educational experience with banking, Freire states that:

> knowledge is a gift bestowed by those who consider themselves knowledgeable [teachers] upon those whom they consider to know nothing [students]. Projecting an absolute ignorance onto others, a characteristic of the ideology of oppression, negates education and knowledge as processes of inquiry. The teacher presents himself to his students as their necessary opposite; by considering their ignorance absolute, he justifies his own existence.[4]

Thus, we, as teachers, set ourselves up as omniscient and often infallible experts who have a huge cache of facts and information from which students can frequently make withdrawals. In most cases, we do not wait for students to make the withdrawal; we conveniently direct-deposit the information into students' accounts through lectures, worksheets, and textbooks. Students are at the mercy of the banker, who creates all the rules as to how the bank and the information deposited therein shall be organized, managed, and dispensed. We social studies educators, many of us who at some time or other have practiced this banking concept of education, often let our personal choices and values affect how students think about social issues in the curriculum. Social studies educators often fall into the trap of defining the social studies curriculum solely through our own vision of our own ideological correctness. The following example, offered by Henry Giroux in Peter McLaren's *Life in Schools,* is illustrative of this problem:

> A middle class female teacher is horrified by the blatant sexism exhibited by her male students. Predictably, the teacher presents her students with a variety of feminist tracts, films, and other curricular materials. Instead of responding with interest and gratitude for this political enlightenment, however, the students demonstrate only scorn and resistance. The teacher is baffled; the students' sexism appears only further entrenched. As Giroux points out "the teacher falsely assumes the self-evident nature" of the correctness of her position; she has refused to allow students to "tell their own stories, to present and then question the experience they bring into play." She has denied her students an op-

portunity to question sexism as a problematic experience; she is, in other words, simply telling them once again what to think as middle class/institutional authority so often does.[5]

In the banking concept of education, the teacher is often seen as the expert and authority who imparts knowledge to students and expects them to adopt the prescribed perspectives and practices. This approach essentially reduces students to the role of passive learners and places them at the mercy of the teacher's philosophy and ideas. This approach limits the students' role in the learning and teaching process. In effect, the student is without a voice as to what happens in the classroom.

THE PEDAGOGY OF PAULO FREIRE

Paulo Freire has developed an approach to education that focuses on resistance to the dominant forms of education that reinforce the status quo in society. Central to his perspective is the idea that there is no such thing as a neutral educational process: "Either education functions as an instrument used to integrate the younger generation into the logic of the present system and bring conformity to it, or education becomes the practice of freedom." Freire believes that education is the means by which humans deal "critically and creatively with reality and discover how to participate in the transformation of their world."[6]

Freire's ideas are in direct opposition to the prevalent paradigm of education that views knowledge as neutral, value-free, and objective, existing totally outside human consciousness. Knowledge, in this sense, is separate from how people use it, and learning becomes simply the discovery of static facts and the description and classification of those facts. Freire offers a different point of view of knowledge by arguing that there should not be an artificial and obtrusive dichotomy between subjectivity and objectivity, or between reflection and action. Knowledge is not and cannot be neutral.[7]

Teaching for democracy and transformation has direct implications for social studies educators. Freire has stated that a progressive educator, one who teaches for transformation, must reject the dominant values imposed on the schools because those dominant values (a banking education) must be transformed. This process absolutely requires social studies teachers to assume a political position that denounces the myth of pedagogical neutrality. The implication is that social studies teachers are not just knowledgeable about the social studies disciplines and their integrative nature, but they also have an understanding of the political and ideological context of their environment.

To understand Freire is not just to focus on the political nature of knowledge. An important component of his conception of knowledge is that knowledge must not be structured to be prescriptive in nature. Among social studies educators, a common and dangerous practice is to prescribe specific ways that knowledge is to be conceived. Recipes for action are almost always provided to teachers and students to enable them to act on knowledge. From teacher education programs and in-service workshops to social studies classrooms, knowledge is often given legitimacy by teachers and students only if prescriptive recipes are provided and carefully followed.

Freire believes that prescriptive recipes for action tend to "domesticate the mind." His critical approach to knowledge insists that meaning (regardless of the author's intent) can never be prescribed outside the historical context in which such meanings were generated.[8] Freire's perspective encourages teachers and students to engage in a struggle to gain their meaning from the ideas they are confronted with and produce their own knowledge that has specific meaning in the context of their own lives.

The desire and demand for prescriptive methods from teachers are put into perspective by critical theorist Henry Giroux.[9] According to Giroux, the problem of prescription often causes teachers to be viewed as technocrats. As evidence, he cites the proliferation of prescribed "teacher-proof" curriculum materials. The underlying rationale in many teacher-proof packages is that teachers have the role of simply carrying out predetermined content and instructional procedures. The method and aim of many curriculum packages are to legitimate management pedagogies; that is, knowledge is broken down into discrete parts and standardized for easier management and consumption by students and teachers. The theoretical assumption behind this pedagogy is that the behavior of the teacher needs to be controlled and made consistent and predictable across different schools and student populations. It organizes school curriculum around instructional and evaluation experts who do the "thinking," while teachers, who are reduced to being "trained," are doing the "implementing" by focusing only on "what works." The effect is not only to deskill teachers but also to remove them from the process of reflection and routinize the nature of learning and classroom pedagogy.

A recipe-based curriculum is at odds with the premise in the next section: teachers *and* students should be actively involved in planning a curriculum suited to the school's cultural and social contexts.

PLANNING WITH STUDENTS

We as social studies teachers are besieged by a plethora of publishers who construct teacher-proof curricular packages. The "new social studies" materials of the 1970s are evidence of this trend that affected publishers' beliefs about social studies teachers into the 1990s. Applied to the social studies classroom, a pedagogy influenced by the ideas of Freire takes the problems and needs of students themselves as the *starting point.* A Freirien pedagogy provides students with the means to articulate, examine, analyze, and attach meaning to their own experience and knowledge.

We social studies teachers can emphasize student experience as central to everything that happens in the social studies classroom. We can understand, validate, and analyze student experience. That is, social studies teachers must make knowledge of the social studies meaningful to students before it can be critically analyzed. By grounding the social studies curriculum in experiences of students and their political, economic, social, and cultural settings, teachers enable students to attach the experiences they bring to the class to the concepts and themes of the social studies curriculum. Ahlquist states that too much social studies teaching reaches far into the past as a beginning point for understanding events, rather than looking at the experiences of the students in their world. Thus, many social studies curricula and classes are deadly, from the student's point of view.[10] If we social studies teachers ignore the students' political, economic, social, and cultural settings, we are invalidating the very space in which students live, learn, and dream.

Integrating student experience into the curriculum can be done only when students are given the opportunity to plan what they will learn with the teacher. Student experience will not become an integral part of the curriculum if students do not have a hand in determining and planning what will be studied. As we plan for social transformation, we can plan with students rather than for students.

As we look at the content and context of social studies instruction, we might begin by asking students, What do we know about what we are studying? Students bring a wealth of experience into the classroom. Often, they have had direct experience with racism, prejudice, environmental issues, hunger, and violence, to name but a few issues. For example, William Bigelow uses historical concepts as points of departure to explore themes in students' lives and, in turn, uses students' lives to explore history and contemporary society. In his classroom, the Cherokee Indian Removal was studied via role play of major players of that time period who were combining to push the Cherokees west of the Mississippi against their will. Students discussed how and why this happened. They were then asked to write about a time when their rights were violated and capture how they felt and what they did about the injustice. In a "read-around format," students then read their stories to the class and look for a "collective text" or portrait of what emerges from the read-around. This type of activity helped students find social meaning in their own experiences and understand how their individual and collective experiences can be used as windows into the past, present, and future.[11] By building on what students already know, the past becomes inextricably linked to the present.

But it is not enough to only talk about what we know. If we use our experiences only to define what we know, then we are risking a very limited, parochial social studies curriculum. It is just as important to ask, What do we not know? Planning with students can become very insightful when students *and* teachers spend time exploring the limits of our own expertise. It can be very exciting for students and very enlightening for teachers to freely talk about what they do not know about a given subject. Not only does it serve as a point of departure for students but also it indicates that the teacher is not a huge bank of knowledge to be accessed by students.

Asking what we do not know on a topic only allows us to share our collective ignorance. Where do we go from here? What students and teachers need to consider is, What do we want to find out about what we don't know? On any given topic, there can be a multitude of information we can study. Knowledge, in almost any area of study, geometrically increases on a yearly basis, making it increasingly difficult to know much about anything.

To make sense of this incredible growth of knowledge, students and teachers need to learn that in any given area of study there is a certain subjectivity in determining what we choose to study or, more important, what we choose not to study. Welton and Mallan have defined this process as "selective neglect."[12] This idea is centered on the belief that, because total coverage of any topic is impossible, students and teachers can begin to answer the question, "What do we want to find out about what we don't know?" by first selecting topics that they do *not* plan to study. When students and teachers generate a long list of questions to which they do not know the answers, focusing on special questions can get rather intimidating, difficult, and frustrating. Thus, selective neglect allows students and teachers to openly discuss what they are not interested in studying. Students can get a handle on posing problems that they do not know but that they wish to study. This process can provide very interesting insights into the collective interests of the class and provide students and teachers with interesting information as to why they are choosing to study specific problems.

Once students and teachers have decided what they want to find out, they need to determine how they can find information and what resources they have to find the information. Once students ask how they can find the information, they realize very quickly that the problems they pose for study ultimately determine the resources they use. They also realize that these resources are often not available in the social studies textbook or within the confines of the social studies classroom. This search for information often takes students and teachers to places and people they may never have considered before.

Most students are satisfied when they find these resources. They believe that they are close to being finished. In a transformative social studies curriculum, when students find the resources, they are just *beginning* their journey. When posing a problem, students must not assume that they will actually solve anything or reach a final solution. Rather, a problem posed, more often than not, is a problem *not* solved. If we pose problems such as how change affects the community or what the linkages are among people in the community and poverty or global warming, we need to help students become comfortable with a sense of ambiguity about their own answers. That is, whatever "answers" we come up with are not solutions but pieces of a larger, yet incomplete, puzzle that helps us gain insights into the human condition.

Rather than focusing exclusively on the answers, students need to discuss how they can present and share their findings. After all, the real power in solutions exists not only in a narrow belief of one's correctness but also in presenting the ideas in ways that invite consideration, scrutiny, and questions. The solutions to any problem become meaningful only when the "answer(s)" are brought before the bright—and often harsh—light of critique in ways that are accessible by many people.

Finally, if we believe that social transformation is the outcome of a social studies curriculum, then we need to challenge students to ask what specific proposals they can make to implement their findings. This difficult and challenging experience is, at times, frustrating, but it also should be seen as an opportunity for social change. We must be compelled to implement our ideas, make choices, and develop commitments, even though they may be subject to revision, ridicule, or rejection. To do otherwise is to risk a continuation of the status quo, stagnation, and ultimately the demise of a democratic society. Students who are posing problems can learn what it feels like to implement a vision, act on that vision, and begin to transform their world.

THE IMPORTANCE OF STUDENT CRITIQUE

Antonio Gramsci has argued that every teacher is always a pupil and every pupil a teacher. This statement does not mean that instruction is chaotic and lacks structure. Rather, Gramsci is introducing a teacher-student relationship that goes beyond the traditional elitism, authoritarianism, and ademocratic culture of many social studies classrooms. The idea that the teacher is always a learner who openly and enthusiastically encourages student critique places teachers in the role of critically examining the nature of their relationship with students and other oppressed groups.[13]

As mentioned earlier, Freire has argued that there is no such thing as a neutral educational process. Education either functions as an instrument that is used to educate children into the conformity and logic of the present system, or it becomes a "practice of freedom," the means by which humans deal critically with their world and transform their world.[14] He implies that all teaching is partisan. With this reality comes the importance for teachers to be crystal clear about their own social visions. The central question for social studies teachers is what kind of citizens and society they want. If we do not have an answer, teachers are reduced to technicians who are participating in a political experience with absolutely no idea of its goals or consequences.

Teachers who do not allow for student critique are authoritarian. The instructional choices of these teachers affect students, but the students are not provided an opportunity to critique the choices of the teachers. If we believe that planning with students is important, then we must allow students opportunities to learn analytic and evaluative skills that provide for social critique.

Evaluation with a problem-posing curriculum places the emphasis on the idea that students can learn to evaluate their own learning. Wallerstein lists several questions that can begin this student-centered evaluative process: Did the classroom come to life with emotion, laughter, and personal stories? Did these emotions and stories foster student understanding of the issues discussed? Was any action taken by students? What did students learn about themselves and their collective work as a class? How would students do the task differently? What new problems did the investigation uncover that can be pursued further in the curriculum? Wallerstein emphasizes that evaluation reflects transformation so students can "become actors in their own worlds."[15]

In addition to this student involvement, teachers need to be rigorous models of self-evaluation. Evaluation of this kind is continuous. Rather than happening once or twice a semester, it is built into the daily and weekly activities of the class. In other words, classroom discussions should have as a goal to consistently evaluate how the classroom community is feeling and how the instruction is meeting the stated goals established by both teachers and students. Students should be responsible for providing a critique of the instruction that promotes a free and open exchange of ideas, not a narrow, selfish laundry list of how their personal needs are either met or not addressed. More important, students should reflect not only upon the nature of the instruction but also upon their role in creating, promoting, and sustaining a classroom environment that supports a community of learners and teachers.

A social studies classroom where students are free to provide informative and substantive critique of the pedagogy of the classroom can provide students with living proof that fundamental change based on constructive criticism is useful, informative, and possible. Student critique emphasizes a social studies teacher's humane and democratic values in the classroom.

TEACHING FOR DEMOCRACY AND TRANSFORMATION

The ideas of Paulo Freire are practical and powerful for social studies educators. To teach for transformation challenges social studies teachers and students to create a vision of hope and promise grounded in the principles of equality and democracy. Teaching for democracy by creating a democratic environment in the classroom should be a goal central to all social studies teaching.

A Freirien curriculum promotes a democratic dialogue in the social studies classroom. Democratic dialogue begins when we involve students in planning their curriculum and when we relinquish power to students. Kenneth B. Clark, distinguished professor of psychology at the City University of New York, has challenged educators to work toward teaching for democracy and transformation. He speaks directly to social studies educators when he insists that "children must be helped to understand the genuine meaning of democracy from the earliest grades."[16]

One of the greatest challenges for social studies teachers who are teaching for democracy and transformation is to create opportunities for students to experience empowerment and to develop the capacity and ability to enter into relationships with students—that is, to be able to collaborate with students rather than coerce them. Obstacles to creating such relationships are often within the teachers themselves. Relationships of domination are fundamental to the structure and norms of schooling and our experiences with students and administrators. Whether we teach in a K–12 or university classroom, these dominant and authoritarian relationships lie deep within teachers. This relationship has been imprinted within us, as many of our own experiences as students in our K–12 schooling and certainly in our university liberal arts and teacher education programs can be characterized as predominantly ademocratic.

Teachers who are transformative have a clear understanding of the domination that is a product of their personal educational experience and their daily environment in the school. They are aware how this domination works against democracy in the classroom. The struggle therefore becomes an external and internal struggle to overcome domination and relinquish power.[17] The main challenge for social studies teachers is to establish a democratic dialogue in an institution that is inherently ademocratic.

If a democratic dialogue is to take place in the social studies classroom, teachers should become competent at listening to students. The Freirien educator is a critical, probing listener rather than a mechanical answer-giver with a preestablished curriculum. Wallerstein insists that we must (1) listen for deeper understanding, (2) listen inside class, and (3) listen outside class.[18] When listening for a deeper understanding, teachers must be cognizant of students' personal histories. A classroom discussion about family that assumes only a traditional nuclear arrangement can be devastating to children of a single-parent family if the teacher is not sensitive to students' personal histories and their emotions about those histories. Encounters with social studies issues such as homelessness, hunger, child abuse, alcoholism, prejudice, and violence have the potential to affect how students view themselves, their families, and their teachers. Wallerstein discusses how important it is for teachers to listen to and uncover sensitive student emotions or "hidden voices" that students bring to the classroom. These hidden voices have the power to block learning and alienate students.

To begin to uncover these hidden voices, teachers must listen in class. Listening in class begins with allowing students to share their concerns: What are their fears? What makes students happy, sad, or angry?[19] In a discussion of an issue in the classroom, we might ask, Has something like this ever happened to you? Have you ever felt or thought something similar? How does this information make you feel? What can you do? How would you prevent. . . ? What are you going to do when. . . ? How would you change. . . ? Students need to feel comfortable about expressing their feelings and concerns in class. These types of questions can help students begin to feel comfortable and inform teachers on a deeper level how students are feeling and what they are thinking.

One way a teacher can begin to develop a collective sense of trust that can help students express their feelings is to ask students to do an anonymous write-around about an event in their school or personal life, an issue that is of widespread interest to students (e.g., music or sports), or an issue in the social studies curriculum. After the students anonymously write their answers, feelings, reactions, or what they know or would like to know, their papers are collected and distributed to the class. Make sure no one gets his or her own paper. Students are then asked to anonymously respond, in writing, to any or all of the written statements of their peers. After the students are given opportunities to respond this way to several papers other than their own, their responses are read aloud by students in the class. The discussion that follows about these statements can be very enlightening and revealing for both students and teachers.

Listening outside class demands that students become observers of their community and world.[20] Students use skills of observation, interviewing, and document analysis. For example, ask students to carefully observe their surroundings and interview people in the community about an issue being discussed in the social studies curriculum. Ask students what they notice about human interactions in various community settings and the differences of opinion that result. By observing and interviewing people from their community, they can compare notes, look for issues and trends that arise, discuss how and why people are thinking differently on issues, and look for supporting or conflicting information.

We can also encourage students to look at issues and events from the perspectives of those most immediately involved in global events. We can ask students questions like what they would want to see achieved in their lives if they lived in Somalia, Bosnia, or Iraq or how the history of the Gulf War changes when written from the perspective of a citizen of Iraq or Kuwait. Listening outside class challenges teachers and students to confront the real issues of the world and make them part of an exciting transformative curriculum.

CONCLUSION

Teaching for transformation and democracy is inspired by the critical pedagogy of Paulo Freire. Freire believes that human beings, while part of the larger ongoing creation of history, are in an evolving process of creating themselves and defining their own realities. Freire denounces traditional education as an oppressive banking system in which teachers deposit information into students, as though they were making deposits into a bank account. Freire proposes that students and teachers participate in creating a dialogue in which reality is recognized, understood, and transformed in a democratic classroom. Teachers and students are partners in a search to understand events by relating the existing information of the social studies to students' own experiences.

In the social studies classroom, where democracy is often taught but rarely practiced, Freire's perspectives can be exciting and challenging. This process requires social studies teachers to assume a political position that denounces the "myth of pedagogical neutrality." Freire's perspective encourages teachers and students to engage in a mutual struggle to produce their own knowledge that has specific meaning in the context of their own lives.

When Freire's perspective is applied to the social studies classroom, problems are posed with students that focus on their experiences and needs; the students themselves are the starting point for critical inquiry in the classroom. Teaching for democracy and transformation provides students with the means to articulate, examine, analyze, and attach meaning to their own experience and knowledge. As we plan the social studies curriculum for democracy and transformation, it becomes critical that we plan with students rather than for students.

It is the business of social studies teachers to focus on preparing students for the responsibilities of citizenship; the central question that social studies teachers must answer before they plan a curriculum is what kind of citizens and society they want. The response speaks volumes regarding what we do in the classroom. If we are serious about teaching for democracy, we need a social studies curriculum that reflects the principles of democracy that we are trying to teach.

Teaching for democracy by using student experiences and involving students in the planning and development of the curriculum is risky. Democracy in the social studies classroom requires commitment and responsibility from teachers and students, presents daily infinite challenges, invites controversy, constantly involves contradiction, and places teachers and students in situations with no clear outcomes, expectations, or answers. Is this not what confronts each and every one of us in a democratic society?

The children of today "live in a world characterized by a staggering volume of information, varying sets of values, and a growing interdependence among nations. Children are citizens now, with rights, responsibilities and a confusing array of choices before them."[21] We social studies teachers need to encourage our children to confront the problems of the day, reflect on the issues confronting democracy, study the principles of democratic societies, question the choices our government makes, and transform the world in which they live. If we social studies teachers are serious about preparing students to become "active, responsible, citizens for maintaining the democratic values upon which this nation was established," then we must put students in classrooms that are inherently democratic.[22] We need to teach the democratic principles of equality, freedom, and justice in our social studies classrooms not only by our words but also by our deeds. Social studies teachers would do well to consider the pedagogy of democracy and transformation of Paulo Freire.

NOTES

[1]Paulo Freire, *Literacy, Reading the Word and the World* (South Hadley, Mass.: Bergin & Garvey, 1987).

[2]Paulo Freire, *Pedagogy of the Oppressed* (New York: Continuum, 1970), p. 58.

[3]Ibid., p. 59.

[4]Ibid., p. 58.

[5]As quoted by Peter McLaren, *Life in Schools* (New York: Longman, 1989), pp. 227–228.

[6]Richard Shaull, foreword to *Pedagogy of the Oppressed* by Paulo Freire, p. 15.

[7]Marilyn Frankenstein, "Critical Mathematics Education: An Application of Paulo Freire's Epistemology," in *Freire for the Classroom*, ed. Ira Shor (Portsmouth, N.H.: Boynton/Cook Publishers, 1987).

[8]William B. Stanley, *Curriculum for Utopia* (Albany: State University of New York Press, 1992), p. 127.

[9]Henry A. Giroux, *Teachers as Intellectuals* (South Hadley, Mass.: Bergin & Garvey, 1988).

[10]Roberta Ahlquist, "Critical Pedagogy for Social Studies Teachers," *Social Studies Review* 29 (1990): 56.

[11]William Bigelow, "Role Plays: Show, Don't Tell," in *Rethinking Our Classrooms: Teaching for Equity and Justice,* ed. Bill Bigelow, Linda Christensen, Stan Karp, Barbara Miner, and Bob Peterson (Milwaukee, Wis.: Rethinking Schools, 1994), pp. 114–115.

[12]David A. Welton and John T. Mallan, *Children and Their World,* 2d ed. (New York: Houghton Mifflin, 1981).

[13]Giroux, p. 203.

[14]Freire, *Pedagogy of the Oppressed.*

[15]Nina Wallerstein, "Problem-posing Education: Freire's Method for Transformation," in *Freire for the Classroom,* ed. Ira Schor, p. 44.

[16]Kenneth Clark, "Unfinished Business: The Toll of Psychic Violence," *Newsweek* (January 11, 1993): 38.

[17]Seth Kreisberg, *Transforming Power: Domimation, Empowerment and Education* (Albany: State University of New York Press, 1992), p. 154.

[18]Wallerstein, p. 35.

[19]Ibid., p. 36.

[20]Ibid.

[21]NCSS Task Force, "Social Studies for Early Childhood and Elementary School Children Preparing for the 21st Century," *Social Education* 53 (1989): 15.

[22]Ibid., p. 14.

CHAPTER 10

Put Up or Shut Up
The Challenge of Moving from Critical Theory to Critical Pedagogy (A Formative Assessment)

GLORIA LADSON-BILLINGS

It is my intent to make this chapter highly experiential and deeply personal, as opposed to theoretical and dispassionate. This choice is not an indictment against theory or an attempt to privilege experience. Rather, the limits of time and space require me to choose between the two, and I believe I can make a more compelling argument by focusing on the personal. Lest someone accuse me of working out of a less than rigorous and atheoretical paradigm, for the record, my thinking about these issues is informed by and grounded in the work of Freire, Apple, Giroux, McLaren, Aronowitz, and Shor, as well as the not so highly recognized efforts of Ellsworth, Lather, (Septima) Clark, (Fannie Lou) Hamer, and (Myles) Horton.[1]

Many scholars—both researchers and practitioners—have been intrigued by the challenge of critical theorists to develop an emancipatory pedagogy. What this pedagogy looks like, how it is implemented, and how it can be assessed are all unanswered questions in most school settings. And, although this pedagogy is highly touted in the academy, there, too, we find few models of critical pedagogy. But instead of a diatribe against the ways that critical theories fail to point us toward critical practices, I want to share an attempt at critical pedagogy in teacher education that is currently underway at the University of Wisconsin–Madison.

WHAT IS CRITICAL THEORY(IES) AND WHAT DOES IT HAVE TO DO WITH TEACHING?

Although we often hear about critical theory, in reality there are various critical theories. Many have their origins in the work of what has come to be known as the Frankfurt School, which represents the work of theorists such as Horkheimer, Adorno, Marcuse, and Habermas.[2] Their work was an attempt to "reevaluate capitalism and the Marxist explanation of class domination and reformulate the meaning of human emancipation."[3]

Unlike Marxists, members of the Frankfurt School did not believe that domination of the working class by the bourgeoisie is achieved purely through the economic structure. Rather, they argued that the production of a mass culture, through media, arts, education, literature, and education, would serve as the vehicle through which ruling-class interests would best be served. Contemporary theorists associated with this work include Freire, Giroux, Aronowitz, and Shor. They argue that societies harbor many forms of domination and oppression. They see education and schooling as a part of the struggle to overcome dominations of all sorts so that each person can grasp the meaning of individual personal existence and future life. The tool for overcoming dominations, according to critical theorists, is the acquisition of critical knowledge, which can be used to develop critical literacy.[4] Critical theorists in education argue that schools need to "challenge the established practices, institutions, and ways of thinking and conceive new and alternative possibilities."[5]

Less recognized for their critical work than the Frankfurt School, but just as significant, are a number of African American scholars and theorists who raised questions about the ways schooling reproduced racist constructions and academic inequality. Two of the better known in this tradition are W. E. B. Du Bois and Carter G. Woodson. Du Bois was challenged in his critique of schooling by Booker T. Washington, who argued that blacks needed a manual trade education to become self-sufficient. Du Bois, by contrast, argued that a manual trade education was just the tool that the power structure would use to keep blacks in second-class citizenship. Woodson's classic, *The Miseducation of the Negro,* pointed out how ill-equipped most schools were in meeting the needs of African American learners.[6] In it, he critiques both the institutional and structural constraints and the educated blacks who become complicit with the power structure. Except for some archaic expressions and terms, Woodson's book reads like a contemporary analysis of schooling for African Americans. The spirit of their conceptual work was made a pedagogical reality by teachers such as Septima Clark and Esau Jenkins, who worked to promote adult literacy in the citizenship schools of the South during the modern civil rights movement and the liberation schools that flourished in northern cities as a result of black nationalist organizations such as the Black Panthers.[7]

However seductive notions of critical theory may seem, they have had minimal impact on the schooling of most students. Cuban argues that, despite cries for reform, schools have changed very little over the past century.[8] Critical theory's dilemma lies in how to get teachers—who have been educated in and inducted into patterns of tradition and hierarchy that reproduce inequality—to teach in critical, emancipatory ways. The advantage that scholars like Woodson and Du Bois had was that their message was aimed at people who understood (and experienced) the ways that education failed to produce human liberation. African American teachers often recognize that they have succeeded despite their schooling. Thus, the work of helping to prepare teachers as critical pedagogues falls to teacher educators.

CRITICAL THINKERS THINKING CRITICALLY ABOUT TEACHER EDUCATION

In the middle to late 1980s, faculty in the Department of Curriculum and Instruction at the University of Wisconsin–Madison began a series of informal meetings to discuss growing concerns about teacher education. Paramount among these concerns was the failure of students to demonstrate a clear understanding of and commitment to principles of human diversity, equity, and social justice. Indeed, a recent internal evaluation of the ongoing undergraduate program indicated that students were "tired of having multicultural education shoved down their throats" and felt that everyone talked about multicultural education but "no one showed them how to do it!"

A second concern was for the continued fragmentation of the academic and professional coursework. Students were faced with increasing course requirements from both the university and the state credentialing agency, the Department of Public Instruction. However, this loose configuration of courses failed to help students develop a coherent understanding of pedagogy. Indeed, taking all of these courses did not even produce a more intellectually disposed person.

The third major concern was the disjuncture between coursework and field experiences, which was exacerbated by the typical "buyers' market" that exists between the university and local school districts. So overwhelming is the university's need for cooperating teachers that almost any warm body will do. Thus, students receive very uneven experiences based on where they do student teaching and with whom they are placed.

But the discussions at the university were not about the logistics of credit hours, course sequence, and student teaching placement. Rather, these brown bag conversations were an attempt to wrestle with the knotty problematics of the undergirding philosophical, theoretical, and conceptual tenets on which to construct a teacher education program. I believe that I can say that the prevailing political sentiment of the group was leftist (after all, we are talking about Madison). However, the theoretical lenses through which most members of the group view their work ranged from critical to postmodern. To keep the weekly discussions from degenerating into gripe sessions or ego enhancers, individual group members were asked to suggest or write position papers that considered the dominant theoretical perspectives extant in teacher education. Out of some of these presentations, Zeichner analyzed the theoretical and conceptual grounding of the current University of Wisconsin–Madison program. His work revealed at least four competing perspectives that operated within the ongoing program: an *academic* tradition that emphasized teachers' knowledge of subject matter and their ability to transform that subject matter to promote student understanding, a *social efficiency* tradition that emphasized teachers' abilities to thoughtfully apply a knowledge base about teaching that has been generated through research on teaching, a *developmentalist* tradition that stressed teachers' abilities to base their instruction on their direct knowledge of their students, and a *social reconstructionist* tradition that emphasized teachers' abilities to see the social and political implications of their actions and to assess their actions and the social contexts in which they are carried out for their contribution to greater equality, justice, and humane conditions in schooling and society.[9] Although each of these traditions can have a multicultural component, it was the fourth—social reconstructionist—that we as a faculty felt we needed to work toward. This commitment to a social reconstructionist perspective marked the beginnings of a program we instituted, "Teach for Diversity."

ORGANIZING A PROGRAM OF CRITICAL PEDAGOGY

Teach for Diversity (TFD) is an elementary certification plus master's program designed to prepare teachers to teach in *multicultural,* social reconstructionist ways. Although the program was the brainchild of a variety of faculty, its program proposal was written and submitted to the State Department of Public Instruction by Ken Zeichner, and its administration and direction are handled by Mary Louise Gomez and Gloria

Ladson-Billings. The program is a fifteen-month cohort program open to twenty-five students each year. The program requires two summers and two semesters of full-time graduate school enrollment. To describe the program in a coherent manner, I explain some of the preprogram planning and the sequence in which students participate.

Preprogram Planning

To ensure a successful program, the program directors invited representatives from a variety of stake-holding constituencies to participate in a dialogue about the city's changing demographics and the need for a teacher-education response. These representatives included the school superintendent and members of her management team, teacher union representatives, and representatives from community-based organizations. I believe I can safely say that our proposal met with enthusiasm for the concept and some skepticism about our ability to deliver.

Our second task was to convince individual elementary principals of the worthiness of this project. At the elementary principals' meeting, we outlined requirements for participation. Interested schools needed to have a diverse student body and at least one-third of its faculty who were willing to interrogate their own practice and work in a new kind of collaboration with the university. We asked interested principals to complete an application form, and we volunteered to make a presentation to their faculties. We found three sites that met our criteria and were willing to work with us.

The application process for prospective candidates in TFD has two steps. Initially, applicants must send a three-page statement of purpose, a copy of their undergraduate transcripts, scores on the state mandated PreProfessional Skills Test (PPST), and three letters of recommendation. This information is reviewed blind by a committee of faculty and local teachers, and each applicant is ranked. The top twenty-five to twenty-seven applicants who meet minimum graduate school requirements are offered admission to the program and required to formally apply to the graduate school. Admission to TFD requires that applicants meet all graduate school admission requirements. The graduate school's grade point average requirement of 3.0 (on the last sixty undergraduate credits) has limited our ability to admit as diverse a pool as possible. However, TFD cohorts have been noticeably more diverse than those of the ongoing undergraduate program.

While we were negotiating with schools and teachers to establish new working relationships, teams of faculty and teachers were meeting to construct new courses aimed at addressing school subjects in an integrated, critical way. The three "methods" courses were, Literacy and the Arts; Math, Science, and Environmental Education; and Health, Physical Education, and Social Studies. These courses relied on prior subject matter knowledge of the students and a willingness to rethink what it might be to teach this subject matter effectively to all students.

The First Summer

TFD students begin an eight-week summer session to initiate their program. The first summer consists of two academic courses, a field experience, and a seminar to integrate the coursework and field experiences. The first course, "Teaching and Diversity," is offered during the first four weeks. Taught from a postmodern perspective, it challenges all of the assumptions that students may have about issues of difference and diversity. It is designed to help them think broadly about how subjectivity, positionality, and language structure the categories we construct and create notions of "the other."

The second four-week course, "Culture, Curriculum, and Learning," is taught from an anthropological interpretivist perspective. Students begin reading the literature of educational anthropology and examine the role of culture and language in education. Students have experiences with ethnographic research and conduct a mini-ethnography.

The summer field experiences are placements in community-based recreational and educational programs such as Salvation Army day camp, a summer day camp program for homeless children, and neighborhood centers. The thinking underlying this placement is that prospective teachers should have an opportunity to meet children in a setting in which the children are competent. Thus, their later interactions with children in schools may cause them to ask important questions about why such differences in competency exist and ultimately to challenge the ways schools help to construct that incompetence. The summer seminar becomes the place to discuss emerging and evolving notions of diversity, equity, and social justice. The summer ends with students receiving their school placements for the upcoming school year.

Fall Semester

During fall semester, the TFD cohort is divided into three subcohorts. Although the entire cohort continues to take classes together, groups of seven or eight students are assigned to a school building. A faculty member assigned to each of the buildings serves as student teaching supervisor and seminar leader. This practice is different from the ongoing undergraduate program, in which supervision and seminar leadership are done primarily by graduate students. The TFD cooperating teachers are asked to make decisions about the placement and utilization of the students. Thus, students may be in collaborative work arrangements with each other and spend time in "special" classes such as art, music, and physical education, as well as compensatory programs such as Chapter 1, ESL, and special education.

The students take the three methods courses on Monday and Tuesday of each week. On Wednesday, Thursday, and Friday, they are in their school sites participating in the practicum aspect of the program. Instead of the one hundred hours of practicum experienced by the undergraduate students, TFD students spend approximately twenty weeks (fifteen to twenty hours each week) in the practicum. One day a week, they participate in a practicum seminar. Students also are required to participate in five hours of community service per week. This service often is conducted in the neighborhood and community placements where students participated during the summer. The focus of the fall semester is to help students develop some pedagogical skills while they come to a deeper understanding of the school as a community institution.

Spring Semester

During the spring semester, students remain in their school sites. Teachers, students, and university faculty determine whether to move students to different classrooms to obtain different experiences and perspectives. Their schedules now require them to participate in full-time student teaching, Monday through Friday. On one afternoon per week, the students attend a university course, "Inclusive Schooling." This is the first course in which TFD students are in class with students from the ongoing certification programs. Comments from the instructor suggest that TFD students are distinctive, at least in the university classroom. They are more likely to challenge the ideology of both the teacher and the course material, more likely to raise critical questions, and more likely to support their points with experiences from their own beginning teaching. The TFD students also continue their field experiences seminar during this semester. By this time, they are exhibiting a fair amount of leadership and take responsibility for the form and substance of the seminar.

The Final Summer

Like the first summer, the final summer consists of two academic courses: "School and Society" and "Child Development." Both courses are offered outside our department, in the Educational Policy Studies Department and the Educational Psychology Department, respectively. However, the major task of the summer for most students is completing the master's paper. Because of the truncated nature of the program, students are not expected to complete a master's thesis. The program does not supply them with the necessary tools of inquiry to undertake conventional research. They have had an opportunity to examine and explore "action research" and are encouraged to develop an action research paper or project or to conduct library or archival research.

BEING CRITICAL ABOUT A CRITICAL PEDAGOGY PROJECT

With each subsequent semester, TFD improves. Now in its second cohort year, we can see marked improvement in the performance, attitudes, and dispositions of the current group as compared with the first cohort group. We also can see marked improvement in the organizational and administrative supports we have provided. However, from my perspective, all is not well with TFD. The primary challenge is the intensification of faculty work required by such a project. As a codirector, course instructor, and faculty supervisor–seminar leader, I am engaged in every phase of the program. In addition, I still teach graduate courses, advise doctoral and other master's students, and serve on numerous department, school, and university committees. To allow me to work with TFD exclusively would cost the department more than it is able to commit at this time—perhaps at any time. Thus, TFD faculty are required to work very hard and are very vulnerable to burnout.

Whether TFD graduates are different from our undergraduate teacher education graduates is difficult to say. We do know that the very nature of the program attracts a different kind of student, one with expressed commitments to principles of equity, diversity, and social justice. Haberman argues that this is half the battle.[10] To have better teachers means we need to recruit better people. We do believe that very fine people come into TFD. However, some of the shortcomings I see are located in both the individuals and in the program. They include the following concerns.

Prospective Teachers' Lack of Appreciation for the Complexity of Teaching

Some of our TFD students come to the program with enthusiasm and marvelous ideas about issues of equity and social justice. They believe that teaching can provide a venue for expressing that enthusiasm, and they are correct. However, often they have naive conceptions of what it means to teach young children. Some prospective teachers believe that if you tell students about the brutality of slavery, the horrors of Japanese internment, or the scandal of Indian removal, they will understand it, appreciate it, and be moved to some type of social action. Often the prospective teachers do not take into consideration their students' lack of experience and background with these issues or their students' skill levels.

Helping our prospective teachers break down their ideas into manageable pieces that tie into the everyday experiences and interests of young children is an important part of the field experiences seminar and integrated methods courses. Prospective teachers sometimes are amazed to learn that it takes much more time to develop a simple concept than they planned. Very often, prospective teachers have lost touch with the "child's view" of the world and the idea that something that reflects their passion does not necessarily capture the passion of youngsters.

Our prospective teachers also struggle with the multiplicity of things that occur simultaneously in the classroom. While a teacher is explaining a concept, three students may leave for English as a second language instruction, another student attends Chapter 1 support, and three other students attend a learning disabilities class. When these students return, they may be confused about what is happening in the class and have difficulty reentering the flow of classroom activities. Even if no student has to leave for a program, various things are likely to be occurring within the classroom. Someone has to go to the bathroom, someone else needs a pencil sharpened, and still another someone has lost her milk money. Each of these things is the most important thing to these individual children at that particular time. Our prospective teachers sometimes are overwhelmed with kids "being kids."

Prospective Teachers' Struggle to Translate Complex Social Issues into Meaningful Curriculum

As previously mentioned, many of the people attracted to Teach for Diversity have been and continue to be social activists. They care about issues of equity, social justice, health, the environment, and human rights. However, standing before a group of third-graders, many seem confused about how to develop meaningful curricular and instructional strategies that best express these concerns.

One prospective teacher wanted students to understand how capitalism creates inequalities. He chose to give students inequitable amounts of candy. At first glance, this lesson idea seemed to be appropriate. However, he had not adequately prepared the students for the learning activity, and the squabbling over who got how many and what kind of candy became the focus of the students' attention. Issues of social inequality never got raised.

Another prospective teacher was more successful with his attempts to excite children about endangered species. He planned in a very deliberate fashion to introduce one animal a day. Each day, he wore a T-shirt that had a picture of the animal. He planned games, songs, literacy, math, science, and social studies activities around that particular animal. Over time, his first-grade students began to realize that there were lots of animals that were endangered. One student remarked, "I'll be glad for the day when you come here with a plain T-shirt." The teacher's concrete display (the T-shirt) made a powerful statement that students could understand. He did not try to make them "get it" in one class period. He understood that, over time, the children would begin to understand that our biodiversity was being seriously affected by the pending loss of so many animals.

Prospective Teachers as Ideologues—Unwilling or Unable to Understand Challenges to Their Views

One of the reasons we, as teacher educators, were attracted to Teach for Diversity was the opportunity to work with adults who had opinions and perspectives on a variety of issues. However, we did not anticipate working with prospective teachers whose commitment became dogma. Because someone believes that children should be "free to express themselves" does not mean that we allow them to "choose" not to wear a jacket out to recess in below-freezing weather. Because one has chosen vegetarianism does not make eating meat a sin. For some prospective teachers, Teach for Diversity was to become their bully pulpit, on which their personal ideas would be advanced. Reminding them about and refocusing their energies on the children in the classrooms in which they were learning to teach became a regular task.

Another way these ideological positions were manifested was in the coursework. In one of our cohorts, two of the students chose to attend a public lecture given by a well-known conservative speaker. The students asked to share what they heard at the lecture to give their classmates a feel for the speaker's perspective on particular issues. Throughout their presentation, their cohort members responded angrily to them—almost as if the speakers had no right to express ideas that ran counter to their own. Still another student reacted negatively because one of the assigned readings had the word *zen* in it. The article itself had nothing to do with religion, but the student saw it as an affront to his religious beliefs. A third student wanted to do a curriculum project on holistic healing.

Although we thought helping elementary students think critically about health care had some potential, we could not see how the prospective teacher planned to fit the project in with what students were learning. The prospective teacher became very upset with the program, insisting that it did not support "diversity" and that she was teaching the "truth."

Prospective Teachers' Overconcern with Discipline and Order

Most student teachers struggle with classroom management issues. Those same children who seem individually so delightful can seem like horrible monsters as a group. Classroom management relies heavily on the relationship that teachers have with students. Thus, the cooperating teacher who is seen as the "real teacher" may be accorded deference because of her experience and expertise, while the student teacher occupies a lowly status and has difficulty exercising any power and authority. As a way to compensate for that lack of power and authority, some of our prospective teachers seem to become fixated on maintaining order.

Visits to classrooms organized around discipline and order are difficult to make. "Sit down," "put that away," "be quiet," and "listen to me" become the major communicative phrases. This overreliance on maintaining order and discipline serves to mask the prospective teachers' insecurities about teaching. If they can just keep the students seated and quiet, they might appear to be teaching. However, no experienced classroom observer is fooled by quiet, seated children. Questions about the quality of the instruction often send these prospective teachers into a discourse on badly behaved children.

Conversely, Some Prospective Teachers' Complete Lack of Regard for a Sense of Order

Although we do not want teachers to believe that teaching is only about getting students to be seated and quiet, we do want prospective teachers to understand that the classroom must have some sense of order to function smoothly. Some of our prospective teachers lose control of the classroom and have no idea what to do. So, they do nothing. The students continue to talk over the teacher and each other. Some engage in behaviors that are a danger to themselves and others. Like their colleagues who are rigid in their classroom management techniques, they end up blaming the students for the disintegration of classroom order.

Program Intensity—Almost to the Detriment of the Development of Critical and Reflective Practitioners

We say that one of the hallmarks of this program is the development of critical, reflective teachers. However, from the time the prospective teachers arrive in June until the time they leave in August of the following year, the TFD participants are on a fast-moving train. In an attempt to get them through both certification and degree requirements, almost every moment of their time is scheduled. Their family and social lives take quite a toll for them to participate in this program, which does not make for healthy personal social situations. The program participants hardly have any time to think about what is happening to them as a result of their participation in the program. The prospective teachers are so overwhelmed with the demands of classroom teaching and the rigors of university coursework that many are not inspired to think deeply about teaching and its social purposes. Their main demand is for some rest. Thus, we may be defeating our own expressed purposes by organizing the program this way. Are we merely trying to get people to finish teacher certification quickly, or are we trying to help prepare certain types of teachers—those with a disposition toward critical and scholarly thought?

Program "Holes"

Because we are working with a fifteen-month time frame, we realize that we cannot cover all of the areas that are part of undergraduate teacher education. We accept that as a limitation with which we can live. But we have omitted some areas that I see as essential to the kind of work in which we claim to be engaged. One area of concern is our limited attention to second language acquisition. With the growing number of children who populate our schools who have languages other than English as their first language, language acquisition must be a strong part of a teacher preparation program. We have aspects of second language learning in some of our coursework, but not nearly enough to help students know what to do when non–English-speaking children appear in their classrooms.

Because our program offers students a master's degree with their certification, students are required to write a master's paper. A second hole in our program I perceive is the lack of a strong enough research methodology background. Some of our students would like to undertake some empirical studies as they pursue their degrees. Our "regular" master's students have an opportunity to take quantitative and qualitative inquiry courses and research design courses. They can develop credible research projects. The TFD participants often are limited in what they can "research" because they have not had an opportunity to learn about competing research paradigms and ethical issues confronting educational researchers. To this date, we have restricted the scope of what our program participants can research and write. Their choices are typically archival (or library) research or action research in which they examine their own practice.

Another program hole has to do with the instances of nonintegration and incoherence that appear from time to time. We suggest that the program is an integrated, coherent approach to teacher preparation, and in many aspects we do an excellent job. The cohort structure means that students get to know a group of fellow teacher candidates intimately. Ideas expressed in one setting can be extended and continued in another. Much of the faculty has met together to discuss what they are teaching and how it relates to other things being taught. The "methods" teachers have attempted to pull together a unified course requirement of a curriculum project that integrates the subject areas covered. However, some of the state-mandated requirements are courses and experiences that are beyond our control as a program. Some courses seem unrelated and irrelevant to the participants' experiences. At this point, we have no answer for these kinds of bureaucratic, organizational problems.

Professional Development

What we envisioned as one of the ancillary benefits of the program was the opportunity for more professional development for the cooperating teachers and schools in which our program participants were placed. The truth is that few of these opportunities have been made evident. Some of us have conducted staff development sessions, and at least one of us has maintained a working group of teachers interested in action research. Perhaps the primary reason for this lack of professional development stems from the ways that schools are organized. Even though we placed between six and eight additional adults in a school, these adults tended to have fewer skills and more needs than six to eight experienced teachers. Thus, the cooperating teachers were taking on more work and actually had less time for their own professional development. A program such as Teach for Diversity needs the financial support to be able to provide teachers with release time to work on their own professional development issues. Schools and school districts have to value professional development opportunities as important chances for teachers and other educators to grow and mature in the profession—not just fillers for the obligatory staff development day.

What I have detailed here are a few of the obvious ways that I see the program failing to function at its best. However, these shortcomings are not an indictment of the TFD concept or its implementation. Rather, this chapter is an attempt to look critically at what it might mean to help teachers become critical pedagogues—to ask questions about difference and inequity. For TFD students, race, class, gender, ability, and sexual orientation are important sites of contestation. They are not swept under the rug in an attempt to foster a more palatable teacher preparation program designed for a mythical school setting. However, moving from critical theory talk to critical pedagogical action requires a large investment in human and fiscal resources. University of Wisconsin–Madison has committed itself to bringing critical pedagogy out of the academy classrooms and into the public school practices of novice teachers. Despite our shortcomings, we have attempted to "put up." I presume that means we are not yet required to "shut up."

NOTES

[1]See Paulo Freire, *Pedagogy of the Oppressed* (New York: Seabury Press, 1970) and *Education for Critical Consciousness* (New York: Seabury Press, 1973); Michael Apple, *Ideology and Curriculum* (Boston: Routledge and Kegan Paul, 1979) and *Education and Power* (Boston: Routledge and Kegan Paul, 1982); Henry Giroux, *Schooling and the Struggle for Public Life: Critical Pedagogy in the Modern Age* (Minneapolis: University of Minnesota Press, 1989);

Peter McLaren, *Life in Schools* (Albany, N.Y.: Longman Press, 1989) and *Schooling as a Ritual Performance* (New York: Routledge, 1994); Stanley Aronowitz and Henry Giroux, *Education Under Siege: The Conservative, Liberal and Radical Debate Over Schooling* (South Hadley, Mass.: Bergin and Garvey, 1983); Ira Shor, *Critical Teaching and Everyday Life* (Boston: South End Press, 1979); the autobiography of Myles Horton written with Judith and Herb Kohl, *The Long Haul* (New York: Doubleday, 1990); the autobiography of Septima Clark by Cynthia Brown, *Ready from Within* (Tenton, N.J.: Africa World Press, 1990).

[2]Their most well-known writings include Max Horkheimer, *Eclipse of Reason* (New York: Seabury Press, [1974] 1974); Theodor Adorno, *Negative Dialectics* (New York: Seabury Press, [1969] 1973) Herbert Marcuse, *One Dimensional Man* (Boston: Beacon Press, 1964); Jurgen Habermas, *Towards a Rational Society* (Boston: Beacon Press, 1968) and *Knowledge and Human Interests* (Boston: Beacon Press, 1971).

[3]Y. Pai, *Cultural Foundations of Education* (Columbus, Ohio: Merrill, 1990), p. 143.

[4]Stanley Aronowitz and Henry Giroux, *Education Under Seige* (South Hadley, Mass.: Bergin and Garvey, 1981).

[5]Pai, p. 145.

[6]Carter Goodwin Woodson, *The Miseducation of the Negro* (Washington, D.C.: Association Press, 1933).

[7]Cynthia Brown, ed., *Ready from Within* (Trenton, N.J.: Africa World Press, 1990).

[8]Larry Cuban, "Reforming Again, Again, and Again," *Educational Researcher* 19 (April 1990).

[9]Kenneth M. Zeichner, "Teacher Education for Social Responsibility," paper presented at the annual meeting of the American Educational Research Association, Chicago, 1991, p. 4.

[10]Martin Haberman, "The Rationale for Training Adults as Teachers," in *Empowerment Through Multicultural Education,* ed. Christine Sleeter (Albany: State University of New York Press, 1991).

CHAPTER 11

Community, Displacement, and Inquiry
Living Social Justice
in a Social Studies Methods Course

EDWARD BUENDIA
SHUAIB MEACHAM
SUSAN E. NOFFKE

A university methods course, with its traditional tendency to emphasize the "practical" needs of prospective teachers, seems at first glance an unlikely place to promote living social justice issues through teaching. Reports of efforts to integrate feminist pedagogy within secondary teacher education or critical pedagogy within social studies methods classes or elementary education programs are full of instances of resistance and accounts of barriers, as well as hopeful signs.[1] Many studies that discuss critically oriented teacher education have focused on either the conceptual flaws or the knowledge gaps of preservice teachers related to issues of race and culture.[2] Others have discussed the implications of preservice teacher identity for the practices in which these students are likely to engage as teachers.[3] Few works, however, have attempted to connect specific social studies methods and curriculum to the content knowledge, practical needs, and experiential knowledge of preservice teachers with a focus on issues of social justice. We attempt in our methods course to help students know themselves and critically examine their social world, but we do so with a valuing of the importance of also learning how they can work through similar issues with their students. Rather than as a study of preservice teachers, our efforts have been framed as action research with a focus on our own practices as teacher educators—our attempts to "practice what we preach."[4]

In this chapter, we describe both the theoretical conceptions and the practical aspects of a critical approach to preservice social studies teacher education—one that emphasizes social critique as well as inquiry in teaching and learning to teach, as it has emerged through action research on our practice. In our work over the past three years, we have attempted to integrate a critical perspective on social studies content (e.g., "alternative" tellings of history, multiple interpretations of economics, and geography) with an emphasis on active learning methods, and we have tried to do so in such a way as to pedagogically live out our beliefs about how a person learns to learn about the social world.

The theoretical and curricular tensions explored here center on three areas: (1) a community ethos wherein personal narratives and dispositions are shared and valued, (2) critical content and methods that foster an unsettling displacement of the beliefs and historical conceptions that have informed prior personal and national identity construction, and (3) an examination of the beliefs that bound assumptions about such identities and that translate into the social studies curriculum. A key issue for our work has been how linkages can be made between these displaced beliefs and progressive teaching methods. That is, at the same time as we have tried to be responsive to the ways in which preservice teachers construct their understandings of whose knowledge is of most worth,[5] we have also tried to focus on and value the "methods" for social studies instruction.

This chapter includes background information on the course, as well as specific examples of what we have done in our class sessions with preservice teachers to help foster these ends. Because we believe that the ability to "live social justice" in teaching practice is dependent on both ideological commitments and concrete pedagogical practices, we include references to the kinds of resources available to use to such ends. Such a material base, we argue, is central to the process of seeing teaching both as inquiry and as knowledge production. Finally, we address the constraints and tensions that both we and the students encounter in attempting to define and practice critical social education. Our aim is to provide a theoretical framework for our efforts, to describe the necessary material bases for such practices, and to advocate an ethos of struggle that frames the construction of practice as filled with tensions and contradictions, as well as hope.

THE "METHODS" COURSE

The social studies methods course is part of a block of teaching methods courses in an elementary teacher certification program at the University of Illinois. The program is structured such that seniors, as well as a few master's students, participate in two practicum settings, lasting eight weeks each, and one student teaching experience, lasting sixteen weeks, over the course of a full academic year. From August through February, the preservice teachers are involved in university coursework Mondays, Thursday afternoons, and Fridays, with the remaining time spent learning and gradually assuming responsibilities in their field experiences. The social studies methods course, language and literacy, science, and general methods courses comprise the last series of courses in the certification program.[6] The general methods course continues as a student teaching seminar throughout the last third of the year, concurrent with full-time classroom experience.

The students who have participated in the program have been primarily young, white, female, and from rural, small city, or suburban settings. Despite their seeming homogeneity, they have brought to the course a broad range of perspectives that have been minimally represented in the teacher education literature. The representation of males, people of color, and ethnic minorities in the program has been small.

The social studies methods course has been in a state of evolution over the last four years.[7] During the 1993–1994 academic year, it functioned primarily as a course in the "principles and practices of social studies education," although a good deal of attention to issues of cultural pluralism was incorporated into readings and class activities. A separate one-credit course—developed in response to an evaluation of program needs, focused on addressing issues of cultural diversity, special education, and the uses of technology in the classroom, and taught by Shuaib—was an added part of this block of university coursework. In the fall of 1994, however, at Sue's suggestion, the separate course was redefined. The diversity segment was reassigned to the social studies course (cotaught with Shuaib), and the technology portion was added to the general methods course. This configuration has remained intact ever since.[8]

Alongside programmatic alterations, the course has also undergone pedagogical modifications over the last four years. Changes in the graduate students coteaching the course (from Shuaib to Ed) and feedback from preservice teachers have prompted variations in the pedagogical strategies and organizational structures. Each of us constructed aspects of the course from our experiential bases and ideological concerns, and each brought different teaching skills. Input from preservice teachers resulted in greater attention to the rhythms of the students' field experiences, as well as greater clarity in how our coursework "applied" to their own concerns.

Several cooperating teachers who participate in the program have also contributed to the eventual form and content of the course through a series of meetings that culminated in the development of a "social inquiry" component as a major course assignment.[9] These inquiries have enabled students to do observations and interviews in a variety of contexts—for example, in local churches, at homeless shelters, and in women's centers—and some have examined local media. These activities, as well as others dealing with films, oral history, and neighborhood study, for example, are designed to take students out into the community and encourage them to cross "borders" in their personal experiences. The inquiries also worked to help them see and practice social education as an *active* process of investigation into the social world. Although the specific methods and activities addressed in class sessions have changed over time, the social justice platform of problematizing teaching practices and raising questions pertaining to diversity and equity have remained central aspects of the course.

BUILDING AND CONNECTING WITH COMMUNITIES

The theoretical framework that underpins the methods course encompasses an integrative and recursive process of fostering a community through building relationships, of problematizing and displacing the beliefs and conceptions of both preservice teachers and ourselves, and of reconceptualizing teaching as a process of inquiry and production. Interwoven through these tenets and practices is the assumption that all of these are enacted within multiple tensions that silence and privilege particular views and ways of knowing. The concept of community, though, is a cornerstone of the course. It forms a basis for the processes of continual displacement and reconceptualization, but it is also shaped by them.

Our concept of community has been multilayered. At one level, we have attempted to foster a classroom community ethos in which preservice teachers would feel capable of taking risks in discussing issues and topics (e.g., racism, social inequality) that have often been left out of the polite and procedural discussions within teacher education programs. We spend a great deal of time examining our own and the preservice teachers' biographies, experiences, and beliefs about education, self, and others. Dialogical forms of communication, such as small and large group discussions and individualized e-mail, are used as pedagogical practices for collectively linking and problematizing conceptions of epistemology, of identity, and of difference within the social studies curriculum. We have also worked to establish a common weekly lunch time, when students and faculty can gather to share both ideas and experiences. The process of interacting over readings and examples of social studies lessons, as well as the process of just getting to know one another a bit more personally, becomes a means of dialoguing across and against our backgrounds and biographies.

The scope of community, however, did not stop with merely locating our identities and those of the preservice teachers in our course. The experiential and epistemological frameworks of the children and communities in which these preservice teachers would potentially teach were also brought into the discussion of the social studies curriculum and classroom practice. We attempted to avoid a monologue about communities and children of color by facilitating a dialogue between our classroom community and these other communities. The voices of local African American clergy,[10] of a librarian from the branch serving part of the African American community, and of progressive African American and white teachers, for example, which sometimes involved visits to area sites, provided multiple perspectives on topics such as the place of race and culture within classroom practices and curriculum and the interconnections between race and social and economic inequality.

These efforts at both building and expanding community have tended to emphasize elements of struggle and change, rather than conformity and comfort. Our struggle in the methods course has frequently paralleled the students' efforts in their field placements to create and sustain communities, rather than institute "management plans." Here, too, the contribution of cooperating teachers in sharing their concrete examples of useful strategies for community building has been a vital resource. Yet the very concept of community also needed to be continually problematized to address the often concurrent pressures for unanimity and compliance. Living social justice issues in our classroom, as in theirs, meant that difficult issues could not be avoided for the sake of harmony. The community in our methods course, like those outside it, was at times a painful reminder of the difficulties and hard work involved in reaching across differences.

Broadening our own and the students' conceptualizations of community did not stop with site visits, guest speakers, or discussions. Students were also involved in learning about their community through social inquiry.[11] They were encouraged to interview local businesspeople, such as the owner of a local Korean American grocery store or announcers from the local African American radio station; to attend community places of worship, such as one of the community's African

American churches or Jewish synagogues; or visit any of the social agencies that served the larger community, for instance, a local shelter for women or homeless people or boys and girls clubs.

The purpose of these inquiries was, first, to broaden our students' understanding of what and who our community is by having them investigate the diverse segments that compose the larger whole. Our assumption was that the experiences and backgrounds of our students oftentimes provide them with a view of only a narrow segment of the community. Second, the process of doing social inquiries for themselves was intended to provide them with a model for engaging their own students in inquiry about their community and world. We hoped that the possibilities of social inquiry for their own practice—conducting interviews, observing events, or examining artifacts—would be more evident after they had experienced it themselves. Third and most important, their interactions with community members with similar and yet qualitatively different experiences, investments, and issues were intended to be challenges—what we have termed *displacements* of preconceptions about a unitary "American" norm. In other words, the aim, in part, was to uproot beliefs about American identity and experience to make room for other ways of seeing and acting in the social world.

DISPLACEMENT OF SELF AND MEANING

The process of displacement took place through other practices within the course, as well, particularly in our classroom activities, readings, and discussions. The use of revisionist historical texts and the practice of critically interrogating conceptions of pedagogy overlapped with the social inquiries and the voices of community people. Takaki's *A Different Mirror: A History of Multicultural America,* Zinn's *A People's History of the United States: 1492–Present,* and Rethinking Schools' *Rethinking Columbus* all functioned to displace the historical conceptions of America and the American identity that many of our students were taught and had embraced as the American narrative.[12] Students' readings of these texts have often resulted in an epistemological disequilibrium in which the conceptions and images of self and nation are displaced from their position of moral and judicial righteousness. Comments such as "I can't believe Columbus did that!" and "I never knew we did that to the Native Americans!" are common responses, as the "discovery" of America and the "westward movement" are reframed in these texts as invasion, colonization, and attempts at genocide. Of primary importance in the reaction to these readings is the increasing salience—often a response to a disbelief of what they read—of questions such as "How does he [the author] know?" and "Why weren't we told this [in school]?" Such questions provide an entry point into discussions of evidence and narrative in history, as well as of selectivity in the school curriculum.

The practice of critical social studies education carries with it a strong sense of responsibility. The epistemological disequilibrium that results from the community experiences and the reading and discussion of texts often displaces much that students have come to believe about American identity and experience, and it can be paralyzing. Students frequently find themselves in a quandary as they grapple with what they should teach tomorrow. Consequently, we have struggled to define and live a "practice of hope" that provides our students with concrete pedagogical alternatives to what some have come to see, if not name, as "reproducing the master narrative."

This practice of hope has entailed connecting our students through readings to communities of practitioner-researchers who are involved in defining alternative frameworks and models for their classroom practice and curriculum, both local and farther afield. Over time, we have selected materials representing a broad range of issues, but always ones that highlight strategic actions for change in clear terms. For example, alongside the historical content, texts such as Perry and Fraser's *Freedom's Plow;* Campbell's *Choosing Democracy: A Practical Guide to Multicultural Education;* Levine, Lowe, Peterson, and Tenorio's *Rethinking Schools: An Agenda for Change;* and the Rethinking Schools group's *Rethinking Our Classrooms* have provided important links to conceptual and practical alternatives.[13] Steffy and Hood's *If This Is Social Studies, Why Isn't It Boring?* provides teachers' insights of the struggle, messiness, and possibility of constructing an inquiry-oriented social studies curriculum.[14] Students have shared, in "literature circle" format, their reactions to works such as Paley's *Kwanzaa and Me,* Ladson-Billings's *The Dreamkeepers,* and Delpit's *Other People's Children.*[15] In addition, articles from the journals *Rethinking Schools, Teaching Tolerance, Feminist Teacher,* and *Radical Teacher* provide students with teaching examples and sources for materials. These periodicals often complement other materials, such as *Social Studies and the Young Learner, The Social Studies,* and children's magazines such as *New Moon, Muse,* and those from the *Cobblestone* group, letting our students see ways to adapt ideas but also see themselves as part of a larger community of social educators with a shared agenda.

Of central importance in this process, too, has been the presence, in the field and in our university classroom, of local cooperating teachers who provide examples of how both social justice issues and social inquiry play themselves out in their practice. Many of these teachers read similar works; one group at a local school held regular study groups over several of the readings from the class. These teachers, many of whom see themselves as deeply engaged in teaching as part of social struggle, are present as more than role models or dispensers of alternative technical knowledge, although these roles are indeed important. Rather, they are colleagues and resources in the process of "Learning to Teach against the Grain."[16]

Although such teachers and texts provide alternative conceptualizations of self and meaning that also serve as models for what might be done in classrooms, we feel a strong need to present teaching alternatives in our own classroom as well. They provide a direct experiential base for seeing what else can be done in a course's pedagogical practices and immerse students in alternative frameworks for theorizing and enacting their classroom teaching. This pedagogy has been conceptualized as looking outward, recognizing the students our preservice teachers will eventually teach and also the potential constraints of the public educational system. We have attempted to model practices and curricula that resist the marginalization of the voices, experiences, and backgrounds of the many.

Examples have included our students' participation in democratic grading structures, in which we collectively defined the parameters and evaluation criteria for their coursework, and participation in critically oriented simulations. One simulation served as a means of modeling how economic concepts such as mode of production and division of labor could be explored in ways that demonstrate the tensions in various economic models. The structure of this activity entailed dividing our students into production groups whose task was to produce paper flowers. The groups included an assembly line, in which each member had a specific task in producing a predefined flower; an independent artist collective, in which each artist had full control over her or his own flowers' design and production; an environmentally responsive group who had control of design and production but was limited to recycled paper as raw material; and a democratic cooperative, in which their shared vision of design, shared labor, and shared profits formed the underlying ethos. Students conducted the simulation, examined the conceptual learning that took place, and participated in a discussion on the conceptual and pedagogical possibilities for doing simulations with upper- and lower-grade classes.

In another class activity that dealt with the creation of theme or topic units, especially for young children, we began by having the students examine their shoes for place of manufacture. The information was then transferred to a class chart as well as a world map. This simple "shoes" activity was again a concrete example of how concepts and skills were not neutral bodies of knowledge to be "taught" to children. Rather, they were rich opportunities for developing critical thinking. The charting process and the examination of the world map are not merely "basic skills," they are a stimulus to great questions: Why are so few of our shoes made in the United States? Who are the people who make our shoes? What are their lives like? We examined a wide range of children's literature on various themes or topics and also planned a section dealing with music in social education. Pieces such as Sweet Honey in the Rock's "Are My Hands Clean" were examined as ways to raise critical issues about the lives of the people who actually make the things we wear and use. In several local classrooms, such topic units do not avoid important controversial issues, for example, discussions of the use of child labor in the production of popular U.S. consumer goods.

Thus, students not only read about but also experience how hegemonic conceptualizations, capitalism in this case, could be critically interrogated with children. Moreover, we hoped to demonstrate that the practical aspects of teaching are also political, theoretical, and personal. Our conceptions of curriculum, we emphasized, are reflections of how we make sense of the world. The shared experience of actually doing lessons together provided not only practical ideas but also a common basis for inquiry into the messages constructed by curriculum and teaching. The "practical" in teaching becomes a primary vehicle for critical thought and action.

Our students' strongly felt need for teaching ideas has to be taken seriously.[17] As meanings are displaced, there is an even stronger necessity for specific resources. Especially in the latter part of the course, we spend a great deal of time helping them locate materials or providing suggestions for ways to think through their lessons. But we do so with a clear eye to how activities and materials are but beginning points for the transformation of practice based on insights gained in *doing* social education with children, as well as on ideological frames. Learning to live out the struggle for social justice, a major part of critical social education, is as much a process of construction, needing a material base in practices, as it is a set of beliefs.

TEACHING AS INQUIRY AND PRODUCTION

We believe that teachers (including student teachers and ourselves) need to see their pedagogical practice as political, personal, and theoretical activities in which they do have considerable latitude, although there are clearly varying degrees and kinds of constraints. Facilitating a connection between these dimensions of practice was a key element in our gradual reconceptualization of teaching as inquiry and production. A recursive element of the course was to provide students with the opportunity to collaboratively theorize their practice by defining if and how particular materials and content could be used in their teaching. The overarching goal was to displace the conception of teaching as merely the implementation of prepackaged materials and techniques and to promote a view of teaching as mediation and production through inquiry.

Children's literature was one medium for facilitating this process. Students were regularly given children's nonfiction and fiction (including historical fiction) and asked to determine if and how particular concepts and content should be part of the curriculum. They were frequently prompted with questions such as "What concepts does this book highlight?" "What social issues are addressed?" and "How would you decide whether and how to use it?" Students examined titles such as Mills' *The Rag Coat,* which tells the story of a young girl's connection to her father, who dies from miner's cough, and to her immediate community through her patchwork coat.[18] The children's literature examples were often selected to represent alternative tellings of history or to highlight a particular group whose perspectives, history, and culture have not always been part of the standard curriculum. *The Rag Coat,* for example, opened up issues of working-class history and of groups struggling for economic survival, as it centered on the interconnections between a child's personal growth and the social world. As literacy, particularly "whole-language" approaches, has come to play an increasing role in elementary school classrooms, it becomes even more important that the social content of books be examined in such a way as to open up the broader social sphere. Here the linkages between critical social education and critical literacy are important to remember.[19]

We would often bring armloads of instructional materials to class: trade books, children's magazines, games, simulations, local curriculum guides, textbooks, and various versions of "standards." Although these materials were frequently selected to represent the "best" of what is available, such materials were not included to be "accepted" as ready-made best practice. Rather, the analysis and planning from these instructional materials was intended to be a means for continual learning—inquiry into practice as well as production of new meanings of classroom practice. The strategic use of commercial materials, including textbooks— frequently part of the world of beginning teachers—becomes a means of production of the pedagogy of social justice.

Our intent, then, was to have our preservice teachers see themselves as both inquirers into and creators of their practice. Planning, teaching, and evaluation were presented as a circular process of inquiring, problematizing, and negotiating between and among multiple dimensions. Knowing what content and concepts to teach was articulated as a process of displacing and suspending—or holding at bay—the dominant meanings about a concept or theme and engaging themselves and their students in an inquiry into a wide range of experiences and perspectives. This inquiry concurrently entailed negotiating the voices and interests of their children, the community, district guidelines, and their own biases and beliefs. Planning and evaluation were expanded from a narrow and technical orientation to include the problematizing of their curricular conceptions, especially along the lines of identifying and responding to privileged and, most important, silenced voices.

We have attempted to shift curriculum away from fixed and monolithic conceptualizations, instead emphasizing its responsiveness to context and process. In this way, the construction of curriculum cannot be seen as something done outside the classroom, the products of which teachers can choose to either embrace or avoid. Rather, curriculum is literally "what happens" in classrooms as teachers and students construct experiences and meanings. Our characterization of teachers' work embodies a process of struggle between the practices that have historically been promoted by educational institutions (including ours) and those that they as teachers create.[20] Determining who will and will not benefit from particular decisions and practices is vital to conceptualizing, enacting, and evaluating instructional materials and methods.

CONSTRAINTS AND STRUGGLES

This description of our course is a representation of what has been a simultaneous process of working through tensions and building relationships with our students. The narrative of the chapter has an obvious "absent presence" of the voices of our students. Although we could have "used" excerpts from their course notebooks, course evaluations, and private communications, by gaining the usual guarantees of anonymity, we decided early on in this project that we would focus on *our* practice. Information from the students gleaned from such "data" sources was crucial in formulating our actions, yet we acknowledge that the project was not fully collaborative. We hope that what is reported here is a first step toward engaging students in research over how to approach the issues and also toward engaging other colleagues in teacher education in such work. Although some may regard this stance as a flaw in our approach to action research, we felt that the task of documenting and interrogating our practice as teacher-educators was a substantial beginning point to further efforts, as well as a reflection of the kinds of constraints teacher-educators face in examining their own practice.

In teaching the course, we have grappled with many of the same tensions and constraints our students face as teachers. Personal tensions, for example, were common sources of conflict. Our desire to promote a safe and humane classroom environment that fosters the exchange of ideas and perspectives was often at odds with our concern with challenging dominant conceptions of difference. This conflict often left us wondering when and how to pursue discussions of race and social inequality. In our reflections on our teaching, we often questioned ourselves on whether we had pushed some students too hard on themes of teaching practices that highlighted race, gender, and class, with the result that in some students shut down. At the same time, we were aware that some of the students, in part because of their identities but also as a result of prior experiences, were impatient with "waiting" for others on issues they felt very ready to address. Because of the structure of the program, it also became particularly important that we attend to the phases of their classroom work, as well as the demands of other coursework, in planning class sessions.

In addition—and not inconsequentially parallel with the teaching tasks of our students—we needed to be reminded of the multiple points of entry into critical discourse. The visits to an African American church, for example, provided good evidence that some students who had limited experiences with African American students found that the common ground of their religious faith gave them ways to see connections rather than otherness. The struggle for a critical perspective could not be grounded in our vision of "what matters". Rather, we needed, as teachers in general do, to understand the students and the potential connections to be made. Yet our quandary had another side, articulated in concerns about not pushing hard enough. Although we wanted our students to learn, to grow, and to see themselves as emerging, capable practitioners, ones who look for connections, we equally realized that their credentialing also licensed them to do potentially great harm.[21] The search for connections needed to be framed, not as a way to subsume difference under similarities, but rather as a way to see how social justice issues for the other are bound up with our own.

Alongside this personal tension, the professional question of which methods to include in the course was also a preoccupation. Like any classroom teacher, the constraints on the amount of time available to teach the course translated into making decisions about which methods would and would not be discussed in the course. We grappled with what cultural capital would best serve the interests of our preservice teachers and also, and most important, their future students. Questions such as "What types of methods and skills will our preservice teachers need to be able to be 'successful' in their teaching?" were counterbalanced with "What practices will best facilitate their students' empowerment?" We therefore struggled to engage in our own inquiry into multiple parties' (e.g., community members, classroom teachers, and district personnel) positions and negotiate between our preferences for methods constructed within a social reconstructionist framework[22] and those more in line with the social efficiency orientations so prominent in many schools,[23] perhaps made more prominent by the increase in efforts toward centralized assessment. Our students needed to learn to deal with state and national "standards," as well as textbooks and drill and practice orientations to social studies skills. Our feeling continues to be that critical orientations to social study must develop practices that both allow for critique of technical-rationalist assumptions embedded in practice and, at the same time, develop tangible alternatives.

Although personal and professional tensions and the politics both embody weighed heavily on our reflections, structural constraints were also a source of discordance. One struggle was the displacement of our course within the larger teacher education program. The course's attempt to advocate for critical questions about pedagogy and democratic practices as legitimate classroom discourse was sometimes muffled by the larger program's emphasis on mastery of techniques, on the "survival" needs of the students, or on acceptance of versions of "good practice." Our discussions of problematizing voice and framing curricular conceptions as inquiry were suppressed by the focus of other courses within the block on decontextualized skills and strategies or on the need to implement the "findings of research." Other aspects, such as the program's competency-based evaluation scheme, also undermined conceptions such as democratic evaluation or teaching as inquiry by privileging predefined solutions to pedagogical questions. This aspect was problematic not so much because our version of "truth" was not accepted programwide but because students were not engaged in analysis of multiple frameworks that would let them see, and begin to evaluate for themselves, the assumptions and intentions of various approaches to curriculum and instruction. We have, as a result, added a course session that attempts to provide such a framework.

Our time constraints share similarities with those encountered within the students' teaching placements. The lack of cohesive vision within the teacher education program has been partly a function of time; just learning each others' perspectives, let alone trying to create cohesion, has seemed, at times, to be a task far beyond those hours that fit neatly into professorial course loads. Communication with teachers, with students, and with other course instructors takes time. Although larger-scale efforts at program revision are underway, including substantial opportunities for planning with teachers, substantive discussions of program goals, especially over social justice issues, have had to be continually re-identified so that visions of teaching are not lost in bureaucratic demands.

We have been able to make some adjustments in the influence of university coursework by changing the spring segment of the course to a pass-fail grading system. This seemingly minor change releases students from the sometimes overwhelming influence of grading on the development of responses to issues with no clear-cut resolution. Quite logically, in an era of strong competition for jobs on graduation, concern with "getting the right answer" for a grade can work in tandem with desires for ready-made solutions—for "things that work" in their everyday classroom practice.

Finally, our positions as graduate students and junior faculty limited the amount of time we could realistically spend in students' classrooms and schools as we attempted to better understand their questions about practice. We were busy graduate students and professors, with demands and agendas affecting the time we had available to work through our planning and enactment of the course. It takes time to identify cooperating teachers who are familiar with and modeled inquiry-based social studies with a social justice orientation. The very crucial support for this model of social studies takes time to develop. As a result, the amount of experimentation our students did was initially minimal. However, there are promising signs. The voices of cooperating teachers, as well as our own emergent understanding of the context of student teaching, have led to an increase in alternative practices in their course and field assignments. In the most recent semester, for example, the number of students selecting social studies topics for the thematic unit required by their general methods course increased greatly. But it is not only in the selection of "topics" but also in the development of an inquiry orientation that the most progress has been seen. We remain, after years of work, very optimistic.

MOVING ON IN INQUIRY

Our classrooms, in the teacher education program and in the local school districts, continue the struggle for meaningful community. At the beginning of the sixth year, the social studies methods course is beginning to be able to name time as a benefit, not only a constraint. The inquiry assignments, the substance and form of the class, and the continuity of instructors mean that the course has developed a "history." Local teachers and graduating student teachers share their experiences with incoming students and make our work have a ring of familiarity. Although displacement is still a strong feeling on the part of many of the students, we have a wealth of prior experiences to point to and to learn from. There have also been new materials, such as *Beyond Heroes and Holidays* and *Integrating Socially,* which have given the course new ways to make connections between the ideals and the practices.[24]

But what continues to frame the course and to therefore shape our understandings of community and displacement is the conceptualization of teaching as inquiry and production. The study of teaching, the study of and with children, and the study of ourselves form the basis of a practice of social education that is continually under production. In an era when teachers' work is deeply embedded in contradictory efforts toward both site-based management and standardization, this vision is, we believe, vital to continually directing social education toward greater social justice.

NOTES

[1]Susan Adler, "Forming a Critical Pedagogy in the Social Studies Methods Class: The Use of Imaginative Literature," in B. Robert Tabachnick and Kenneth

Zeichner, eds., *Issues and Practices in Inquiry-Oriented Teacher Education* (London: Falmer Press, 1991), pp. 77–90; Landon Beyer, ed., *Creating Democratic Classrooms: The Struggle to Integrate Theory and Practice* (New York: Teachers College Press, 1996); Frances Maher, "Gender, Reflexivity and Teacher Education," in B. Robert Tabachnick and Kenneth Zeichner, eds., *Issues and Practices in Inquiry-Oriented Teacher Education* (London: Falmer Press, 1991), pp. 22–34.

[2]Joyce King, "Dysconscious Racism: Ideology, Identitiy, and the Miseducation of Teachers," *Journal of Negro Education* 60 (1991): 133–146; Gloria Ladson-Billings, "Coping with Multicultural Illiteracy: A Teacher Education Response," *Social Education* 55 (1991): 186–189, 193; MyLuong T. Tran, Russell L. Young, and Joseph D. DiLella, "Multicultural Education Courses and the Students Teacher: Eliminating Stereotypical Attitudes in our Ethnically Diverse Classroom," *Journal of Teacher Education* 45, (1994): 183–198.

[3]James Banks, "Teaching Multicultural Literacy to Teachers," *Teaching Education* 4, (1991): 135–144; Kenneth Zeichner, *Educating Teachers for Cultural Diversity* (East Lansing, Mich.: National Center for Research on Teacher Learning, 1992).

[4]Jennifer Gore, "Practicing What We Preach: Action Research and the Supervision of Student Teachers," in B. Robert Tabachnick and Kenneth Zeichner, eds., *Issues and Practices in Inquiry-Oriented Teacher Education* (London: Falmer Press, 1991), pp. 253–272.

[5]In work such as this, it is important to invoke one's ideological roots.

[6]The students currently take their arts, kinesiology, and math methods coursework during the previous academic year.

[7]Prior to the work presented here, the work of Wallace Strong as an assistant in the course added much to our understandings and to the basic approach of the course.

[8]In subsequent work on the elementary teacher education program, attention to special education has been integrated into coursework.

[9]Although many of the cooperating teachers have enriched our thinking about the course, we'd like to acknowledge the particular contributions of Barbara Gillespie-Washington, Vicky Cromwell, and Marcella Vancil in developing social inquiry ideas.

[10]The commitment of the pastors of Canaan Missionary Baptist Church, Reverend B. J. Tatum and Reverend Harold Davis, in welcoming our students to their church community is gratefully acknowledged.

[11]H. Millard Clements, William R. Fielder, and B. Robert Tabachnick, *Social Study: Inquiry in Elementary Classrooms* (New York: Bobbs-Merrill, 1966).

[12]Rethinking Schools, *Rethinking Columbus* (Milwaukee: Rethinking Schools, 1992); Ronald Takaki, *A Different Mirror: A History of Multicultural America* (Boston: Little, Brown, 1993); Howard Zinn, *A People's History of the United States: 1492–Present* (New York: Harper, 1980/1995).

[13]Duane E. Campbell, *Choosing Democracy: A Practical Guide to Multicultural Education* (Englewood Cliffs, N.J.: Merrill/Prentice Hall, 1996); Daniel Levine, Robert Lowe, Bob Peterson, and Rita Tenorio, *Rethinking Schools: An Agenda for Change* (New York: New Press, 1995); Theresa Perry and James W. Fraser, eds., *Freedom's Plow: Teaching in the Multicultural Classroom* (New York: Routledge, 1993); and Rethinking Schools, *Rethinking Our Classrooms: Teaching for Equity and Justice* (Milwaukee: Rethinking Schools, 1994).

[14]Stephanie Steffy and Wendy Hood, *If This Is Social Studies, Why Isn't It Boring?* (York, Minn.: Stenhouse, 1994).

[15]Lisa Delpit, *Other People's Children* (New York: New Press, 1995); Gloria Ladson-Billings, *The Dreamkeepers: Successful Teacher of African American Children* (San Francisco: Jossey-Bass, 1994); Vivian Paley, *Kwanzaa and Me* (Cambridge: Harvard University Press, 1995).

[16]Marilyn Cochran-Smith, "Learning to Teach Against the Grain," *Harvard Educational Review* 61 (1991): 279–310.

[17]Erica McWilliam, *In Broken Images: Feminist Tales for a Different Teacher Education* (New York: Teachers College Press, 1994).

[18]Lauren Mills, *The Rag Coat* (Boston: Little, Brown, 1991).

[19]Paulo Freire, *Pedagogy of the Oppressed* (New York: Herder & Herder, 1970); Ira Shor, "Monday Morning Fever: Critical Literacy and the Generative Theme of 'Work,' " in Ira Shor, ed., *Freire for the Classroom: A Sourcebook for Liberatory Teaching* (Portsmouth, N.H.: Heinemann, 1987), pp. 104–121.

[20]McWilliam.

[21]Joyce King, "Dysconscious Racism: Ideology, Identity, and the Miseducation of Teachers," *Journal of Negro Education* 60 (1991): 133–146; Susan E. Noffke, Shuaib Meacham, and Edward Buendia, "History, Culture, & Community: Comfort, Conflict, and Change in an Elementary Social Studies Methods Course," paper presented at the annual meeting of the American Educational Research Association as part of the symposium *Talking About Diversity and Making Change: Bridges Between Coursework and Fieldwork in Teacher Education*, New York, April 1996.

[22]See William Stanley, *A Curriculum for Utopia: Social Reconstructionism and Critical Pedagogy* (Albany: State University of New York Press, 1992).

[23]See Herbert Kliebard, *The Struggle for the American Curriculum: 1893–1958* (New York: Routledge & Kegan Paul, 1995).

[24]Julie Hamston and Kath Murdoch, *Integrating Socially: Planning Integrated Units of Work for Social Education* (Portsmouth, N.H.: Heinemann, 1996). Enid Lee, Deborah Menkart, and Margo Okazawa-Rey, eds., *Beyond Heroes and Holidays: A Practical Guide to K–12 Anti-Racist, Multicultural Education and Staff Development* (Washington, D.C.: Network of Educators on the Americas, 1998).

RESOURCES

The materials listed here are representative of some of the things we have shared with the methods course students. The first listings focus on a long period in U.S. history, roughly from early industrialization through the 1930s, under the general theme of "working people." Works highlight lives in the cotton mills in Lowell, Massachusetts, in the 1830s, in the labor movement of the turn of the century, in post-Reconstruction America, and during the Great Depression. Rather than marking them off into discrete historical periods, often really a reflection of events and priorities in the dominant society, this clustering is intended to emphasize the continuities and changes in "working people's" lives, with particular emphasis on children's lives and perspectives. They are grouped according to types of materials rather than specific subtopics. The final section lists general sources of materials that tend to highlight social justice issues.

Children's Trade Books

The grouping here by genre is not meant to imply age group or to create a distinction in a literary sense between fiction and non-fiction, but rather, the type of literature often suggests particular kinds of instructional strategies. The works can for the most part be used with all age groups, albeit in different ways. The "stories" being told in all kinds of writing provide opportunities for critical examination of questions such as "Whose story is being told?" "How do stories get written?" and "What sorts of things are left out?".

Picture Books

Eve Bunting, *Train to Somewhere* (New York: Clarion Books, 1996), illustrated by Ronald Himler, 32 pp. The orphan trains, which carried children from New York City to small towns and farms from the mid-1850s to the late 1920s is the focus for the story of fourteen orphan children, heading west in 1878. The poignant belief of a young girl, who is the last child left on the train, that her mother will come to claim her forms a backdrop for the stories of the various children and the reasons that brought people to adopt them.

Elizabeth Friedrich, *Leah's Pony* (Honesdale, Pa.: Boyds Mills Press, 1996), illustrated by Michael Garland, 30 pp. A young girl on a Great Plains farm in the 1930s. People's collaboration at "penny auctions" to save others' possessions from the bank auction plays a role in the story.

Jacob Lawrence, *The Great Migration* (Washington, D.C.: Rappahannock Press in association with The Phillips Collection, 1993), with poem "Migration," by Walter Dean Myers, 48 pp., illustrations from Lawrence's narrative panels, "The Migration of the Negro," painted in 1940–1941.

Kate Lied, *Potato: A Tale from the Great Depression* (Washington, D.C.: National Geographic Society, 1997), illustrated by Lisa Campbell Ernst, 32 pp. This book was written by a then eight-year-old, based on a family story of her grandparents and her aunt Dorothy, who passed the story on to her. The family story begins as the bank takes away their farm in Iowa and tells of their journey to Idaho to pick potatoes, the eventual finding of a job, and the passing on of the story. Good for family history, as well as understanding that era.

A. Emily McCully, *The Bobbin Girl* (New York: Dial Books, 1996), illustrations by the author, 34 pp. The life of a ten-year-old girl who works in the Lowell Mills. Working conditions and the women's efforts at education and organizing are highlighted.

Lauren Mills, *The Rag Coat* (Little, Brown, 1991), illustrations by the author, 32 pp. After a young girl's father dies of miner's cough, she receives a coat patchworked by the Quilting Mothers so that she can attend school.

Margaree K. Mitchell, *Uncle Jed's Barbershop* (New York: Scholastic, 1993), illustrated by James Ransome, 34 pp. A young girl's uncle works to start his own barbershop in the rural, segregated South of the 1930s. The impact of racism, poverty, and the Depression delay but do not defer his dream.

Chapter Books

Particia A. Cochrane, *Purely Rosie Pearl* (New York: Delacorte Press, 1996), 135 pp. A 12-year-old girl and her extended family work as migrant pickers during the 1930s. Hardships and strength of families play central roles.

Holly Littlefield, *Fire at the Triangle Factory* (Minneapolis: Carolrhoda Books, 1996), illustrations by Mary O. Young, 48 pp. The events of March 25, 1911, focusing on two young girls, one Jewish and one Catholic, who work in the shirtwaist factory. Author's note and afterword provide historical background. Beginning reader.

Doreen Rappaport, *Trouble at the Mines* (New York: Thomas Crowell, 1987), illustrations by Joan Sandin, 85 pp., bibliography. The story of Mother Jones and a miner's strike in Arnot, Pennsylvania, from December of 1898 to February of 1900, centering on a young girl. The role of children and women in the strike is highlighted.

Harriette G. Robinet, *Mississippi Chariot* (New York: Aladdin Paperbacks, 1994), 117 pp., bibliography. Set in the 1930s, the story revolves around a young boy's efforts to free his father, who is serving a term on a chain gang for a crime everyone knows he did not commit. The harsh realities of sharecropping contrast with the tight-knit efforts of the family. Interesting implicit examination of the "trickster" theme in African American literature.

Ouida Sebestyen, *Words by Heart* (New York: Bantam Doubleday Dell, 1979), 162 pp. A young girl's triumph at a Bible verse memorization contest forms a backdrop for the struggles of an African American family in a predominantly European American community in Kansas in the years just before World War I. The brutal realities of racial oppression are clear and moving, but equally compelling is the story of the girl's learning values that combat as well as sustain.

Mildred D. Taylor, *Roll of Thunder, Hear My Cry* (New York: Bantam Books, 1976), 210 pp. First of a series of well-known books about the Logan family and their struggles in the early to middle part of this century. Adds a great deal to understanding both economic and racial oppression and the strength of family across generations in confronting oppression. Other titles include *Let the Circle Be Unbroken, The Road to Memphis, Mississippi Bridge,* and *The Well* for older readers and *Song of the Trees, The Gold Cadillac,* and *The Friendship* for younger readers.

Ann Turner, *Dust for Dinner* (New York: HarperCollins, 1995), illustrations by Robert Barrett, 64 pp. A dust bowl family loses their farm and heads west in search of work. Beginning reader.

Yoshiko Uchida, *A Jar of Dreams* (New York: Macmillan, 1981), 131 pp. A Japanese American family in California during the Depression years teaches a young daughter the value of her heritage. Economics and racially motivated violence play roles in the story.

Information Books

Probably no list of nonfiction books for young readers would be complete without reference to the works of Milton Meltzer. Relevant to this theme are *Bread and Roses: The Struggle of American Labor, 1865–1915* (1967), *Brother, Can You Spare a Dime? The Great Depression, 1929–1933* (1969), and *Violins and Shovels: The WPA Arts Projects* (1976), but his works on African American and Hispanic history also contain important related material. A full listing of his work can be found in *Nonfiction for the Classroom: Milton Meltzer on Writing, History, and Social Responsibility,* E. Wendy Saul, ed. (New York: Teachers College Press, 1994).

Susan Campbell Bartoletti, *Growing Up in Coal Country* (Boston: Houghton Mifflin, 1996), 127 pp. Life in Pennsylvania around the turn of the century. Photos, oral-historical text, legacy, and bibliography.

Kathryn T. Cryan-Hicks, *W. E. B. Du Bois: Crusader for Peace* (Lowell, Mass.: Discovery Enterprises, 1991), illustrated by David H. Huckins. Picture book biography series, 48 pp.

Joan Dash, *We Shall Not Be Moved: The Women's Factory Strike of 1909* (New-York: Scholastic, 1996), 165 pp. Photos, documents, excerpts from real people's lives, bibliography, and index.

Russell Freedman, *Kids at Work: Lewis Hine and the Crusade Against Child Labor* (New York: Clarion Books, 1994), 104 pp., Hine's photos, historical postscript, bibliography, and index.

Joy Hakim, *The Age of Extremes* (part of the History of US series) (New York: Oxford University Press, 1994), 192 pp. Many illustrations, documents, timeline, bibliography, and index.

Betsy Harvey Kraft, *Mother Jones: One Woman's Fight for Labor* (New York: Clarion Books, 1995), 116 pp. Lots of period photos and documents, further resources, and index.

Judith Pinkerton Josephson, *Mother Jones: Fierce Fighter for Workers' Rights* (Minneapolis: Lerner Publicatons, 1997), 144 pp. Photos, period drawings, source notes, and index. Very thorough, yet interesting text.

A. P. Porter, *Jump at de Sun: The Story of Zora Neale Hurston* (Minneapolis: Carolrhoda Books, 1992), 96 pp. Many photos, notes, bibliography, and index.

Jerry Stanley, *Big Annie of Calumet: A True Story of the Industrial Revolution* (New York: Crown Publishers, 1996), 104 pp., excellent photos. The book describes the strike of copper miners in the Upper

Peninsula of Michigan in 1913. Final chapter and afterword help to situate the incident within larger labor struggle. Bibliographic notes and index.

Jerry Stanley, *Children of the Dust Bowl: The True Story of the School at Weedpatch Camp* (New York: Crown, 1992), 86 pp. Many photos, with information about the dust bowl region, the journey to California, migrant life. Afterword with information about the educator responsible for the camp school, as well as bibliographic information and index.

Andrea Warren, *Orphan Train Rider: One Boy's True Story* (Boston: Houghton Mifflin, 1996), 80 pp. Background information, period photographs, oral-historical basis, and contemporary information on the child's life subsequent to his 1926 ride. Bibliography and index.

Richard Wormser, *Growing Up in the Great Depression* (New York: Antheneum, 1994), 124 pp. Through text, extensive quotes from documents, and oral-historical material, the causes and impact of the Depression on the adult world are evident, but there is a particular focus on the lives of children. Includes a chapter "Growing up Rich," as well as bibliography and index.

Janeele Yates, *Zora Neale Hurston: A Storyteller's Life* (Staten Island, N.Y.: Ward Hill Press, 1993), 96 pp. Time line, bibliography, and index.

Other Resources
Randy Albeda, Nancy Folbre, and the Center for Popular Economics, *The War on the Poor* (New York: New Press, 1996).

William Bigelow and Norman Diamond, *The Power in Our Hands: A Curriculum on the History of Work and Workers in the United States* (New York: Monthly Review Press, 1988) (Also available through NECA).

Nancy Folbre and the Center for Popular Economics, *The New Field Guide to the U.S. Economy* (New York: New Press, 1995).

Music
The struggle for social justice in U.S. history is a movement rich in music. Besides the many resources available through the Smithsonian Institution ("Wade in the Water: African American Music Traditions," "Don't Mourn—Organize," "Smithsonian Folkways American Roots Collection" (easy access at http://www.si.edu/folklife/education/40062.html), see:

Songs for Social Justice, Network of Educators on the Americas.

Peter Blood and Annie Patterson, *Rise Up Singing* (Bethlehem, Pa.:

A Sing Out Corporation, 1988). Also available through the Highlander Center.

Keith McNeil, and Rusty McNeil, *Working and Union Songs* (Riverside, Calif.: WEM Records, 1989).

Teaching with Primary Source Documents

The following are commercially produced materials. The National Archive is very busy with a lot of interesting materials, including oral-historical works, documents, and photographs. Write to them, or see these at http://www.nara.gov/nara/nail.html (August 14, 1997). The Library of Congress also has fascinating material available through the Web or directly, including some very rich oral history material from the 1930s.

JoAnne B. Weisman, ed., *The Lowell Mills Girls: Life in the Factory* (1991); Juliet H. Mofford, ed., *Talking Union: The American Labor Movement* (1996); Jeanne M. Bracken, ed., *The Orphan Trains: Leaving the Cities Behind* (1997); Janet Beyer and JoAnne B. Weisman, eds., *The Great Depression: A Nation in Distress* (Carlisle, Mass.: Discovery Enterprises, 1995).

Jean M. West, ed., *Child Labor in America,* Vol. 3 of Teaching with Primary Sources Series (Peterborough, N.H.: Cobblestone Publishing, 1996), 104 pp. Activities and documents, as well as issue of *Cobblestone* on "The History of Labor."

These titles are from the Perspectives on History Series. The booklets contain materials for students. There is a separate educator's guide to the series that covers the overall approach used, teaching materials for particular kinds of documents, and suggestions for using the many books in this series. This company has also produced interesting plays, including *Working in Darkness: A Play about Coal Mining,* which can be produced in full, done as readers' theater by a class, or used as a starting point for a simulation or role play.

Films

The social inquiry aspect of the course included the option of viewing and critiquing films as a way for teachers to continue to extend their knowledge. The suggested list included children's films, such as *You Must Remember This* and *Words by Heart* (Wonderworks series). We also suggested other films, including *Matewan, The Killing Floor, The Milagro Beanfield Wars, Salt of the Earth,* and *Norma Rae,* as ways for all of us to understand the tensions and contradictions in working people's struggles. The documentary *The Uprising of '34*, available from Icarus Films in New York, is particularly good.

Special Issues of Periodicals

"Working-Class Studies," *Radical Teacher,* No. 46 (Spring 1995).

"Labor History" and "Oral History," *Magazine of History* 11, No. 2 and No. 3 (Winter and Spring 1997).

"What Are Public Works?" "The Great Depression," "Radio Days," and "The History of Labor," *Cobblestone: The History Magazine for Young People* 4, No. 8 (August 1983); 5, No. 3 (March 1984); 9, No. 10 (October 1988); and 13, No. 8 (October 1992), respectively.

Useful Organizations and Periodicals

Democracy and Education
Institute for Democracy in
Education
313 McCracken Hall
Ohio University
Athens, OH 45701

Feminist Teacher
Ablex Publishing
Greenwich, CT

Highlander Center
1959 Highlander Way
New Market, TN 37820

Labor's Heritage (Quarterly of the George Meany Memorial Archives)
10000 New Hampshire Ave.
Silver Spring, MD 20903
(Volume 2, No. 1, 1990, was accompanied by a teacher's guide and simulation, "The Company Store." The journal itself is rich in useful photographs and documentary sources.)

New Internationalist
P.O. Box 1143
Lewiston, NY 14092
(The issue on child labor, No. 292, July 1997, is particularly relevant.)

Radical Teacher
Boston Women's Teachers' Group
P.O. Box 102, Kendall Square Post Office
Cambridge, MA 02142

Rethinking Schools
1001 E. Keefe
Milwaukee, WI 43212

National Coalition of Education Activists
P.O. Box 679
Rhinebeck, NY 12572

Teaching for Change
Catalogue from Network of Educators on the Americas
P.O. Box 73038
Washington, DC 20056–303
http:www.teachingforchange.org/
(August 14, 1999)

CHAPTER 12

Social Struggles
Schools and Universities Collaborating for Social Justice in Conservative Times

DAVID W. HURSH
REBECCA GOLDSTEIN
DERRICK GRIFFITH

In 1932, when the Great Depression was at its deepest and the radical left was at its strongest, George Counts, socialist educator, asked, "Dare the school build a new social order?"[1] At first, it seems ludicrous to ask this same question regarding social studies when hope for egalitarianism is bleakest. But it is precisely now, when conservative and corporate efforts to push education even further toward meeting the needs of business and traditional curricular conceptions, that the political and contested nature of education becomes most apparent.

In this chapter, the three of us, a professor and two doctoral students, describe our efforts, in collaboration with two teachers and several master's students, to develop a high school seminar that counters the conservative thrust toward individualism, competition, and uncritical preparation for work. Instead, we desire to promote in students the collaborative analysis of their own social situation and education. Before providing the details of those efforts, we want to situate our work within the larger context of historical and contemporary social struggles.

Throughout the twentieth century, different social factions have promoted conflicting conceptions of education. During the 1920s and 1930s, Counts, Dewey, Brameld, and other social reconstructionists differed with the proponents of social efficiency.[2] The social efficiency movement aimed to model schools after industry; principles of scientific management would form the basis for teaching and the organization of schools. Students would be selected and tracked, according to Snedden, a dominant proponent of scientific efficiency, for "their probable destinies," which, not surprisingly, corresponded to the students' race, class, and gender.[3]

In contrast, Dewey, Counts, and the other reconstructionists were interested not in preparing students for some societal slot but in developing "the kinds of intelligence that would lead to a command of the conditions of one's own life and ultimately social progress."[4] Schools would be models of democracy in which integrated and authentic learning occurred.

CONTEMPORARY STRUGGLES IN CONSERVATIVE TIMES

Similar conflicts continue today. Throughout the industrialized world, corporate and conservative interests are demanding that society and schools meet the needs of business. The conservative agenda focuses on redefining rights, equality, knowledge, culture, and the purposes of education. Apple has documented how, since the Reagan administration, the conservative restoration has been rolling back the gains in personal rights made over the last century, such as the right to a minimal standard of living, as evidenced in the elimination of guaranteed welfare support, political representation, and education.[5] Instead, conservatives hold property rights as more significant and redefine justice as eliminating "unjust and unfair regulations of private property rights" and as promoting the ability to profit within freely functioning markets. Justice is whatever the market delivers. Justice is situated within "an ideology of individualism . . . which emphasizes individual responsibility within a free market economy and, thereby, defends the notion of the minimal state on moral as well as efficiency grounds."[6]

Perhaps the most blatant example of this view is Dinesh D'Souza's *The End of Racism: Principles for a Multiracial Society,* in which he calls for the repeal of the Civil Rights Act of 1964.[7] Arguing for property rights over personal rights, he asserts that "private employers should be able to discriminate on the basis of race without penalty." African Americans, he declares, are not unemployed or underemployed because of discrimination or structural inequalities but because they do not "act White." He claims that inequality will end when blacks learn to "act White."[8]

By calling for blacks to "act White," D'Souza is also promoting white (and we must assume he means upper-middle-class) culture as culturally correct. This debate over privileging one culture over another—or whether we should examine our experience in terms of class, race, and gender within the social structure—frames the dispute over multiculturalism.

Defining justice as property rights rather than personal rights redefines equality as the ability to compete in the marketplace. As implied by D'Souza, individuals become responsible for obtaining the required skills and cultural attributes to gain employment. The emphasis on individual competition within the marketplace also suits national corporate needs. Schools are to be reformed, writes Undersecretary of Education Marshall Smith, to meet "ever changing challenges of international competition and a changing marketplace."[9] This outlook leads to the reorganization of schools so that they reflect corporate interests. In spring 1996, the nation's governors held an educational summit in the headquarters of a corporate giant, IBM, a leader in computer production. A working paper, developed in cooperation with IBM's CEO, stated:

> We believe that efforts to set clear, common, and community-based academic standards for students in a given school district or state is a necessary step in any effort to improve student performance. We are convinced that technology, if applied thoughtfully and well integrated into a curriculum, can be used to boost student performance and ensure a competitive edge for our workforce.[10]

Governmental and privately funded groups, such as the National Center for Education and the Economy, focus their reform efforts on developing student knowledge and skills to make them more productive workers. This emphasis on education for work has shifted the educational goal away from the humanities and critical thinking toward incorporating "appropriate" workplace behaviors and so-called traditional values. Not only is education redefined primarily in terms of economic growth but also the long-term struggle to expand personal rights, such as rights to education, voting, and health care, is being rolled back so that property rights can be expanded. In sum, the conservative view reconceptualizes justice as property rights.

Although we find a lot wrong with the educational system, we find abhorrent the conservative agenda of blaming education for our economic problems and restructuring education to improve the economy. We abhor the prominence given to the economy in conceptualizing education because the causes of our economic problems are rooted in government and corporations rather than in educational policies. The attack on the educational system is used to support more general policies that make it increasingly difficult for the nonelite to argue for equality. The promotion of property rights is part of a larger policy to reconstruct social relations as individual competition rather than the common good.

In contrast, we want to argue for developing schools where teachers and students raise questions of whose knowledge should be in the curriculum and of how power and inequality are maintained, and in the process create new knowledge. Schools should become places where, as Michelle Fine suggests, students give voice to their own concerns and use history, political science, and other social sciences to make sense of their own lives.[11] We want to define justice not as the ability to compete within the market but as countering the oppression that operates through exploitation, marginalization, powerlessness, cultural imperialism, violence, and oppressive ecological consequences of others' actions.[12] Justice defined in this way promotes the common good. Further, we want to link these conceptions of justice to notions of developing practical judgment in students. Stanley, building on the ideals of the reconstructionists, writes that we should focus on developing the social and communal conditions and practices necessary to acquire knowledge sufficient to guide our social actions. Within this context, democracy is not understood as a core value but as a regulative ideal or a way of life in which humans interact to determine what should be their ends and the best means to attain them.[13]

Although the goals of a critical, reconstructive pedagogy are often described, they are less frequently attempted. In the second half of this chapter, we describe the seminar itself and the program within which it exists. We represent our efforts to encourage students to analyze their own social and educational system and the difficulties in accomplishing it, given the culture of schools in which the students have been silenced and knowledge has been reduced to memorizing textbook material for the test.

SCHOOLS AND UNIVERSITIES COLLABORATING FOR EDUCATIONAL REFORM AND SOCIAL JUSTICE

Two years ago, the Rochester City School District, community-based organizations, and institutions of higher education, including the University of Rochester, formed a coalition: The Rochester Educational Access Collaborative (REAC). Its formal mission is to increase the number of underrepresented and underserved students who complete four-year college degrees. The core of the project is a comprehensive program that supports students' progress from middle school through high school and college and back into classrooms and community-based organizations as community education workers: teachers, para-professionals, counselors, librarians, and technicians. Any participant who completes a college degree and state certification in teaching or counseling is assured employment by the Rochester City School District.

The centerpiece of the project is transforming the middle and high school experiences of students. The secondary school reforms are linked to teacher education reforms at the Warner Graduate School of Education and Human Development at the University of Rochester. The goal is to enhance the linkages between secondary schools, the community college, and four-year postsecondary institutions to ease students' transitions from one educational stage to another. A second effort is the development of the Teaching and Learning Institute (TLI), a magnet program designed to prepare students for careers in education, which began in fall 1995 at a city high school with the development and implementation of a ninth-grade seminar on education. In the remainder of this chapter, we focus on the seminar and our participation in it.

The seminar on education is the official responsibility of two high school teachers, but over the summer a group of teachers, educational activists, and graduate students developed the course objectives. The goals of the course were developed during the year by high school and university faculty and master's and doctoral students, who collaborate in teaching the course. The course aims to (1) provide students with the "study skills necessary to become adept at learning and to continue in pursuit of a teaching career," (2) "understand the experience of teaching and learning," and (3) "examine the institutional structure of education and schooling as well as the working environment of teachers and students."[14] During the first several weeks of the course, the high school teachers, with graduate students assisting, took primary responsibility for introducing the course and teaching a unit on learning styles. After about a month, the graduate students began implementing units they had designed; the first, "Faces of You, Faces of Me," focused on themes of identity and difference and their relation to learning. The second, "Studying Your Own School," led students to situate their own school within a wider examination of the institutional structure of schools and the environment for teachers and students.

The master's students also enrolled in a university seminar, led by Hursh, that concentrated on understanding the goals and history of the overall project and educational reform and on developing the units and lessons for the TLI seminar. The doctoral students also enrolled in a university seminar, also led by Hursh, with other doctoral students involved in collaborative reform of schools and society. A goal for both the master's and the doctoral seminars was to research the problems and possibilities of critical pedagogy in reorganized schools. At the end of the semester, the master's students wrote an analysis of the cultural changes needed in the school to develop a magnet program in which teachers collaborate in developing the program's structure, courses, and lessons. In this chapter, written in collaboration with two doctoral students, we focus on the rationale for our pedagogical practices and describe some of the lessons taught and learned.

In planning for our teaching, we wanted to shift the focus away from education as preparation for work and the curriculum as received knowledge to focus on the students' lives and the ways they understand school and society. We hoped the students would experience the process of developing their own questions and finding answers to those questions that are unique to their experience. We wanted them to realize that their questions were as valuable as those provided by a textbook or teacher. We wanted them to learn to work together, to come to appreciate the value of one another's questions and perspectives, and to appreciate the power of collaboration. Finally, we wanted the students to feel that they could participate in deciding the class goals and procedure.

In focusing on the students' experiences, we were also opposing the silencing of students and "the disempowering effects upon students of the conventional 'top-down' power structures of schools and classrooms." Instead, we welcomed the benefits of students' conversation and debate over schooling, self, and society. We wanted students to raise questions about the effect of race, ethnicity, and gender on academic success and agreed with Kenway and Modra that "cultural difference and their associated power relations must be acknowledged and critically addressed in schooling."[15]

During the semester, we learned both the possibilities and difficulties of attaining our goals. Some students resisted our efforts as just as irrelevant as their previous school experience. Others, even if they were failing academically, embraced education as the process of teachers' transmission of knowledge to students. Still others held the seemingly contradictory stance of rejecting Eurocentric curriculum as irrelevant to their lives while also rejecting readings from African American authors as irrelevant to passing the state exams.

OVERCOMING SILENCE, ADDRESSING DIFFERENCES

The twenty-eight students in the every-other-day, forty-two-minute seminar reflected the student population in the district: mostly African American, some Latino/a, and a few working- or middle-class students of European descent. The students enrolled in the program for a variety of reasons but primarily because they correctly perceived that magnet program teachers collectively give students more attention.

If we wanted the students to have a voice in their own education and to use the classroom to gain a better understanding of their world, we would have to understand why students often choose to be silent. Students are not silent because they have nothing to say. Students, as Fine reminds us, are silent because they have been discouraged in schools from contributing their experiences, knowledge, and opinions. Therefore, some students become silent because they have become apathetic about school. Other students told us they were bored. Sometimes students did not participate because they were thinking about their lives outside school: jobs, friendships, and activities. But students sometimes move beyond silence; they actively resist learning what the school offers. Students, writes Herb Kohl, sometimes actively choose not to learn the dominant curricular knowledge. This behavior is not simply laziness but an active process.[16]

> Learning how not to learn is an intellectual and social challenge; sometimes you have to work very hard at it. It consists of an active, often ingenious, willful rejection of even the most compassionate and well designed teaching. It subverts attempts at remediation as much as it rejects learning in the first place.[17]

Students employ not learning in order to maintain their own identities in opposition to schools and schooling. By not learning, students reduce the impact traditional curricular content and practices have on them.

Given that many of the students either have been silenced, have become disengaged from school, or choose to actively resist schooling, we began with low-risk seminar activities focusing on the theme of "getting to know you." Students interviewed each other, talked in small groups, wrote in their journals, and got to know each other. Teachers, who participated and observed, learned about the students' concerns and experiences.

One day in a small group discussion, a student asked Derrick: "Mr. G., is it OK to be racist? My entire family is, but I think it's wrong."[18] The student, who is black, posed this to a group of students, all of whom, except for one young man, also were black. In another classroom, this student's question might have been gently pushed aside; in others, he might have been reprimanded for being off task. Worse, he might have been dismissed altogether. For many educators, notes Michelle Fine,

> to examine the very conditions that contribute to social class, racial, ethnic, and gender stratification in the United States, when they [the teachers] are relatively privileged by class usually and race often, seemed to introduce fantasies of danger, a pedagogy that would threaten, rather than protect, teacher control. Such conversations would problematize what seems like "natural" social distinctions, potentially eroding teachers' authority.[19]

In contrast, we valued this student's question. It might be seen as a way of directing the discussion away from the class topic of learning styles; however, we saw the question as an opening to challenge current notions of identity and difference. Not only did it mean that students themselves were struggling with many of the same questions we were but it also meant that we were succeeding with the students. This student felt safe enough to ask the question and was hoping to talk about something personal and political. We had opened a "dangerous space."

Another dangerous space was provided in the classroom after the seminar, when students returned during their lunch period for the opportunity to talk with college students and raise questions about race, gender, and politics. Some of the students returned to the classroom, where they wanted to deal with more than just eating and the everyday banter of high school life. Whether the topic was what teachers needed to do to make a project more interesting, the Million Man March, acting and talking black or white, loving one's race as being racist (posed by a young black woman), and the difference between naming oneself black or African American, lunchtime had become a space in which teachers and students alike grappled with very personal and political issues.

The questions raised during the seminar and lunch encouraged us to start a new unit named "Faces of You, Faces of Me." In this unit, we wanted students to continue to examine the questions they had previously raised. They asked and we discussed questions like: Are stereotypes the cause of acting "black" or acting "white"? What does it mean to be Hispanic?

How do people learn to create particular identities and then remain attached to them? Why is it important to classify yourself and to classify others?

Following the "faces" unit, we moved on to examine the institution of schooling and the lives of teachers and students. In both units, we worked to promote students' confidence that they could be not just consumers but creators of knowledge. Students often, according to Freire, experience schools as a place where "banking occurs," where the teacher

> leads the students to memorize mechanically the narrated content. Worse yet, it turns them into "containers," into "receptacles" to be filled by the teachers. The more completely she fills the receptacles, the better a teacher she is. The more meekly the receptacles permit themselves to be filled, the better students they are.[20]

In a classroom that "banks" students, the teacher is viewed as the holder of "true knowledge," and the students are containers to be filled. The banking model sees knowledge as a commodity deposited into students, much like money is deposited in a bank account. In turn, that same knowledge creates and supports social practices that locate our students outside knowledge production.

Because students were likely "banked" in many of their previous classes, they had little chance to become partners in their own education. Even though as ninth-grade students in a new school they were in a unique position to question schools and practices within schools, they had had few experiences to see themselves as anything other than receivers of knowledge.

In social studies, the students often resisted curricular content that neither was on the tests nor conformed to their conceptions of history as names and dates. Many students would rather stick with what is familiar, even if they hate it, rather than risk trying something new. As Derrick said one day regarding his own social studies classes, "All my students want me to do is bank them!" His students, he said, were afraid that they would not be able to succeed on the state-mandated tests. One student even asked Derrick if "his way" would help them on the tests.

In contrast, we tried to develop what Gloria Ladson-Billings calls "culturally relevant teaching. " According to Ladson-Billings,

> culturally relevant teaching is a pedagogy that empowers students intellectually, socially, emotionally, and politically by using cultural

referents to impart knowledge, skills, and attitudes. . . . Moving between the two cultures lays the foundation for a skill that the students
will need in order to reach academic and cultural success.[21]

In the "Study Your Own School" unit, once we overcame silence and
resistance to alternatives to traditional banking practices, we faced the
additional difficulty students had in imagining alternatives to the current
organization of schools and the educational process. We began the unit
by presenting to the students a thirty-minute video portraying students'
experiences at Central Park East (CPE), the well-known New York City
public high school. To our surprise, the students responded negatively to
CPE. One student was adamantly against having two-and-a-half-hour
classes. When we asked her why, she said that they would be too boring;
she had enough trouble sitting through a forty-minute class. We thought
that from the video they would see the students engaged in discussions
and hear their descriptions of their projects. Instead, the students saw
only longer versions of their own classes. They could not imagine that
school could be different; CPE was only a variation on the traditional
theme.

We had underestimated the students' comprehension of schooling.
While we as educators perceived the alternative structures and methods
implemented at CPE as advantageous, the students realistically and
rightfully reacted with concern. It is not that they did not appreciate the
differences; they could not conceive of them as real.

The problem did not lie with the students but with our own percep-
tions of what would be preferable. To students who had never experienced anything different, there were no advantages. In our efforts to
present an alternative, we forgot to begin with the students. We therefore
thought of other ways we might present alternatives to the students. We
suggested that they interview students from a local school that, like CPE,
is a member of the Coalition of Essential Schools and has extended class
periods, performance-based assessment, and classes with small student-
to-teacher ratios. We asked the students if they were interested in interviewing students from the other school and could commit themselves to
forming groups of three to develop questions, interview students, take
notes, and present what they learned. They agreed to do so.

After a week of interviewing the students, we again asked the students
if they would like to interview students, teachers, and administrators in
their own school. They then developed their own topics—athletics, funding, tracking, and teaching—and, after forming groups, developed their

own questions. Over a period of several weeks, the students, in groups of three or four, interviewed students, teachers, administrators, and university faculty.

As the students conducted the interviews, they were presented with alternatives to tracking, standardized testing, and textbooks. But often they were convinced that the traditional standard curriculum content and assessment methods were the appropriate standards by which to be judged. The students wanted to believe that by acquiring the official knowledge of school—the same knowledge that minimized the students' own knowledge—they would succeed. Furthermore, tracking was legitimate, perhaps because they were now all in the college-bound track, and, as some students stated, they did not want to be slowed by other students. Last, in a school that boasted a graduate on an Olympic team and several professional athletes, many students saw athletics as a very possible route to college and perhaps the only one.

The students' defense of tracking, testing, and textbooks as they entered discussions about identity, ethnicity, and education reveals the difficulty of developing classrooms and schools in which students become active critical learners. The educational structure supports students in clinging to the notion that schools are places that support meritocratic competition.

Our semester with the students revealed the difficulties and complexities of shifting the focus from individual competition to raising questions about rights and the common good, from preparing for work to examining identity and education, and from looking for the answers as provided by the teachers and texts to seeing knowledge as problematic and collaboratively produced by students and teachers. The task of developing critical, collaborative communities is not achieved overnight but undertaken only for the long haul, by raising questions and depicting a different vision for school and society than the one now dominant.

The task also requires that we engage in the process together, with no predetermined answers, and listen to the students. For example, the students responded to the video about Central Park East differently than we expected. They did so not because their understanding was inferior to ours but because we had not understood the influence their current school experience had on the way they perceived the world. Furthermore, by listening to the students and engaging in discussion, we learned how they comprehend issues of identity, race, and ethnicity. The students did not endorse D'Souza's call to "act white" but openly debated the relationship between culture and academic and economic success. While we can't claim to have reached our goals, we can claim to be on the way to becoming a community of learners more concerned with supporting the good of the community.

NOTES

[1]George Counts, *Dare the School Build a New Social Order?* (Carbondale and Edwardsville: Southern Illinois Press, 1932).

[2]John Dewey, *Democracy and Education: An Introduction to the Philosophy of Education* (New York: Free Press, 1916). Theodore Brameld, *Patterns of Educational Philosophy Divergence or Convergence in Culturalogical Perspective* (New York: Holt, Rinehart, and Winston, 1971). For descriptions of the reconceptionists, see Herbert Kliebard, *The Struggle for the American Curriculum: 1893–1956* (New York: Routledge, 1986); and William Stanley, *Curriculum and Utopia: Social Reconstructionism and Critial Pedagogy in the Postmodern Era* (Albany: State University of New York Press, 1992).

[3]David Snedden, "Vocational Education," *New Republic,* Vol. III (May 15, 1915): 40.

[4]John Dewey, "Education vs. Trade Training: Dr. Dewey's Reply," *New Republic,* Vol. III (May 15, 1915): 42.

[5]Michael Apple, *Official Knowledge: Democratic Education in a Conservative Age* (New York: Routledge, 1993).

[6]Michael Peters, "Individualism and Community: Education and the Politics of Difference" *Discourse* 142 (April 1994): 66.

[7]Dinesh D'Souza, *The End of Racism: Principles for a Multiracial Society* (New York: Free Press, 1995).

[8]As quoted by George Fredrickson, "Demonizing the American Dilemma," *New York Review of Books* 42 (16) (October 19, 1995): 1016.

[9]Marshall Smith and Brett Scoll, "The Clinton Human Capital Agenda," *Teachers College Press* 96 (Spring 1995): 389–404.

[10]*Education Week* 15 (February 14, 1996): 17.

[11]Michelle Fine, *Framing Dropouts: Notes on the Politics of an Urban Public High School* (Albany: State University of New York Press, 1991).

[12]Iris Young, *Justice and the Politics of Difference* (Princeton, N.J.: Princeton University Press, 1990).

[13]William Stanley, "Curriculum and the Social Order," this volume.

[14]Syllabus for course.

[15]Jane Kenway and H. Modra, "Feminist Pedagogy and Emancipatory Possibilities," in Carmen Luke and Jennifer Gore, eds., *Feminism and Critical Pedagogy* (New York: Routledge, 1992), p. 143.

[16]Herbert Kohl, *I Won't Learn from You: And Other Thoughts on Creative Maladjustment* (New York: New Press, 1994).

[17]Ibid., p. 2

[18]Rebecca Goldstein, notes from TLI journal, 1996.

[19]Michelle Fine, *Disruptive Voices: The Possibilities of Feminist Research* (Ann Arbor: The University of Michigan Press, 1992), p. 123.

[20]Paulo Freire, *Pedagogy of the Oppressed* (New York: Continuum, 1970), p. 523.

[21]Gloria Ladson-Billings, *The Dreamkeepers: Successful Teachers of African American Children* (San Francisco: Jossey-Bass, 1994), pp. 17–18.

CHAPTER 13

Diverting Democracy
The Curriculum Standards Movement and Social Studies Education

E. WAYNE ROSS

This chapter examines the current curriculum standards movement and argues that it misleads us with a simple solution to a complex problem and, as a result, diverts us from attending to the conditions of schools and how they might be reenvisioned in more democratic ways. Recent educational reform efforts aim to create a national education system with uniform content and goals. The current movement toward educational standards is a rationalized managerial approach to issues of curriculum development and teaching, which attempts to explicitly define curricular goals, design assessment tasks based on these goals, set standards for the content of subject matter areas and grade levels, test students, and report the results to the public. The intent is to establish standards for content and student performance levels.

Virtually all of the subject matter–based professional education groups have undertaken the development of curriculum standards over the past several years. Encouraged by the positive response to the standards in other discipline areas, social studies educators have taken up the development of curriculum standards with unparalleled zeal. There are now separate (and competing) national standards for U.S. and global history, geography, economics, civics, and social studies. The lobbying agenda of the National Council for the Social Studies has been dominated in recent years by efforts to have "social studies" included in Goals 2000 legislation and to develop standards for the social studies curriculum.

The intent of this chapter is threefold. First, it briefly surveys the curriculum standards movement, with particular attention to efforts directed at the social studies curriculum and related disciplines. Second, it examines the historical tensions between centralized and grassroots curriculum development. Third, it discusses assumptions underlying the curriculum standards movement within social studies education. It argues that curriculum standards, as they are presently pursued, promote standardized school knowledge, divert attention from teachers' roles in curriculum development, and skew the discourse of curriculum reform away from issues of equity. In closing, the chapter explores democratic alternatives to curriculum standards.

THE PARADE OF CURRICULUM STANDARDS

In the 1990s, educational reform efforts have emphasized the development of "world-class" national curriculum standards. The purposes of schools have been linked directly with increasing the economic productivity of the nation in an effort to respond to the increasing competitiveness of the global marketplace. The impetus for this movement in the United States can be traced to the meeting of the nation's governors in the 1989 education summit in Charlottesville, Virginia. The summit led to the development of the federal legislation that became the Goals 2000: Educate America Act, which was subsequently passed by Congress and supported by the National Governors Association (then headed by the future president, Governor Bill Clinton).

In the wake of the governors' summit, educators in virtually every subject area undertook development of curriculum standards. Curriculum standards have been developed for English, mathematics, science, social studies, art, and physical education. For social studies, no fewer than six curriculum standards projects are competing to influence the content and pedagogy of social studies classrooms.[1]

The curriculum standards movement represents an important shift in emphasis for educational reform. *A Nation at Risk* linked American educational performance with the decline in the "once unchallenged preeminence [of the United States] in commerce, industry, science and technological innovation." The report's recommendations focused attention on raising expectations for student learning.[2] The National Commission on Excellence in Education encouraged states and local schools to adopt tougher graduation requirements (e.g., requiring students to take more of the basic subjects), extend the school year, and administer standardized achievement tests as part of a nationwide, but not federal, system of examinations. Concern for student performance standards (what students should be able to do, such as evaluating historical evidence) has now been transformed into specific content standards, which identify what information students should analyze. National curriculum standards and widespread support for assessments tied to national standards raise concerns about a national education policy that supplants state and local curriculum reform efforts and about the development of a rigid system of national standards, curricula, and assessments.

GOALS 2000

The Goals 2000: Educate America Act was signed into law by President Clinton in April 1994. The act established eight national education goals—six goals that had been identified at the 1989 education summit, plus two goals regarding the roles of teachers and parents, which were added by Congress.

1. All children in America will start school ready to learn.
2. The high school graduation rate will increase to at least 90 percent.
3. All students will leave grades 4, 8, and 12 with demonstrated competency in challenging subject matter, including English, mathematics, science, foreign languages, civics and government, economics, arts, history, and geography.
4. Teachers will have access to programs for the continued improvement of their skills.
5. Students in the United States will be first in the world in mathematics and science achievement.
6. All adults will be literate.
7. Schools will be free from drugs, firearms, alcohol, and violence.
8. Every school will promote involvement of parents in their children's education.

In addition, the legislation established three panels: a nineteen-member National Education Standards and Improvement Council to certify various curriculum standards, an eighteen-member National Education Goals Panel to monitor progress toward the goals, and a National Skill Standards Board to develop work-related standards, testing, and certification systems.

The eight goals are broadly stated and engender little disagreement. The question is whether there is a commitment to providing the resources necessary to reach them. The legislation does not significantly increase federal spending on education. Of the $105 million allocated for the first year, 87 percent was to go toward financing model projects. That translates into $2.11 for each of the nation's 43 million elementary and secondary school students.[3] Notably absent from the goals list is any mention of the issue of unequal funding among (and within) school districts. Failure to address issues of funding and equity raise questions about the meaningfulness of goals such as the "opportunity to learn" standard. The law allows states to take action to provide all students with an opportunity to learn; however, adoption of any standards and strategies is voluntary, and no federal funds were allocated to encourage states to take up the issue of equitable resources.

At present, the most important question regarding national standards is not about their existence (they are here) but rather the meaningfulness of the standards. Who is defining the standards and for what purpose? How do national curriculum standards affect local control of schools? How do national curriculum standards affect teachers' work? Will the standards lead to a new battery of assessments? After a brief historical overview of the tensions between centralized and local control over curriculum, this chapter explores these questions within the context of the social studies curriculum.

HISTORICAL TENSIONS BETWEEN CENTRALIZED AND GRASSROOTS CURRICULUM DEVELOPMENT

The current national debate over curriculum standards has deep roots in the history of education in the United States. Curriculum development and reform efforts have long harbored a tension between, on the one hand, approaches that rely on centralized efforts that lead to a standard curriculum and, on the other, grassroots democratic efforts that provide greater involvement for teachers, parents, students, and other local curriculum leaders in determining what is worthwhile to know and experience. Curriculum centralization has resulted from three major influences: legal decisions; policy efforts by governments, professional associations, and foundations; and published materials. Examples of the latter two influences follow.[4]

INFLUENCE OF NONGOVERNMENTAL AND GOVERNMENTAL POLICY EFFORTS[5]

The centralizing influence of educational policy on curriculum can be seen as early as 1839, in Henry Barnard's first annual report as secretary to the Board of Commissioners of Common Schools in Connecticut, which raised the question of what the common school curriculum should be.[6] Educational reform efforts in the 1890s attempted to define the nature of the school curriculum and featured efforts by both intellectual traditionalists (e.g., W. T. Harris and Charles Eliot) and developmentalists (e.g., Charles DeGarmo and Frank McMurry) to exercise control through a centralized curriculum.[7]

The social studies curriculum has been heavily influenced by policies of curriculum centralization. In 1918, the National Education Association (NEA) Commission on the Reorganization of Secondary Education stated seven broad aims of secondary education that moved away from the traditional subject matter curriculum. Their report, *Cardinal Principles of Secondary Education,* identified aims such as health, command of fundamental processes, worthy home membership, worthy use of leisure time, citizenship, vocation, and ethical character. Like the more recent Goals 2000, its aims were characterized in a very broad way, making them difficult to oppose.

The roots of the contemporary social studies curriculum are evident in the 1916 report of the NEA Committee on the Social Studies. The current pattern of topics and courses in social studies is largely the result of recommendations of the 1916 committee, whose influence was enhanced when the American Historical Association joined in the social studies movement with the formation of the AHA Commission on Social Studies in 1929. In addition to using the term *social studies* to refer collectively to history, economics, political science, sociology, and civics, the committee's recommendations established the dominant curricular scope and sequence in secondary social studies.[8]

These examples illustrate the influence of professional organizations on the school curriculum through nonmandated educational policy. Efforts to centralize the curriculum through government mandates also have a long history. The debate over vocational education in the early 1900s embodied rhetoric similar to today's concerns for economic competitiveness. One assessment of the educational situation at the time argued that schools were failing to provide students with "industrial intelligence" and called for a shift in the orientation of secondary schools from "cultural" to vocational education.[9] The subsequent campaign for vocational education was modeled after Germany's dual system and ultimately produced the Smith-Hughes Act of 1917. Smith-Hughes fostered the transformation of the American high school from an elite institution into one of mass education by mandating that the states specify training needs, program prescriptions, standards, and means for monitoring progress. The dual system of education created by Smith-Hughes was reconceptualized in 1990 with the passage of the Perkins Vocational and Applied Technology Act, which provides a major incentive for the development of work education programs that integrate academic and vocational studies. The new law supports grassroots curriculum development by allocating 75 percent of its funds directly to local schools, rather than to the states, and by giving priority to communities with the highest rates of poverty. This approach supports local grassroots initiatives of people who know best the needs and characteristics of economically distressed communities.[10]

Curriculum frameworks produced by states are often accompanied by mandated standardized tests that ensure the "alignment" of classroom practices with state frameworks (e.g., the Regents Examinations in New York State). These frameworks are intended to influence textbook publishers and establish standards by which to assess students, teachers, and schools. In many cases, state curriculum frameworks represent a major step toward state control of what knowledge is of most worth.[11] Although states (and, as we shall see, current curriculum standards projects) deny that these frameworks amount to "curriculum," their practical effects are the equivalent, particularly when frameworks, standardized tests, and textbooks are aligned.[12]

I have just hinted at the large-scale centralizing influence of education policies on curriculum. Resistance to curriculum centralization has always existed because of the strong tradition of local school control in the United States, which has generally extended to curriculum development and implementation. The influence of John Dewey's philosophy of education has been a major resource for the resistance. Dewey argued that acquaintance with centralized knowledge must derive from situational concerns; that is, inquiring students must attain disciplinary knowledge in ways that have meaning for them.

William H. Kilpatrick's project method is an example of a grassroots approach to curriculum development that is clearly different from centralized curricula and based upon Dewey's philosophy.[13] The project method is very similar to the contemporary notion of thematic units, in which learning is approached as integrative, multifaceted, collaborative, responsive to students' varied needs, and organized around a particular theme. In the project method, students and teachers took on a greater role in determining the curriculum because they were deemed to be in the best position to understand the personal and contextual foundations from which a meaningful and relevant curriculum could be constructed. Projects were pursued in small groups or as whole-class experiences.

Knowledge from the disciplines could be brought to bear on the project when it was perceived as relevant. The essence of the project required teachers and students to develop the idea together. If students were fascinated by zoos, for instance, all subjects (traditional and modern) could be related to a deepened understanding of zoos.[14]

PUBLISHED MATERIALS

Textbooks have also been a major force in standardizing the curriculum. For more than sixty years, teachers have relied on textbooks as a primary instructional tool. In 1931, Bagley found that American students spent a significant portion of their school day in formal mastery of text materials.[15] A 1978 study of fifth-grade curricula found that 78 percent of what students studied came from textbooks, and a 1979 study found that textbooks and related materials were the basis for 90 percent of instructional time in schools. In their review of research on the social studies curriculum, Marker and Mehlinger found that about half of all social studies teachers depend upon a single textbook and that about 90 percent use no more than three.

Many states adopt textbooks on a statewide basis.[16] Three large "adoption states" (California, Florida, and Texas) exert an enormous influence on the content of textbooks used nationwide. The textbook industry is highly competitive, and the industry is dominated by a small number of large corporations; as a result, textbook companies modify their products to qualify for adoption in one of these states. As a result, the values and politics of adoption committees in those states influence curriculum nationally.[17]

To reach the widest range of purchasers, textbook publishers promote values (overtly and covertly) that maintain social and economic hierarchies and relationships supported by the dominant socioeconomic class.[18] James W. Loewen illustrates this at length in his analysis of U.S. history textbooks. For example, in a discussion of how history textbooks make white racism invisible, he notes:

> Although textbook authors no longer sugarcoat how slavery affected African Americans, they minimize white complicity in it. They present slavery virtually as uncaused, a tragedy, rather than a wrong perpetrated by some people on others. . . . Like their treatment of slavery, textbooks' new view of Reconstruction represents a sea change, past due, much closer to what the original sources for the period reveal, and

much less dominated by white supremacy. However, in the way the textbooks structure their discussion, most of them inadvertently still take a white supremacist viewpoint. Their rhetoric makes African Americans rather than whites the "problem" and assumes that the major issue of Reconstruction was how to integrate African Americans into the system, economically and politically. . . . The archetype of African Americans as dependent on others begins . . . in textbook treatments of Reconstruction. . . . In reality, white violence, not black ignorance, was the key problem during Reconstruction.[19]

In his analysis of the history of curriculum centralization, Schubert notes 1958 as a key turning point in educational policy making. That year, the National Defense Education Act helped to import disciplinary specialists to design curriculum packages for schools. In the social studies, these curriculum innovations were collectively called the New Social Studies. The purpose of the New Social Studies was to "capture the main ideas and current approaches to knowledge represented by the academic disciplines."[20] These curriculum projects focused on inquiry methods and the "structure of the disciplines" approach. Although social studies specialists helped in the development of New Social Studies materials, the curricular focus was on the academic disciplines. These materials were not "teacher-proof," but they are exemplars of teachers-as-curriculum-conduit thinking.[21] Developers, who were primarily experts in academic disciplines, viewed teachers as implementers, not active partners in the creation of classroom curriculum. Strategies for promoting the New Social Studies, as well as other subject matter projects from this era, focused on preparing teachers to faithfully implement the developers' curricular ideas. For example, schools could not adopt and use the project *Man: A Course of Study* unless teachers were specially trained.[22]

Although the development and dissemination of the 1960s curriculum projects were well funded, they failed to make a major impact on classroom practices. Some have argued that the "failure" of the projects is attributable to technical problems, such as inadequate training of teachers to use the packages or lack of formative evaluation. In contrast, proponents of grassroots democracy in curriculum explained that the failure was due to the blatant disregard of teachers and students in curriculum decision making. This point is especially ironic, inasmuch as those who promoted inquiry methods with the young neglected to allow inquiry by teachers and students about matters most fundamental to their growing lives—that is, inquiry about what is most worthwhile to know and experience.[23]

In the past thirty years, support for educational reform from industry, private foundations, and the federal government has clearly produced a more capitalistic, less educator-oriented, and ultimately less democratic network of curriculum policy makers.[24] The following section examines the impact of the current curriculum standards movement on social studies, in light of the historical patterns and tensions just discussed.

STANDARDIZING AMERICA: CURRICULUM STANDARDS AND SOCIAL STUDIES EDUCATION

This section examines two interrelated aspects of the curriculum standards movement and its effect on social studies education. First, the arguments over what should be taught in social studies are examined. The intention here is not to delve into the details of the turbulent debates over the content of social studies but to examine the assumptions and ideologies that have framed this debate in recent years.[25] The second part of this section looks at how the arguments over the "core knowledge" of social studies divert attention away from conditions of schooling and handicap efforts to transform schools into more democratic institutions.

Politics of Knowledge in Social Studies Education

The social studies curriculum has long served as an ideological and moral battleground in the culture wars. The most dominant social studies curricular reform effort of the past decade has focused on replacing the interdisciplinary, citizenship-oriented focus of social studies with the study of history and geography. Critics of social studies have advanced Hirsch's cultural literacy argument,[26] which holds that participation in a culture requires common reference points for all participants, and have criticized the social studies curriculum's emphasis on inquiry, decision making, current issues, global education, and feminist and multiculturalist approaches.[27]

Seixas points out that "building a common national historical vocabulary is by no means a politically neutral project; it is not an accident that its most prominent defenders have been associated with conservative political positions."[28] Seixas notes that this project is explicitly nationalist in that the "uncritically accepted cultural unit with which a common vocabulary is sought is the nation."[29] The effort to replace social studies with traditional history and geography is based on a "cultural transmission" approach to education, whose purpose is to "raise up future generations of citizens who will guarantee cultural survival" rather than the use of social science techniques or reflective inquiry to develop social critiques.[30] The latter approaches have been hallmarks of social studies education, if not its successful achievement.

Who is defining the social studies curriculum standards and for what purpose? As part of what came to be called the Reagan Revolution, a relatively small but well-financed group of academics, educators, and government officials effectively defined the terms of the debate over American education for the past thirteen or so years. This "neo-nativist network," as Cornbleth and Waugh label them, has been deeply involved in the movement to establish national standards and played key roles in history standards projects and Goals 2000.[31]

The fundamental assumption underlying the curriculum standards movement promoted by the neonativists is that uniform content and goals are appropriate, in fact, necessary components of educational reform in a country like the United States, with its vast array of cultural, regional, ethnic, and ideological differences. The goal is to create an ideological consensus around a national identity and return education to "traditional knowledge" in order to preserve a particular notion of a common culture. In a sense, neonativists apply a theory of containment to issues of multiculturalism, diversity, and difference.

The brief and incomplete chronology that follows describes how neoconservative academics with funding from conservative foundations and the U.S. government have influenced or created the central organizations attempting to control the social studies curriculum. The Educational Excellence Network (EEN) was founded by Chester Finn and Diane Ravitch in 1982, with the stated purpose of improving schools and education in the United States. Supported by a grant from the ultraconservative Bradley Foundation, the EEN spawned the Bradley Commission on History in the Schools.[32] The Bradley Commission was chaired by Columbia University historian Kenneth Jackson, and Paul Gagnon, a University of Massachusetts history professor, was executive secretary. The seventeen Bradley Commission members included Ravitch and Charlotte Crabtree, a UCLA education professor. Following its 1988 report, *Building a History Curriculum,* the Bradley Commission was transformed into the National Council for History Education.

In 1987, Crabtree and Ravitch were the principal authors of California's history and social sciences curriculum framework. Crabtree was later appointed to the California Curriculum Commission, an advisory board that makes textbook adoption decisions. That same year Ravitch and Finn published *What Do Our 17-Year-Olds Know?* to advocate teaching a detailed knowledge base in history.[33] In 1988, the National Endowment for the Humanities, under Lynne Cheney, awarded funding to UCLA for the National Center for History in the Schools (NCHS). Crabtree and historian Gary B. Nash served as directors, and Gagnon participated as a staff scholar. At the same time in New York, Gilbert Sewall, who had become a codirector of EEN, used funding from the Donner Foundation (and later the John M. Olin Foundation) to create the American Textbook Council (ATC). The ATC, which included Crabtree, Gagnon, Jackson, and Bill Honig (former California schools' superintendent) on its advisory board, did much to shape the debate of social studies curriculum through its reviews of social studies textbooks and commentary in its publication, *Social Studies Review.*

In 1990, textbooks in the Houghton-Mifflin social studies series, coauthored by UCLA's Nash, were the only K–7 textbooks approved for adoption by the California Curriculum Commission, whose history–social science subject matter committee chair was Crabtree. That same year, the New York Education Department appointed a panel to review its social studies curriculum. That panel included Arthur Schlesinger Jr., whose book *The Disuniting of America* articulated a standardized, common culture that should serve as a basis for the core subjects students study in schools.[34] In 1991, Ravitch became assistant secretary in the U.S. Department of Education Office of Educational Research and Improvement, where Gagnon soon followed. Crabtree's center and the Bradley Commission's successor organization received major grants from OERI during Ravitch's tenure there, including $1.6 million to the National Center for History in the Schools for the history curriculum standards projects, which included Jackson, Nash, and Sewall as advisors.

Although the neonativists have advocated the study of history as the remedy to perceived problems created by social studies, the "medicine" has produced unexpected side effects. The standards for U.S. and world history developed by the national center at UCLA were enmeshed in controversy even before their release. Criticism from advocates of grassroots curriculum development was expected, but the most vociferous and widely publicized attacks on the standards came from neonativists, who promoted a singular national identity by celebrating "perceived common values, while downplaying social inequities and the racial hierarchy that

maintains them."[35] Some of the most vocal critics of the history standards were Cheney and Ravitch, who were responsible, as federal officials, for commissioning their creation. Their criticisms targeted the
teaching examples included in the standards documents; they charged
that the examples were too compensatory of traditionally marginalized
groups and that they undercut the "heroic" figures of the West and the
United States that have traditionally dominated the history taught in
schools. Critics (including ninety-nine U.S. senators) repudiated the
standards largely because they judged that the U.S. history standards
were not celebratory enough and the world history standards did not
offer a more singular focus on Western civilization. Ironically, efforts to
promote a standardized history curriculum in place of social studies is
now plagued by the deconstruction of the historical canon.[36]

> The proliferation of historical subdisciplines . . . challenges the very
> notion of a canon. The new social history, the new working-class his-
> tory, the new educational history, as well as African American history,
> Native American history, feminist history and ethnic history encom-
> pass only a few of the topic areas and methodologies which emerged to
> challenge the traditional historical synthesis in the late 1960s and
> 1970s. . . . The problem is not as simple as deciding which names and
> which dates to include as significant: much of the new history chal-
> lenges the idea that individual people, and one-day or one-year
> "events" provide the important material of history.[37]

Two recent panels established by the Council for Basic Education, a
private group based in Washington, recommended that the history standards be revised and that more emphasis be placed on Washington,
Jefferson, and documents such as the U.S. Constitution and Bill of
Rights.[38]

Nash and Crabtree, codirectors of the national history standards project, defend the standards as the result of a broad-based national consensus-
building process involving teachers, school administrators, state social
studies specialists, academic historians, and representatives of the general public. Whelan has questioned whether consensus building is the
best means to determine the historical understandings most worth knowing and teaching and points out that autonomous, decentralized curricular decision making is more consistent with the fundamental nature of
historical study than the consolidated, consensus-based approach that the
national history standards project represents. He maintains that the very

notion of national curricular standards is contradictory of the essential interpretive nature of history.

> History is not a matter of facts, but a matter of deciding what the facts mean. . . . The notion of national standards seems to be based on the assumption that the study of history is simply about the past with subject matter that is therefore fixed and unchanging. This is a common, but largely misleading assumption, for history is a mode of inquiry which arises from the reciprocal relationship between a historian in the present and whatever she/he endeavors to study in the past.[39]

The discourse of curriculum standards is framed by essentialist assumptions, which, as the history standards illustrate, result in defining the curriculum problem as a matter of historians' reaching consensus about what they will advise teachers to include or exclude from the curriculum. This discourse leads to further standardization of knowledge through textbooks and standardized assessments. What is sacrificed in the process is an approach to teaching and learning that views knowledge as a social construction. Students need much more than facts; they need to understand the relationship between "facts" and whose interests these "facts" serve (a point that will not be lost on any reader of Loewen's recent analysis of U.S. history textbooks). Close examination of the standards discourse leads to the conclusion that the history neonativists want taught in schools is one that does not reflect the nature and diversity of contemporary historical scholarship.

As this brief chronology illustrates, the debate over social studies curriculum has been heavily influenced by a small group of conservative foundations and academics and the federal government, with an eye toward creating ideological consensus around a curriculum that promotes a national identify and strives to preserve the European American dominant culture and promote it as the common culture of all Americans. Cornbleth and Waugh describe this effort as "putting everyone in a covered wagon."

The subtext of the debate regarding standards suggests that there are "cultural" solutions to economic problems that drive much of the current curricular reform effort. At best, the curriculum standards movement offers a simplistic solution to a highly complex problem. The cultural literacy advocates implicitly blame poverty on the failure of schools to produce a uniform culture. The discourse, which focuses attention on curriculum standards and assessments, leaves no room to raise questions about the fundamental economic and political change that is necessary to ensure equity in our schools and in our society.

The Curriculum Standards and the Conditions of Schooling

A fundamental assumption of curriculum standards advocates is that uniform, externally formulated goals and content standards can improve curriculum and instruction. The history of school reform, however, illustrates that changing educational policies is much easier than changing the conditions and operations of schools.[40] Despite many efforts to reform schools in the past ninety-five years, the major features of school remain largely unchanged.

A number of factors account for the stability of schools in the face of repeated reform efforts.[41]

1. Schools are structured and teaching roles defined in ways that make improved teaching performance difficult to achieve. Schools are structurally fragmented with artificial barriers between disciplines and between teachers (e.g., distinct subject matters, narrow time blocks for teaching, teachers working in isolation).

2. The inadequacies of in-service education, which generally asks teachers to leave their classrooms so that they can travel to distant locations to get general advice from people who have never seen them teach.

3. Rigid and enduring norms define what teachers are supposed to be, how children are supposed to act, and what constitutes an appropriate set of expectations for a subject.

4. Conservative expectations for the function of schools. It is difficult for the schools to exceed in aim, form and, content what the public is willing to accept.

5. Reformers typically view teachers as the conduit for the delivery of curriculum. Reformers usually strive to create a uniform program for students regardless of who they are or where they live, which requires centralized decision making. This marginalizes teachers in the curriculum development process.

6. Changes that require new content and new repertoires are likely to be met with resistance by teachers who have not participated in the development of the initiative and/or have defined for themselves an array of routines (regarding what and how to teach) they can efficiently employ.

7. Fragmented efforts at changing schools that fail to account for the multiple dimensions of the ecology of schools (e.g., purposes, structures, curriculum, pedagogy, and evaluation).

Advocates claim that national goals and standards can improve curriculum and instruction. In the discourse of curriculum standards, what counts as "improved" curriculum and instruction?

The curriculum standards movement fails to problematize the structural conditions of schools that affect all teaching and learning. Curriculum standards panels have made assumptions about how teaching and learning can be improved in the social studies classroom without attempting to examine or understand the conditions that shape how teaching takes place, the sense students make of what they study, school norms, or, perhaps most important, the relationship between teachers' aims and what they actually do in the classroom.

The myopic emphasis on defining the content to be taught produces tunnel vision regarding the other dimensions that affect teaching and learning in schools. The consensus approach to defining content standards, as Whelan points out, promotes a rather tedious, superficial debate over the relative attention topics should receive. To this point, the effort to define curriculum standards in social studies has been so dominated by ideological interests, which would emphasize the development of national identity in students, that the depth, diversity, and complexity of historical and social science scholarship are obscured rather than illuminated.

The curriculum standards approach to change not only fails to problematize the conditions of schooling but also has deleterious effects on the structure of schools and on the quality of teaching. National curriculum standards reinforce the curriculum fragmentation and separateness of the departmentalized structure of the secondary school and inhibit interdisciplinary curriculum development at the elementary level through the myriad of distinct disciplinary standards, including the six that address social studies subject matter. The artificial barriers that perpetuate teacher isolation and inhibit reflective practice remain and are reinforced by uniform curriculum standards for each discipline.

The assumption, as with most other school reform efforts, is that the most important outcome of schooling is high levels of achievement on standardized tests. This assumption inhibits consideration of how the intellectual quality of schooling might be strengthened. In the case of social studies education, two complementary intentions are at the heart of efforts to standardize curriculum content. First, as described earlier,

there has been an effort to create a social studies curriculum that is celebratory of Western civilization and that transmits the dominant culture of
the United States in uncritical fashion. Second, U.S. economic competitiveness has been linked to high levels of achievement on standardized
tests, and curriculum standards constitute an effort to improve test results. The curriculum standards movement taps into the cultural norms of
schools as academic institutions that attempt to transmit what is already
known, rather than promoting the development of intellectual institutions that prize inquiry and thought.[42] The recent findings of the National
Assessment of Educational Progress reflect a focus on factual memorization rather than the situated use of history and social science knowledge.[43]

   *National curriculum standards and related efforts undercut teach-
ers' abilities to make professional judgments about what to teach.* If significant change in curriculum is desired, the ways teachers and students
live and work together must be significantly changed. The centrality of
teachers' role as curricular and instructional gatekeepers is well documented.[44] Curriculum improvement depends on teachers being more
thoughtful about their work. To achieve this, the conditions of schooling
must be a central part of any curricular reform effort. Transforming social studies curriculum and teaching via national standards assume that
decisions that are at the very heart of teaching—such as judging what
should be taught about a particular subject in relation to the needs of the
students—can be made by someone or some panel not directly involved
in the particular classroom situation. As with the curricular innovations
of the 1960s, the curriculum standards conceive of curriculum improvement as curriculum installation. Gagnon describes the "right kind of content standards" as laying before the students, the parents, the teachers,
and the teachers of teachers the essential common core of learning that
all students must have.[45] The major questions of what knowledge is to be
included in the history–social studies curriculum and how it is to be organized and used are epistemological and ethical.[46] They are questions of
underlying assumptions about the origins, nature, and limits of knowledge and who benefits or is harmed as a result of the choice of content
knowledge for the curriculum. For Gagnon, however, teachers, students,
and parents are not participants in the conversation about what knowledge is to be included in the social studies curriculum and whom it may
benefit or harm.

   Curriculum standards lead to a national curriculum. Despite de-
nials that curriculum standards equal a national curriculum, the stan-

dards discourse clearly promotes a nationwide "alignment" of standards, state curriculum frameworks, textbooks, and assessment, which amounts to a de facto national curriculum. The "hope of the standards movement" has been described by Albert Shanker, former president of the American Federation of Teachers (AFT), as a common national curriculum linked to high-stakes tests and a new relationship between teachers and students—as test coach and test taker. Shanker argues:

> Without stakes for students, the educational reforms that are proposed in Goals 2000 will not work. Without stakes, nobody has to take education seriously. . . . There's an external standard that students need to meet and the teacher is there to help the student make it. The existence of an external standard entirely changes the relationship of teachers and youngsters, and it changes the relationship of children and parents.[47]

Curriculum standards are intended to serve as the authority on which state curriculum frameworks, textbooks, and assessments are based. Shanker and the AFT argue explicitly that curriculum standards should make it easier for textbook publishers, assessment developers, and teacher educators to create products that are aligned to them. The AFT has encouraged the National Educational Standards and Improvement Council to certify standards that are specific enough to assure the development of a common core curriculum to be used by teachers. Certified standards are to define content (the most important ideas, concepts, issues, dilemmas, and information) and to detail how competent a student demonstration must be to indicate mastery of the content. Interdisciplinary studies are to be eschewed because "when standard setters abandon the disciplines, content suffers" and textbook writers, assessment developers, and teachers have less direction.[48]

Although the AFT and other standards advocates claim that good standards are designed to guide and not limit instruction, after specifying content and performance standards to guide the development of textbooks, tests, and teacher practice, little remains. In fact, the AFT recommends that the common core curriculum defined by standards should account for 80 percent of instructional time in the classroom, "the rest can be filled in by local districts, schools and teachers."[49]

This mechanistic conception of what real curriculum change requires reduces the role of teachers to technicians and fails to consider the differences between the publicly declared formal curriculum and the enacted curriculum brought to life by teachers and students. Curriculum improvement depends on teachers who are more thoughtful about their work. In many ways, curriculum standards perpetuate the central problem Dewey recognized in progressive educators' efforts to improve the curriculum—the intellectual subservience of teachers.

DEMOCRACY, CURRICULUM IMPROVEMENT, AND TEACHER EDUCATION

A primary tension, today and historically, in curriculum reform is between centralized and grassroots decision making. When the curriculum-making process has multiple participants and competing interests, the question arises, *Where ought control reside?* The curriculum standards movement in social studies represents an effort of policy elites to standardize the content and much of the practice of education. Operationally, curriculum standards projects in social studies are antidemocratic because they severely restrict the legitimate role of teachers and other educational professionals, as well as the public, in the conversation about the origin, nature, and ethics of knowledge taught in the social studies curriculum. The curriculum standards movement ignores the most striking aspect of the teacher's role in curriculum development, which is its inevitability.[50] Resources that might have been directed to assisting teachers to become better decision makers have, instead, been channeled into a program dedicated to the development of schemes for preventing teachers from making decisions.

The discourse of standards is a superficial distraction from the real work of making schools better places for students to learn and for teachers to teach. The standards discourse diverts attention away from issues such as inadequate school funding, unsafe school facilities, increasing class size, adequate technology, improving responses to children with special needs, and teachers' roles in curriculum decision making. Although the debate over what to teach in schools is not unimportant, it is a fiscally low-cost (but educationally high-cost) response to changing schools, a diversion that does not address the conditions of teaching and learning that exist in schools today.

ASSERTING THE TEACHERS' ROLE IN CURRICULUM DECISION MAKING

A fundamental assumption of the curriculum standards project is that deciding what should be taught is an unsuitable responsibility for teachers.

Development of national standards encourages centralized curriculum decision making and promotes a view of teachers as conduits for the delivery of externally defined knowledge. The curriculum standards movement in social studies attempts to make both the content and the performance standards in social studies the exclusive domain of disciplinary specialists, policy elites in private foundations, and public officials. Teachers' central role in curriculum decision making is reduced through an approach to curriculum change that aligns standards with mandated state frameworks, assessments, and curriculum materials.

Whether by the teacher-proof curricula of an earlier era or by the highly centralized curriculum change of the standards projects, teachers have been systematically freed from making decisions in the realm of educational authority. By limiting teachers' responsibilities for conceptualizing, planning, and evaluating the curricula they teach, reform efforts like the standards movement and Goals 2000 impose more external control and intervention at the classroom level. This approach to curriculum reform leaves little or no room for teachers to exercise professional judgment about curriculum or to define and enforce professional standards of practice. Although some have argued that the development of curriculum standards creates possibilities to engage teachers in a substantive conversation about ideas and practices, this prospect is unlikely because the standards projects leave no room for teachers at the table. Ironically, or perhaps not, the curriculum standards directly contradict efforts, such as shared decision making, to make schools more democratic, responsive to local needs, and supportive of teacher development and reflective practice.

Curriculum improvement depends on teachers who are more thoughtful about their work. To accomplish this objective, curriculum reform efforts must tackle head-on the conditions of teaching and learning in schools and must embrace, rather than marginalize, teachers as the key element in any transformation of curriculum. Instead of conceiving of teachers as technicians, a mere mechanical component in the process of implementing a formal curriculum, teachers must be understood as key actors in the curriculum creation.

Teachers' roles as both mediators and creators of curriculum must be asserted if significant curriculum improvement is the goal. Reformers must acknowledge the reality of the everyday nature of curriculum development and focus curricular reform efforts on creating supportive conditions for teacher development rather than merely engaging curriculum issues at the policy. Policies that mandate a standardized curriculum and assessments can engender change; the question is whether the change represents progress.

THE ROLE OF TEACHER EDUCATION

Improving social studies education, or any other area of education, requires improving teachers' education in the disciplines and in pedagogy. All the complexities that exist within these domains must be engaged. Dewey clearly recognized that the key to curriculum improvement is the development of teaching as professional work. He argued that teachers should be given to understand that they not only are permitted to act on their own initiative but also are expected to do so, and that their ability to take hold of a situation for themselves is a more important factor in judging them than their following any particular set method or scheme.[51] As Dewey implies, democracy grows through the interaction of complexities, not the production of uniformity.[52]

Although it may be unrealistic to assume that teachers by themselves can bring about fundamental changes in the structure of schools and the curricular and pedagogical practices those structures support, teachers are certainly the linchpins in any effort to transform schools. Teachers are in the best position to address curricular issues and need supportive conditions to do so. Social studies as a field aims to involve students in decision making, problem posing and problem solving about complex social issues. Should not the social studies teachers (as well as other educational professionals) act on these principles in their own lives?

Teacher education is central to improving the curriculum because it can prepare teachers to exercise their professional responsibilities in schools as they also approach disciplinary knowledge and learning in ways that highlight underlying epistemological and ethical assumptions. What is needed in teacher education, however, is more than increased integration of subject matter and pedagogical studies (although that would be useful). Teacher education must focus squarely on how discourse, practices, and social relations in education contend with one another in the formation of professional identities of teachers and the culture and conditions of schools.[53] For example, when curriculum and instruction (ends and means) are conceived as independent entities, as in the discourse of curriculum standards, the role of the teacher in producing the enacted or experienced curriculum of the classroom is obscured or distorted. This discourse justifies a division of labor, which marginalizes the teachers' role in formal curriculum (policy) development and creates unequal participation and power relations.

As an alternative, teacher educators might respond to this circumstance in two ways. First, cultivate an understanding of curriculum not as merely disciplinary subject matter but as the experiences had in the classroom. This approach does not diminish the importance of subject matter knowledge in the education of teachers but it does place the teacher squarely in the center of efforts to transform the curriculum. Second, improving the effectiveness of the personal practical theories of teachers might become the central aim of teacher education. Focusing teacher education on the process of formulating and acting upon practical judgment encourages an active, mediating, creating role for teachers in responding to curriculum and instructional problems. The tacit cultural environment of teaching—the language, manners, standards, and values that influence the classroom and school—is deconstructed as taken-for-granted elements of teaching and schooling are made targets of inquiry for teachers.[54]

GRASSROOTS CURRICULUM DEVELOPMENT

The Deweyan ideal of curriculum as something "created locally by teachers and learners who pursue genuine interests and concerns, realize that those concerns and interests symbolize perennial human interests and draw upon extant knowledge, has been an uphill battle since its inception."[55] Teachers have traditionally understood their power to affect change as stopping at the classroom door and not extending into schoolwide change or communitywide or national educational politics. True educational reform, however, engages policy debates and other struggles beyond the classroom. As teacher Stan Karp argues:

> If we recognize that effective education requires students to bring their real lives into the classrooms, and to take what they learn back to their homes and neighborhoods in the form of new understandings and new behavior, how can we not do the same? Critical teaching should not be merely an abstraction or academic formula for classroom "experimentation." It should be a strategy for educational organizing that changes lives, including our own.[56]

One way to accomplish this goal is by taking advantage of the space for initiatives offered by the introduction of site-based management and shared decision-making reforms in schools. These reforms are not panaceas and bring with them many elements that may potentially further entrench hierarchical relations within schools and between schools and policy elites. Where site councils are given real power and resources, teachers, students, parents, and community members can make significant decisions about the curriculum, instruction, and conditions of schools. Site-based restructuring is underway in many school districts, including large urban districts such as Chicago and Philadelphia. These openings provide the opportunity to develop true grassroots, teacher-initiated curriculum reform. Teachers in Milwaukee, for example, challenged the district's bureaucratic textbook adoption process and its heavy reliance on basal readers. Milwaukee teachers succeeded in winning support for a whole-language alternative to basal readers, as well as resources to provide professional development and alternative materials. The number of teachers using whole-language approaches as a result rose dramatically.[57]

Many key educational issues are determined in the larger context of community, state, and national politics (curriculum standards, voucher plans, privatization schemes). Grassroots curriculum development requires teachers and others to see and act on the connections between classrooms and society. Teachers' efforts in the classroom arc tied to broader efforts to promote democracy. If teachers can find ways to link the two, both will be strengthened.[58]

NOTES

[1]Curriculum standards for social studies include *Expectations of Excellence: Curriculum Standards for Social Studies,* developed by the National Council for the Social Studies in Washington, D.C.; *National Standards for United States History: Exploring the American Experience* and *National Standards for World History: Exoloring Paths to the Present,* both developed by the National Council for History Standards and the National Center for History in the Schools at UCLA; *National Standards for Civics and Government,* developed by the Center for Civic Education in Calabasas, California; and the Geography Education Standards Project developed by the National Council for Geographic Education in Washington, D.C. The development of the geography, history, and civics standards was supported through federal grants awarded by the Bush administration. The social studies standards project did not receive federal funding. Neither social studies nor civics was among the seven subjects listed in the national goals supported by the Clinton administration.

[2]National Commission on Excellence in Education, *A Nation at Risk* (Washington, D.C.: U.S. Government Printing Office, 1983).

[3]Bob Peterson, "Equity Absent in Goals 2000," *Rethinking Schools* 8 (Spring 1994): 6.

[4]For a discussion of the effects of legal decisions on the curriculum, see James A. Whitson, *Constitution and Curriculum* (London: Falmer Press, 1991); and Tyll van Geel, "Two Visions of Federalism and the Control of Curriculum," in *The Politics of Curriculum Decision-Making*, ed. M. Frances Klein (Albany: State University of New York Press, 1991), pp. 42–66.

[5]I am indebted to the work of William H. Schubert for this section. See William H. Schubert, "Historical Perspective on Centralizing Curriculum," in *The Politics of Curriculum Decision-Making*, ed. M. Frances Klein (Albany: State University of New York Press, 1991), pp. 98–118.

[6]Schubert, "Historical Perspectives," p. 101.

[7]For a concise account of the curriculum ferment of the 1890s, see Herbert M. Kleibard, *The Struggle for the American Curriculum, 1893–1958* (New York: Routledge, 1987).

[8]The dominant scope and sequence in secondary social studies is: grade 7, world history and geography; grade 8, American history; grade 9, civics; grade 10, world history; grade 11, American history; and grade 12, American government.

[9]Edward A. Krug, *The Shaping of the American High School, 1880–1920* (Madison: University of Wisconsin Press, 1969).

[10]Arthur G. Wirth, *Education and Work in the Year 2000* (San Francisco: Jossey-Bass, 1992).

[11]For more detailed accounts of how state curriculum frameworks influence classroom practices and teachers' work, see E. Wayne Ross, "Educational Reform, School Restructuring, and Teachers' Work," *International Journal of Social Education* 7 (Fall 1992): 83–92; Sandra Mathison, "Implementing Curricular Change Through State-Mandated Testing: Ethical Issues," *Journal of Curriculum and Supervision* 6 (Spring 1991): 201–212; and Catherine Cornbleth and Dexter Waugh, *The Great Speckled Bird* (New York: St. Martin's Press, 1995).

[12]Martin G. Brooks, "Centralized Curriculum: Effects on the Local School Level," in *The Politics of Curriculum Decision-Making*, ed. M. Frances Klein (Albany: State University of New York Press, 1991), pp. 151–166.

[13]William H. Kilpatrick, *The Project Method* (New York: Teachers College, Columbia University, 1918).

[14]Schubert, "Historical Perspective," p. 107.

[15]W. C. Bagley, "The Textbook and Methods of Teaching," *National Society for the Study of Education Yearbook* 30 (1931): 7–26, cited in Gail McCutcheon, *Developing the Curriculum* (White Plains, N.Y.: Longman, 1995), p. 157.

[16]Gerald Marker and Howard Mehlinger, "Social Studies," in *Handbook of Research on Curriculum*, ed. P. Jackson (New York: Macmillan, 1992).

[17]See H. Black, *The American Schoolbook* (New York: William Morrow, 1967); M. Bowler, "The Making of a Textbook," *Learning* 6 (March 1978): 38–42. For a detailed account of the politics of social studies textbook adoptions in California, also see Cornbleth and Waugh.

[18]Michael W. Apple, *Teachers and Texts* (London: Routledge, 1986).

[19]James W. Loewen, *Lies My Teacher Told Me* (New York: New Press, 1995), pp. 138, 150–151.

[20]Marker and Mehlinger, p. 838.

[21]E. Wayne Ross, "Teachers as Curriculum Theorizers," in *Reflective Practice in Social Studies*, ed. E. W. Ross (Washington, D.C.: National Council for the Social Studies, 1994), pp. 35–41.

[22]Marker and Mehlinger.

[23]Schubert, p. 114.

[24]Ibid.

[25]For detailed case studies of the politics of social studies curriculum making in California and New York, see Cornbleth and Waugh.

[26]E. D. Hirsch, *Cultural Literacy: What Every American Needs to Know* (Boston: Houghton-Mifflin, 1987).

[27]Lynne Cheney, *American Memory: A Report on the Humanities in the Nation's Public Schools* (Washington, D.C.: National Endowment for the Humanities, 1988).

[28]Peter Seixas, "Parallel Crises: History and the Social Studies Curriculum in the USA," *Journal of Curriculum Studies* 25 (1993): 235–250.

[29]Seixas, p. 237.

[30]Robert D. Barr, James L. Barth, and Samuel S. Shermis, *Defining the Social Studies* (Arlington, Va.: National Council for the Social Studies, 1977), quoted in Seixas, p. 237.

[31]See Cornbleth and Waugh for the most complete account of the debate over the social studies curriculum in the past decade.

[32]The role of the Bradley Foundation as the country's leading funder of conservative research, publications, and think tanks (such as the Heritage Foundation, the American Enterprise Institute, and Charles Murray, co-author of *Bell Curve*) is examined in Barbara Miner, "The Power and the Money," *Rethinking Schools* 8 (Spring 1994): 1, 16–21. In his writings, Michael S. Joyce, president of the Lynde and Harry Bradley Foundation, has promoted a "new citizenship," which reconstructs the idea of citizenship as separate from the political sphere. Joyce argues against citizens' involvement in political organizations that design and implement policy and legislative programs and that try to control investment decisions of firms in the workplaces.

[33]Diane Ravitch and Chester E. Finn, *What Do Our 17-Year-Olds Know? A Report on the First National Assessment of History and Literature* (New York: Harper & Row, 1987).

[34]Arthur M. Schlesinger Jr., *The Disuniting of America* (Knoxville, Tenn.: Whittle Books, 1991).

[35]Cornbleth and Waugh, p. 61.

[36]See Michael Whelan, "Right for the Wrong Reasons on National Standards," *Social Education,* 60 (January, 1995): 55–57; Michael Whelan, "National History Curriculum Standards," *Theory and Research in Social Education* 23 (Summer 1995): 278–282; and Seixas.

[37]Seixas, pp. 237–238.

[38]See articles in *Education Week,* November 2, 1994, and October 18, 1995.

[39]Whelan, "Right for the Wrong Reasons," pp. 3, 5.

[40]See Larry Cuban, "Reforming Again, Again, and Again," *Educational Researcher* 19 (January–February 1990): 3–13.

[41]This list is based largely on analysis by Elliot W. Eisner, "Educational Reform and the Ecology of Schooling," *Teachers College Record* 93 (Summer 1992): 610–627.

[42]Eisner, p. 61.

[43]Tamara Henry, "Few Students Understand History Facts," *USA Today* (November 2, 1995): A1.

[44]Stephen Thornton, "Teacher as Curricular-Instructional Gatekeeper in Social Studies," in *Handbook of Research on Social Studies Teaching and Learning,* ed. James P. Shaver (New York: Macmillan, 1991).

[45]Paul Gagnon, "And Bringing Them to the Classroom," *American Educator* 18 (Fall 1994): 15.

[46]Sylvia Wynter, "A Cultural Model Critique of the Textbook, *America Will Be,*" a paper presented at the annual meeting of the American Educational Research Association (April 1992), cited in Cornbleth and Waugh.

[47]Albert Shanker, "Making Standards Count," *American Educator* 18 (Fall 1994): 16, 18.

[48]Educational Issues Department of the American Federation of Teachers, "Making Standards Good," *American Educator* 18 (Fall 1994): 15, 20–27.

[49]Ibid., p. 24.

[50]Thornton.

[51]John Dewey, "The Relation of Theory to Practice in Education," *Third Yearbook of the National Society for the Scientific Study of Education, Part I* (Bloomington, Ill.: Public School Publishing Company, 1904), pp. 27–28.

[52]See "Opinions Class on Curriculum Standards," *ASCD Update* (January 1994): 7.

[53]Stephen Kemmis and Robin McTaggart, *The Action Research Planner,* 3d ed. (Geelong, Victoria: Deakin University Press, 1988).

[54]See Ross, *Reflective Practice.*

[55]Schubert, p. 104.

[56]Stan Karp, "Beyond the Classroom," *Rethinking Schools* 8 (Summer 1994): 24.

[57]Ibid.

[58]I would like to thank Sandra Mathison and David Hursh for their helpful comments on a draft of this chapter.

CHAPTER 14

Promoting Democracy through Evaluation

SANDRA MATHISON

Evaluation in school contexts is ubiquitous: teachers evaluate student learning, principals evaluate teacher performance, curriculum committees evaluate textbooks and curriculum, and consultants evaluate programs. Evaluation is often viewed as something done to teachers, students, and programs, sometimes ritually but often with an implicit expectation of punitive intents and consequences.[1] Evaluation, like many other school practices, is taken for granted and is one means for ensuring the continuation of typical schooling relationships and practices—that is, maintaining the status quo. In the case of schools, this status quo is a hierarchically structured bureaucracy where practices and discourse are determined by external agents such as state-level officials, tradition, and corporations that create curriculum materials and tests. Although much evaluation contributes to the maintenance of this status quo, there is no logical reason why the practice of evaluation is often a conserving act. In this chapter, I explore evaluation as an activity that *can and should* promote democracy within schools, but it is evaluation of a particular sort.

There are many evaluation approaches,[2] not all of which promote democracy and its ideals, even though each is about judging the merit or worth of something, the heart of all evaluation. However, the genre of evaluation called *participatory, collaborative evaluation* is by definition[3] consistent with notions of democracy. Democracy, here, is not simply procedural, such as is evidenced in majoritarianism, where we abide by a one-person, one-vote act to determine what is good or right. Nor is democracy as I discuss it primarily constitutional, such as is evidenced in proceduralism, where majoritarianism is tempered by inalienable moral constraints, such as freedom from cruelty. Rather, democracy here is reflected in Dewey's idea of "a mode of associated living, of conjoint communicated experience"[4] or by the forms of political action and discourse Gutmann and Thompson[5] call *deliberative democracy*. As such, this argument is about the process of creating communities with shared interests and greater clarity about particular value positions and commitment to them. What characterizes the sort of democracy to which I am referring is not actions such as voting but rather an obligation to engage in careful, public consideration of alternatives for the purpose of creating a better way of life.

In this chapter, I first describe what evaluation is generally and then describe participatory, collaborative evaluation in particular. It will become apparent that deliberation is a key feature of participatory, collaborative evaluation, and it is this feature that permits evaluation's contribution to democracy in general and in schools in particular.

THE NATURE OF EVALUATION GENERALLY

The logic of all evaluation entails choosing criteria and standards, measuring the performance based on those criteria and standards, and synthesizing this information to make a judgment about the merit or worth of that which is being evaluated. Making an evaluative judgment requires moving justifiably from definitional and factual premises to evaluative conclusions. This description, of course, makes evaluation appear more rational and linear than it is. Note that this logic underlies all evaluations, but it is not necessarily clearly mirrored in the evaluation process. In the doing of evaluation, this logic may remain hidden and be revealed only through significant mining.[6]

In oversimplified terms, then, the evaluation process involves the following (although not necessarily in this order):

1. Specifying the criteria and standards to be employed in the evaluation[7]
2. Determining the degree to which the evaluand meets or does not meet the established standards (by means of either grading or ranking)
3. Rendering an evaluative judgment of merit or worth

In addition to these attributes, every evaluation is made from some point of view, and a number of points of view might be taken—a pedagogical one, an economic one, an aesthetic one, or a political one, among others. The point of view taken implies that certain criteria, and not others, are employed in the evaluation process. For example, an evaluation of a painting from an aesthetic point of view would consider criteria such as symmetry, color, and harmony; an evaluation of the same painting from an economic point of view would consider criteria such as initial cost, resale value, and likelihood of appreciation. Clearly, a painting might be judged good from one point of view and bad from another.

THE NATURE OF PARTICIPATORY, COLLABORATIVE EVALUATION

Participatory, collaborative evaluation (like all evaluation) has the attributes described in the previous section. What characterizes this approach to evaluation particularly is a commitment to involve a broad range of stakeholders in the evaluation process, both as sources of information (the essence of participation) and as participants in shaping the purpose, substance, and form of the evaluation process and product (the essence of collaboration).

Stakeholders are individuals or groups with a vested interest in that which is being evaluated, the evaluands. If student performance is the evaluand, the stakeholders include students, teachers, educational administrators, and parents, as well as perhaps colleges and employers. With any evaluand, determining who the stakeholders are, the degree of vestedness each has in the evaluand, and how to balance their input is neither straightforward nor simple. How such decisions are made is critical in creating truly participatory, collaborative evaluation.[8]

Evaluator expertise, tradition, folk wisdom, textbook examples, and national standards are commonly used as the bases for directing the evaluation process. For example, criteria (whether stated as criteria, questions, or hypotheses) are adopted from these various sources with little consideration given to their appropriateness in a given context. Participatory, collaborative evaluation, by contrast, explicitly involves stakeholders in making decisions about what criteria, standards, forms of assessment, and points of view are relevant, appropriate, and fair. Judging a social studies curriculum, for example, involves teachers, students, parents, principals, community members, and scholars, among others, in discourse about what social studies is, by what criteria we ought to judge it, and to what degree it must have the qualities we deem valuable.

Participatory, collaborative evaluation (that is, the genuine involvement of stakeholders) requires some means by which stakeholders can express their views about these various aspects of the evaluation. Obviously, one could survey stakeholders about what they believe the criteria and standards ought to be in judging the evaluand at hand. Such needs assessment strategies rely on individual reflection and production of what to base an evaluation on. Seldom, however, is it the case that we determine what we value and how in isolation; more likely, we do so in interaction with one another and from outside sources of information like the media or educational research. Thus, I would suggest that the natural and most productive way of determining the specifics of an evaluation is through face-to-face deliberation.

Rather than taken-for-granted institutional forms driving actions, the deliberative aspects of preparing to do and doing the evaluation provide an opportunity to create institutional practices that require active participation and responsibility for determining what is good and for making it happen. Education is a moral act, and evaluation can increase our collective ability to reason well and justly about the forms of education in schools.

EVALUATION AND DELIBERATION

By deliberation, I mean a dialogue among individuals that assumes a capacity for empathy and a genuine interest in understanding one's own and others' positions, with the possibility of coming to a new common understanding. Deliberation is only one of several means by which we reason about something in hopes of making a decision, and it can be contrasted with two other common forms of reasoning—bargaining and demonstration. Bargaining is a strategy familiar to us in labor-management negotiations that intend to reach a decision acceptable to both sides. There are accepted rules for negotiating, and in general the parties approach one another as adversaries, each side expecting to make compromises that will result in an acceptable although not perfect decision. Each side tries to maximize its own self-interest in what they hope will be a mutually advantageous outcome. By contrast, demonstration relies on authority and tradition to reach a decision. For example, one person shows that through time an enduring understanding has become such and such, and therefore that is what we decide to agree on.

Neither adversarial bargaining nor demonstration has a high likelihood of leading to mutually beneficial and explicitly justified decisions, which, in contrast, deliberation promises. The process of deliberation is regulated by three principles: reciprocity, publicity, and accountability.

"Reciprocity asks us to appeal to reasons that are shared or could come to be shared by our fellow citizens" and that "empirical claims in political argument be consistent with reliable methods of inquiry, as these methods are available to use here and now, not for all times and all places."[9] Deliberation takes place in public forums or is at least disseminated in public forums, and accountability is achieved through challenges to positions and resulting justifications in public forums.

Most books about evaluation do not have an index entry for *deliberation*. It is not an idea that has been considered in quite the way it is discussed here. However, the role deliberation plays in educational evaluation has been highlighted by other evaluation scholars, and so it is not a new idea. House analyzed evaluation as an argument characterized by various types of reasoning.[10] In his monograph, he looks specifically at evaluation as a product, a written document, that employs various forms of reasoning to persuade the audience of the validity of the evaluation.

Other scholars provide a view of deliberation in the context of evaluation as a process.[11] Stakeholder-based approaches to evaluation seek to represent the value positions of those who have a vested interest in a program.[12] Such approaches arise in pluralistic societies where the existence of different interest groups is recognized and prized and the marketplace is seen as the location where resolutions about competing interests are made. In stakeholder-based approaches, the evaluator has the responsibility for determining who the stakeholders are, creating the means for their involvement, determining the relevance of their stake, and deciding how to weight various interests. This approach assumes the evaluator can adopt a value-neutral position representing values but not taking a value position.

Guba and Lincoln's *Fourth Generation Evaluation* goes beyond the representation of stakeholder views approach and assumes a dialectic relationship with the evaluator as the hub of dialogue among program stakeholders. In collecting value positions of stakeholders (including one's own), the evaluator seeks to confront differences and disparities through continuous and repeated dialogue with stakeholders. The evaluator is seen as a stakeholder in much the same way as service recipients, program managers, or program staff are. In this version, the evaluator is a medium for transmitting value positions among stakeholders in an effort to move the understanding of a program forward in beneficial ways. Participatory approaches to evaluation suggest a collaborative relationship between the evaluator and stakeholder.[13] Guba and Lincoln describe this collaboration as "full participative involvement, in which the stakeholders and others who may be drawn into the evaluation are welcomed as equal partners in every aspect of the design, implementation, interpretation, and resulting action of an evaluation—that is, they are accorded a full measure of political parity and control.[14] What all these scholars suggest is that the construct of stakeholders is central to responsible evaluation and that to do valid evaluations, it is important to talk with a variety of people in a variety of roles.

Although the construct of stakeholders is an important, if not fully developed, construct that improves the quality of evaluation, the process of evaluation provides far greater opportunities for genuine involvement of stakeholders. This genuine involvement occurs by making explicit and taking advantage of the fact that deliberation is inherent in evaluation.[15]

Deliberation can and should play an important role at each stage of the evaluation process, although in reality the evaluator may deliberate only with program managers or individually.[16] In practice, many aspects of evaluation as described earlier are taken for granted, and no deliberation occurs. For example, an evaluation of social studies textbooks seldom includes an explication of or deliberation about the point(s) of view various stakeholder groups are assuming. For example, a committee to choose a social studies textbook series may include teachers and parents, as well as other stakeholders. The parents on the committee may predominantly represent the religious right and adopt a fundamentalist point of view that may value creationism, traditional nuclear family structure, and Eurocentric views of history. The teachers on the committee may be a divided group. Some teachers adopt a social studies as history perspective; others adopt a social issues perspective on social studies. Clearly, deciding what the good-making attributes of a social studies textbook series are, given these different perspectives, is not a simple matter. Without deliberation about how to judge the available social studies textbooks as good or bad, this committee cannot come to an agreement about how to justifiably make a textbook selection. These different points of view lead stakeholder groups to invoke different criteria, standards, and means of assessment in judging the value of textbooks considered. So, the religious right parents judge *My Two Dads* to be a poor choice for supporting literature in social studies because of its promotion of non-Christian values (that is, the portrayal of a nontraditional family and homosexuality), some teachers judge it to be a good choice because it provides an opportunity to consider the changing nature of the American family, and some teachers judge it to be irrelevant to the study of history.

In situations with less extreme differences, where stakeholders may adopt the same point(s) of view, folk wisdom, textbook examples, and national standards are often perceived to be adequate and appropriate sources of criteria and standards to be employed in an evaluation. For example, school administrators, teachers, parents, students, and community members might, in general, adopt a pedagogical point of view for an evaluation of a global studies curriculum. In the absence of deliberation, administrators and teachers might assume the state curriculum is the appropriate statement of the criteria for judging the global studies curriculum, whereas community members may think workplace preparation is the more appropriate source for such criteria. Even if the evaluation describes these different perspectives, both groups have grounds to reject or ignore the evaluation because they can contend it was done wrong, that is, the wrong criteria were used. However, deliberating about what the criteria for judging the global studies curriculum ought to be in this evaluation of this curriculum—in this school, at this time, given these stakeholders—might potentially lead to an evaluation in which all groups truly have a stake, which is more likely to create a clearer community vision of what global studies is and ought to be like.

If evaluation—that is, making value judgments that help us decide how to live our lives better—is to be done, then much greater attention must be paid to the role and value of deliberation. Although it is, of course, difficult for stakeholder groups with very different perspectives to deliberate successfully, we should not be deterred from making the effort. As a beginning, deliberations, like the one illustrated in the following dialogue, might reveal the taken-for-grantedness of criteria and how deliberation can lead to the justification of criteria for particular evaluations.

> A: This is a good textbook.
> B: Why?
> A: Well, for one thing, the topics are arranged chronologically.
> B: Why does that make it a good textbook?
> A: Because chronological organization is a good way to judge a textbook.
> B: Why is it a good way to judge a textbook?
> A: Because chronological organization is a good way for judging history textbooks, and this is a history textbook.

B: I will admit that this is a history textbook and that it is organized chronologically, but why is being chronologically organized a good reason for judging history textbooks to be good?

This last question can be stated another way: Why is chronological organization an appropriate criteria for judging history textbooks? Without deliberation between evaluator and stakeholders and among stakeholders, standards remain implicit, unchallenged, and decontextualized. Evaluation that adopts points of view, criteria, standards, and so on in the absence of deliberation among stakeholders is at worst authoritarian and at best irrelevant.

I speak here of the possibilities for evaluation (rather than the practice as it often exists), and this explication of deliberation and evaluation is intended to be prescriptive because *by definition* all deliberation is evaluation and the process of evaluation is deliberative.

DELIBERATION AND DEMOCRACY

Unless deliberation is a core idea in creating and maintaining democracy, the role of deliberation in evaluation would not provide the opportunity for the promotion of democratic ideals. However, deliberation is a foundational idea in democracy, just as in evaluation.

Democracy, here, does not refer to a representational form of government but rather to Dewey's idea of "a mode of associated living, of conjoint communicated experience."[17] As such, this argument is not about political systems as they adhere to nation-states, but rather it is about the process of creating communities with shared interests (although they may be nation-states). What characterizes the sort of democracy to which I am referring here is not an individual exercising the right to vote but rather an obligation to engage in careful consideration and discussion of alternatives, for the purpose of creating a better way of life.

These notions of a democratic community presuppose what Brian Fay calls an "activist conception of human beings"; that is, human beings are "(at least potentially) broadly intelligent, curious, reflective, and willful beings."[18] Fay further tells us that these natural tendencies are awakened in noncoercive contexts and are the result of rational deliberation and persuasion. Through deliberation, we collectively decide how to be and what to do.

Differences of opinion must therefore be settled through deliberation, not by coercion, appeals to emotion, or authority. Is it possible that differences of opinion cannot be resolved through deliberation? Absolutely. Assuming rational deliberation is the basis of democratic communities does not presume that all members of the community agree on all things as a result of deliberating. As Fay explains, "To be rational is to have good reasons for one's beliefs, together with an openness to reconsider alternatives and a willingness to revise one's beliefs if evidence is adduced which fits better with an alternative system of beliefs."[19] Members of a democratic community can disagree as long as they are willing to engage in a discussion about their beliefs, as long as their beliefs are consistent with the best available evidence, and as long as they are open-minded about their beliefs. "Rational people are those who are uncertain of the truth of their beliefs, and who are thus open to revising them if the evidence warrants it."[20]

This deliberation, which characterizes democratic communities as described by Dewey and Fay, is concerned with a right action in particular contexts for particular people, given a specific set of details. The role of deliberation is not to settle a matter, to make a decision, or to take an action that is definitive and immutable. It is a continuous process of assessing the particulars in order to move toward betterment with the implicit expectation that an ideal state does not exist and cannot be attained. Thus, deliberation becomes the heart of democracy because it is the means by which a democratic community maintains its intent and identity, given an indeterminate future.

EVALUATION AND DEMOCRACY

Because deliberation is a primary means by which democratic ideals are promoted and because deliberation is key to the process of evaluation, then evaluation has the potential to contribute to the creation of democracy.[21] Evaluation, if done well, is democratizing. It requires that individuals and groups with vested interests in what is being evaluated engage in genuine deliberation about how to determine if the evaluand is good or bad, right or wrong.

As noted earlier, participatory, collaborative approaches to evaluation provide the greatest opportunity for deliberation, although the typical conceptualization of the stakeholder notion places limits on these approaches' power to democratize.[22] When the intent is merely to represent diverse value positions rather than to discuss those alternative and diverse value positions, the evaluation process becomes primarily a description of the complexity of the educational world. That is why we must move beyond mere representation of stakeholder views to more collaborative approaches to evaluation.

What is needed is an honest and thorough attempt to include all stakeholders, with particular attention to those who are powerless and poor. While we focus our evaluative resources disproportionately on programs intended for the powerless and poor, we are remiss in including them in the acts of creating and evaluating programs intended for their benefit. To be fair, including these stakeholders is often a major challenge. Poor parents whose children receive Chapter 1 services relate to schools and school activities in culturally determined ways that work against their genuine involvement as program stakeholders. Extraordinary effort is required of evaluators to ensure their inclusion and ability to deliberate in the evaluation process. Using the metaphor of an evaluation advisory group, a simple strategy would be to have the powerless (and poor) disproportionately overrepresented in this group. One means of doing this might be to have proportional representation of stakeholder groups. This strategy alone would change the balance of power.

Key also to anticipating the democratizing potential of evaluation is the opportunity for stakeholders to engage in genuine deliberation—that is, the freedom to discuss and reflect on beliefs with an eye to seeking common group values. Creating opportunities for this genuine deliberation requires skills evaluators may not have—that is, the ability to mediate and help stakeholders discuss in fair and open ways. Other fields such as action research, organizational development, or conflict resolution may provide some insight into how genuine deliberation might be created.

The process of evaluation necessarily includes determining point(s) of view, criteria, standards, and means of assessment. Determining what these will be through genuine deliberation by a particular program's stakeholders at a particular time in a particular place suggests the basis of the evaluation will be carefully considered and not merely a reflection of taken-for-granted institutional forms. Plans to evaluate the local social studies curriculum cannot rest on national standards, for example, without explicit discussion of the appropriateness of these standards as criteria for this social studies curriculum. Such national codifications of social studies knowledge and skills may be a useful part of the determination of the value of the local social studies curriculum, but this value cannot be assumed and this position cannot be enforced by a particular stakeholder group. Deliberation demands that students, parents, teachers, and the community, as well as administrators, governments, and funding agencies, take joint responsibility for making judgments about what is right and good in schools. Deliberation requires that we reason about how we judge our schools and the programs and people who work in them and, as a consequence, reason about what we want our schools to be like. Such evaluations require commitment and are not so easily dismissed or falsified as those that do not engage stakeholders in discussion with one another and the evaluator.

Remember, of course, the opportunity for deliberation does not guarantee a consensus value position. What it does guarantee is the disclosure of underlying beliefs, epistemologies, and ontologies. Even if the fundamentalist parents and the teachers, in the earlier example, cannot come to consensus about what criteria to use for judging the available textbooks, the reasons are not evaluation error or stupidity but rather a rational choice to disagree. Any formal evaluation that all stakeholders find valid may have to be abandoned in such a case, but the process of evaluation will have contributed to a greater clarity about who the people of this community consider themselves to be and the social relations they wish to create.

NOTES

[1]This chapter is adapted from Sandra Mathison, "Evaluation as a Democratizing Force in Schools," *The International Journal of Social Education* 11 (1996): 40–48.

[2]Carol H. Weiss, " 'Evaluation and Politics," in *Evaluation and Education: at Quarter Century,* ed. Milbrey W. McLaughlin and D. C. Phillips (Chicago: National Society for the Study of Education, 1991).

[3]See, for example, George F. Madaus, Michael S. Scriven, and Daniel L. Stufflebeam, eds., *Evaluation Models: Viewpoints on Educational and Human Services Evaluation* (Boston: Kluwer-Nijhoff, 1986); and William R. Shadish, Thomas D. Cook, and Laura C. Leviton, *Foundations of Program Evaluation: Theories of Practice* (Newbury Park, Calif.: Sage, 1991).

[4]John Dewey, *Democracy and Education* (New York: Free Press, 1916), p. 87.

[5]Amy Gutmann and Dennis Thompson, *Democracy and Disagreement* (Cambridge: Harvard University Press, 1996).

[6]Robert Stake and his students have questioned this logic in "The Evolving Syntheses of Program Value," *Evaluation Practice* 18 (1997): 89–103. Based on interviews with evaluators, they find evaluators do not describe their work in these terms. I think this finding is reasonable and would suggest that it does not disprove the existence of a general logic of evaluation. What it suggests is that

the logic is deeply embedded in our evaluative discourse. For example, Stake has promoted the use of foreshadowing questions in doing evaluation. An examination of these foreshadowing questions (or hypotheses in the experimental approach to evaluation) reveals evaluation criteria. The measurement of the evaluand's performance is usually transparent in the ways in which evidence is gathered. Standards are perhaps the most deeply embedded aspect of the logic and often are specified only after performance data in relation to criteria (which may change and evolve during the evaluation process) are gathered. The problem of standard setting is serious, and most evaluation does this in situational, contextual ways that do not presume there are absolute, predetermined standards of performance of goodness or rightness.

[7]Criteria and standards are relevant for judging the process as well as the outcomes of a program. For example, a process criterion for a teacher development project might be that the project staff make adjustments to the activities based on the needs, interests, and skills of the teachers involved.

[8]For a more complete discussion of this issue, see Sandra Mathison, "The Role of Deliberation in Evaluation," paper presented at the annual meeting of the American Evaluation Association, Atlanta, 1996.

[9]Gutmann and Thompson, p. 1415.

[10]Ernest R. House, *The Logic of Evaluative Argument* (Los Angeles: UCLA Center for the Study of Evaluation, 1977).

[11]Robert E. Stake, *Program Evaluation. Particularly Responsive Evaluation Occasional Paper No. 5* (Kalamazoo: Western Michigan University Evaluation Center, 1975); Jennifer C. Greene, "Stakeholder Participation in Evaluation Design: Is It Worth the Effort?" *Evaluation and Program Planning* 10 (1987): 379–394. Egon G. Guba and Yvonna S. Lincoln, *Fourth Generation Evaluation* (Newbury Park, Calif.: Sage, 1989).

[12]Carol H. Weiss, "The Stakeholder Approach to Evaluation: Origins and Promise," in *New Directions in Program Evaluation,* ed. Ernest R. House (Philadelphia: Falmer, 1986).

[13]J. Bradley Cousins and L. Earl, "The Case for Participatory Evaluation," *Educational Evaluation and Policy Analysis* 14 (1992): 397–418.

[14]Guba and Lincoln, p. 11.

[15]See Michael Scriven's description of the nature of evaluation in the *Evaluation Thesaurus, 4th ed.* (Newbury Park, Calif.: Sage, 1991); and Paul Taylor, *Normative Discourse* (Englewood Cliffs, N.J.: Prentice Hall, 1961).

[16]See Scriven, "Evaluation Ideologies," in *Evaluation Models: Viewpoints on Educational and Human Service Evaluation,* ed. George F. Madaus, Michael Scriven, and Daniel L. Stufflebeam (Boston: Kluwer Nijoff, 1983), for a discussion of the "managerial ideology."

[17]Dewey, p. 87.

[18]Brian Fay, *Critical Social Science* (Ithaca, N.Y.: Cornell University Press, 1987), p. 64.

[19]Ibid., p. 179.

[20]Ibid.

[21]Of course, evaluation need not be democratizing, but the contention here is that when it is not, it is not evaluation either by design or intent.

[22]A similar argument is made about the stakeholder approach to promotion of social justice by Ernest R. House, "Evaluation and Social Justice," in McLaughlin and Phillips.

Contributors

Edward Buendia is Assistant Professor in the Department of Educational Studies at the University of Utah. Most recently, he has written about the formation of preservice teachers' pedagogical practices, school and curricular processes that shape immigrant students' educational experiences, and the discursive codification of instructional technologies in school settings.

Henry A. Giroux currently holds the Waterbury Chair Professorship in Secondary Education at Penn State University. He received his doctorate from Carnegie Mellon University in 1977. He has taught at Miami University, Tufts University, and Boston University. His books include: *Postmodern Education; Border Crossings; Living Dangerously* (which won the 1995 Gustav Myers Award for one of the best books on Human Rights in North America); *Disturbing Pleasures: Learning Popular Culture;* and *Fugitive Cultures: Race, Violence, and Youth.* His most recent books include: *Channel Surfing: Race Talk and the Destruction of Today's Youth; Pedagogy and the Politics of Hope; The Mouse That Roared: Disney and the End of Innocence; Stealing Innocence: Youth, Corporate Power, and the Politics of Culture;* and *Impure Acts: The Practical Politics of Cultural Studies.* He is currently Director of the Waterbury Forum in Education and Cultural Studies at Penn State University.

Rebecca Goldstein is Assistant Director of Clinical Experiences at the School of Education, Hunter College, CUNY. In addition, she is a Ph.D. candidate at the Warner Graduate School of Education and Human Development, the University of Rochester, Rochester, NY. She is currently writing her dissertation on the interconnection of race, class, gender, sexuality, and power as they shape identity construction in urban class-rooms.

Derrick Griffith received his B.A. in History from the University of North Carolina at Charlotte. He went on to pursue graduate work at the Margaret Warner School of Education at the University of Rochester, earning an M.S. (1995) in Teaching, Curriculum, and Educational Change, with a concentration in Secondary Social Studies. While teach-ing in the Rochester City Public Schools, he continued doctoral studies under the advisement of David W. Hursh.

David W. Hursh is Associate Professor and Director of Teacher Educa-tion at the Warner Graduate School at the University of Rochester. In the 1970s he co-directed an alternative university, directed two private ele-mentary schools (one of which he founded), and was a consultant on race and sex equity. His recent publications include: "The Struggle for Democracy in South Africa: Race, History, and Education" and "Living, Not Practicing, Democracy," both in the journal *Theory and Research in Social Education;* "Critical Collaborative Action Research in Conserva-tive Times," in *International Action Research and Educational Reform;* and "Reforming Schools: From Pious Hope to Democratic Struggle," in *Discourse: Studies in the Cultural Politics of Education.*

Joe L. Kincheloe is the Belle Zeller Chair of Public Policy and Adminis-tration at CUNY Brooklyn College and a professor of Cultural Studies and Education at The Pennsylvania State University. He is the author of many books and articles, including *Teachers as Researchers: Qualitative Paths to Empowerment; Toil and Trouble: Good Work, Smart Workers and the Integration of Academic and Vocational Education; How Do We Tell the Workers?;* and *Changing Multiculturalism: New Times, New Curriculum* with Shirley Steinberg.

Wendy Kohli is Director of Teacher Education at The New School in New York City, where she heads a Master's degree program with an ex-plicit commitment to democratic education and urban school change. Previously she taught at Louisiana State University and SUNY Bing-hamton. Kohli's scholarship has appeared in a range of journals, includ-ing *Harvard Educational Review, International Journal of Social Education, International Journal of Qualitative Studies in Education, Education and Society,* and *Studies in Philosophy and Education.* She is also the editor of and contributor to *Critical Conversations in Philosophy* *of Education,* and has numerous chapters in edited collections. Currently she is working on a book on feminism and educational research.

Gloria Ladson-Billings is a professor in the Department of Curriculum and Instruction at the University of Wisconsin–Madison and a Senior Fellow in Urban Education at the Annenberg Institute for School Reform at Brown University. Her research interests concern the relationship between culture and schooling, particularly successful teaching and learning for African American students. Her publications include *Dreamkeepers: Successful Teachers of African American Children;* the *Dictionary of Multicultural Education* (with Carl A. Grant); and numerous journal articles and book chapters. She is currently the editor of the Teaching, Learning, and Human Development section of the *American Educational Research Journal* and a member of several editorial boards, including *Urban Education, Educational Policy,* and *The Journal of Negro Education.*

Perry Marker is Associate Professor of Social Studies Education and Coordinator of the graduate program in Curriculum, Teaching, and Learning at Sonoma State University in Rohnert Park, California. His scholarship focuses on issues of democratic education and his articles have appeared in journals such as *Theory and Research in Social Education, International Journal of Social Education, The Social Studies, Social Studies Review,* and *Social Science Record.*

Sandra Mathison is Associate Professor in the Department of Educational Theory and Practice at the State University of New York at Albany. Her research focuses on philosophical issues in educational evaluation, including the logic of evaluative thinking, validity, and justice. Mathison has written about these topics in many journals, including *Educational Researcher, Journal of Curriculum and Supervision, Evaluation and Program Planning, Curriculum and Teaching,* and the *International Journal for Social Education,* and numerous book chapters as well. As a basis for research and writing on evaluation, Mathison actively participates in evaluation studies. She has coordinated large-scale national evaluation projects, such as the University of Chicago School Mathematics Project (funded by the Amoco Foundation and NSF, among others) and the Schoolyard Ecology for Elementary Teachers (for the Institute for Ecosystem Studies, with funding from NSF).

Shuaib Meacham is Assistant Professor of Literacy in the School of Education, University of Colorado at Boulder. He specializes in Language and Literacy as well as cultural issues in Teaching and Teacher

Education. His teaching and research are in the areas of literacy, teacher education, and multicultural education, with a specialization in theories and practices of literacy in culturally diverse settings. His dissertation was a qualitative study of the intercultural connections, tensions, and contradictions that occur in literacy instruction in a classroom with over ten different nationalities.

Susan E. Noffke was a teacher of elementary and middle school–aged children in Wisconsin for ten years. She is currently Associate Professor of Curriculum at the University of Illinois at Urbana-Champaign, where she teaches a two-semester sequence of courses that integrate elementary social studies methods with issues of cultural diversity. She works with inservice teachers in graduate courses in action research and curriculum studies, and also in school-based action research groups addressing social justice issues and practices.

E. Wayne Ross is Associate Professor of Education at the State University of New York at Binghamton, where he teaches courses in social studies education, qualitative research, and educational foundations. A former secondary social studies and day care teacher, Ross is also co-founder of the Rouge Forum, a group of educators, students, and parents seeking a democratic society. He is the editor or co-editor of several books, including *The Social Studies Curriculum: Purposes, Problems, and Possibilities; Reflective Practice in Social Studies;* and *Teacher Personal Theorizing: Connecting Curriculum Practice, Theory, and Research,* and author of numerous articles and essays on issues of curriculum theory and practice and the politics of education. He is currently editor of the journal *Theory and Research in Social Education.*

William B. Stanley is Dean and Professor of Curriculum and Social Education at the School of Education, University of Colorado at Boulder. He has been actively involved in educational reform in Louisiana, Delaware, and Colorado. His areas of research include curriculum theory, social education, educational reform, concept formation, and multicultural education. Stanley is a former secondary social studies teacher and has been a faculty member at Louisiana State University and the University of Delaware prior to becoming Dean of Education at the University of Colorado, Boulder. His publications have appeared in numerous journals, including *Theory and Research in Social Education; The Social Studies; Social Education; Educational Theory; Science Education; Science and Education; The Quarterly Journal of Experimental*

Psychology; and the *Journal of Experimental Psychology: Learning, Memory, and Cognition.* He is also the author of *Curriculum for Utopia* (1992). Stanley is an active member of the National Council for the Social Studies/College and University Faculty Assembly, the American Educational Research Association, the Philosophy of Education Society, and the Society for the Advancement of American Philosophy.

Shirley R. Steinberg teaches at Adelphi University in Garden City, New York, and at the Adelphi Urban Campus in lower Manhattan. She is an educational consultant and a drama director. Among the numerous books she has written and edited with Joe L. Kincheloe are *Measured Lies: The Bell Curve Examined; White Reign: Deploying Whiteness in America; Kinderculture: The Corporate Constructions of Childhood;* and *Unauthorized Methods: Critical Strategies for Teaching.* She is the senior editor of *Taboo: The Journal of Culture and Education.*

Author Index

Subject Index

Teacher education (*cont.*)
 program planning, 153–154
 social justice in, 165–179
 texts, 171–172
 traditions in, 151
Teachers (*see also* teaching):
 activism of, 71, 77–78, 81
 as agents of the state, 30–31
 alliances with others, 92–93
 beliefs, 59
 concerns with discipline,
  159–160
 as curriculum gatekeepers, 218,
  220–222
 as democratic leaders, 73
 democratic left, 45
 deskilling of, 138
 as ideologues, 158–159
 as learners, 142
 as reflective practitioners, 160
 as researchers, 127
 roles, 50
 school reform, 45
 surveillance of, 30
Teacher-student relations, 142, 144
Teaching (*see also* teachers):
 activism, 26–27, 45
 alternatives, 172–174
 anti-racist approaches, 50
 with awareness of race, sex, and
  class, 37–38
 child-centeredness, 73
 citizenship, 13, 15
 complexity of, 157
 culturally relevant, 197–198
 democratically, 16–19, 93–95,
  135, 143–146
 discourse of, 30–31, 47
 for empowerment, 121–131
 ideology, 56, 146, 28
 indoctrination, 28, 44–47
 as inquiry, 170, 174–175
 multicultural, 50

 as political, 43–44, 53
 popular culture, 15, 87
 pragmatic, 70
 project method, 74, 208–209
 research on, 49
 social efficiency, 177
 technical act, 97
 traditional patterns in social studies,
  43–60
 for transformation (*see also* critical
  pedagogy), 135, 137, 143–146
 values, 8
Teaching and Learning Institute, 193
Teaching for Change, 188
Teaching Tolerance, 171
Techno-power (*see also* power; power
  relations), 106, 112
Testing, 16, 49, 59, 85, 197, 209
Textbooks, 76, 197, 209–211,
  234–235
Transformative pedagogy (*see* critical
  pedagogy)
True Lies, 88
True Romance, 88
Tracking, 197

University of Illinois, 166
University of Rochester, 193
University of Wisconsin, Madison,
  149, 151–152, 162
Uprising of '34, The, 188
U.S. Chamber of Commerce, 4, 16

Vietnam War, 12–13, 26
Violence, 89, 135, 139, 144
Vocational education (*see also*
  Perkins Act; Smith-Hughes
  Act; work education), 3, 45,
  104, 110, 150

Western civilization, 8, 86, 214
White supremacy, 99
Words by Heart, 187